MW01502982

The Greatest Trials I Ever Had

New Perspectives on the Civil War Era

SERIES EDITOR

Judkin Browning, Appalachian State University

SERIES ADVISORY BOARD

Stephen Berry, University of Georgia

Jane Turner Censer, George Mason University

Paul Escott, Wake Forest University

Lorien Foote, Texas A&M University

Anne Marshall, Mississippi State University

Barton Myers, Washington & Lee University

Michael Thomas Smith, McNeese State University

Susannah Ural, University of Southern Mississippi

Kidada Williams, Wayne State University

The Greatest Trials
I Ever Had

The Civil War Letters of
Margaret and Thomas Cahill

Edited by Ryan W. Keating

The University of Georgia Press
ATHENS

© 2017 by the University of Georgia Press
Athens, Georgia 30602
www.ugapress.org
All rights reserved
Set in 11/13 New Baskerville by
Graphic Composition, Inc., Bogart, Georgia.

Most University of Georgia Press titles are
available from popular e-book vendors.

Printed digitally

Library of Congress Cataloging-in-Publication Data

Names: Cahill, Thomas, 1827–1869, author. | Cahill, Margaret,
–1870, author. | Keating, Ryan W., editor.
Title: The greatest trials I ever had : the Civil War letters of Margaret
and Thomas Cahill / edited by Ryan W. Keating.
Description: Athens, Georgia : The University of Georgia Press, 2017. | Series: New
perspectives on the Civil War era | Includes bibliographical references and index.
Identifiers: LCCN 2017009537 | ISBN 9780820351544 (hardcover : alk. paper) |
ISBN 9780820351551 (pbk. : alk. paper) | ISBN 9780820351537 (ebook)
Subjects: LCSH: Cahill, Thomas, 1827–1869—Correspondence. | Cahill, Margaret,
–1870—Correspondence. | United States. Army. Connecticut Infantry Regiment, 9th
(1861–1865) | United States—History—Civil War, 1861–1865—Personal narratives.
| Soldiers—Connecticut—New Haven—Correspondence. | Women—Connecticut—
New Haven—Correspondence. | New Haven (Conn.)—Biography. | Cahill family.
Classification: LCC E499.5 9th .C34 2017 | DDC 973.7/446—dc23
LC record available at https://lccn.loc.gov/2017009537

Contents

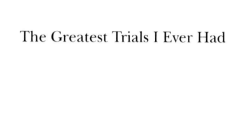

The Greatest Trials I Ever Had

Introduction

ON A COLD NIGHT IN NOVEMBER 1861, Col. Thomas Cahill sat on his mattress, huddled over a small leather writing desk. It is not hard to imagine the scene that evening as the colonel took pen to paper and wrote the first of many letters home to his wife, Margaret. His regiment, the Ninth Connecticut (Irish) Volunteers, had arrived at Camp Chase in Lowell, Massachusetts, two days before. There they joined the Twenty-Sixth Massachusetts and a number of other smaller units, forming the nucleus of Gen. Benjamin Butler's New England Expeditionary Force.[1] The camp was full of men from all over New England, and they were excited—excited to be away from home, excited to be joining the fray against the rebellious Southerners, or maybe just excited at the prospect of slipping over the fence and visiting the local public houses to fraternize with the young women who worked in Lowell's factories.[2]

Housed in "the best of tents . . . [with] plenty of mattresses filled with straw, and a generous supply of blankets and comforts," Cahill described with some dismay the recent journey from New Haven.[3] Soon after their initial muster, his men gained ill repute for their disorderly conduct, and their bad behavior continued, defining their short journey to Lowell. Echoing local newspapers that lambasted the behavior of the Irishmen in the Ninth, Cahill was not optimistic, his language unenthusiastic. While his attitude may have been swayed to a degree by a sense of frustration with the men under his command, his tone reflected underlying emotions that became increasingly evident in his correspondence as the war

---

1. Gen. Benjamin Butler, a Massachusetts Democrat, was perhaps most famous (at this point in the war) for his declaration in the summer of 1861 that escaped slaves be considered contrabands of war. He returned to Massachusetts that fall to raise a brigade consisting of New England regiments for service in the Gulf of Mexico. See Hearn, *When the Devil Came Down*, for Butler's biography and wartime experiences.

2. "The Expedition from Boston; Steamship Constitution at Portland the Trip to the Capes of Virginia, the Weather, the Passengers, and How They Stood the Passage," *New York Times*, November 29, 1861; Daniel O'Sullivan to friend, December 25, 1861, O'Sullivan Collection, held in the private collection of Joseph Kelly, Toms River, N.J.

3. "Camp Chase," *Lowell Daily Citizen and News*, November 9, 1861.

wore on: love and homesickness. When the Ninth Connecticut left New Haven for Lowell on the first leg of a journey that ultimately took them south to New Orleans, Thomas Cahill left his wife, Margaret, and two young children at home. Their letters, written over the course of the war, illuminate not only daily life at home and on the front lines but also the emotional difficulties that came with the absence of a loved one.[1]

Thomas was born in Boston in 1827 "within a stone's throw of Bunker Hill."[5] Both his parents were Irish immigrants who came to the United States long before the Potato Famine that drove hundreds of thousands to flee the shores of the Emerald Isle. His mother, Mary Ann Young, left Ireland with her family when she was only three years old and arrived in New York City on October 1, 1810. At some point the family moved to Boston, where in 1824 seventeen-year-old Mary wed Lawrence Cahill. Their first son, Thomas, was born four years later. The family relocated to New Haven around 1830, where the future colonel grew up.

Thomas married Margaret Lanin in New Haven in the late 1840s, when he was in his early twenties and she was in her late teens. Less is known about Margaret other than that she was born in New York and was of Irish descent. In 1850 the young couple was living with Thomas's mother, Mary, and his three younger sisters, but they moved out soon thereafter to a house on Franklin Street that Thomas purchased sometime in 1850 or 1851.[6] By the time South Carolina seceded from the Union, the family had doubled in size with the arrival of Mary and Eddie, ages two and nearly one. Thomas's sister Ellen lived with the growing family and helped around the house. Both Thomas and Margaret maintained a close relationship with the Irish community in New Haven in the years before the war, developing important connections that ultimately defined their bond to their ethnic and religious heritage. A mason by trade, Thomas found success in his business enterprises in the antebellum period, and by the time war broke out, his personal estate was valued at nearly $2,600, making the family solidly middle class.[7]

---

4. Unfortunately, not all the letters were preserved. In fact, not all the letters were even received by their intended readers. One issue Thomas and Margaret faced throughout the war was finding proper channels for the consistent delivery of their correspondence. It is clear from the collection that at least as many letters were lost by the postal service as remain in the collection.

5. "One of the Documents," *Columbian Register* (New Haven, Conn.), October 6, 1855.

6. Property deeds negotiated between Thomas W. Cahill and Lucius W. Fitch Cahill Collection, held by Charles Sibley, Hamden, Conn.

7. Eighth Census of the United States.

The growth of Cahill's business coincided with the increasingly prominent role he played in New Haven society. In 1860, for example, he was chosen by the New Haven Building Committee to remove the Old Neck Bridge, which spanned the Mill River and connected Fair Haven and New Haven.[8] Government contracts such as these continued after the war, and by his untimely death in 1869 Thomas had amassed a considerable fortune with property valued at $15,000 and a personal estate worth $1,000.[9] During this same period Margaret and Thomas became close friends with a number of prominent men, whose names appeared time and again in their wartime correspondence. Among these were Father Matthew Hart, the head of St. Patrick's Parish, and Harmanus M. Welch, who served as the mayor of New Haven from 1860 to 1863. The two were also acquainted with William Buckingham, a Republican politician who served as wartime governor of the state.

Equally important was Thomas's participation in, and leadership of, Irish American organizations in the city. As the captain of Company E, Second Regiment Connecticut State Militia, a predominately Irish company, the young Irishman had to deal with the repercussions of the rise of Know-Nothing power in the state in the mid-1850s. While xenophobia was a major component of antebellum political and social rhetoric, nowhere did this movement gain more traction than in Massachusetts and Connecticut, where in 1855 state legislators tried to limit immigrant participation in civic life. Following Massachusetts's lead, Connecticut passed a "Militia Act", which disbanded all militia companies composed predominately of foreign-born citizens. The prevailing political climate in the Nutmeg State resonated with the growing national concern surrounding foreign, and especially Catholic, loyalties. Many pointed to the San Patricio Regiment as proof of the potential repercussions that came with relying on immigrant soldiers to defend national interests. The group of men, many of whom were Irish, had deserted the U.S. Army to throw in their lot with Mexico during the Mexican-American war. Though Irish Catholics time and again cited the long history of immigrant soldiers who fought to defend the United States, these reminders did little to soften the blow.[10]

In Massachusetts the disbanded Irishmen protested, at least for a time, refusing to abide by the law. The Irish in Connecticut, however, were less

---

8. Contract between New Haven Building Committee and Thomas Cahill, June 11, 1860, Cahill Collection.

9. Ninth Census of the United States.

10. Callaghan, "San Patricios"; Kurtz, "Let Us Hear No More."

boisterous in their responses, seeking justice in the press and in the voting booths rather than in open displays of animosity. Democratic papers noted in an ironic response to the disbandment that Thomas Cahill was born in the United States and Thomas Coates, Cahill's lieutenant (who would later serve under Cahill in the Ninth Connecticut), was a "naturalized Irishman, who had been an officer of some grade, or drill master, in the United States Army."[11] The soldiers, one newspaper noted, were as "industrious and skillful . . . as any company, and as individuals, they have discharged promptly and faithfully, all duties that are required by law. . . . We have no doubt, they would shed their blood and sacrifice their lives heroically, in defense of American liberty, as any other company in this state."[12] In a private letter to the governor, Cahill sought clarification as to how "the company lately under my command were Detrimental to the Interest of the militia of this state."[13] Citing the onus of the government to prove such accusations before any militia unit was to be disbanded, Cahill made a strong, yet ultimately unsuccessful, plea against this unprecedented act.

Cooler heads soon prevailed. The Know-Nothings lost power and the new administration reinstated the ethnic militia units a year later, in 1856. Soon after the repeal of this law, Cahill began organizing a new unit, the Emmet Guards, named for Robert Emmet, an Irish Republican who had led a failed uprising in Ireland in 1803. Emmet secured a place in history with his "Speech from the Dock" on the eve of his execution when he asked to "repose in obscurity and peace, and my tomb remain uninscribed, until other times, and other men, can do justice to my character; when my country takes her place among the nations of the earth, then, and not till then, let my epitaph be written."[14] Such a link was fitting for Cahill's new unit, composed of men who openly aligned themselves with the Fenian movement, a transatlantic nationalist movement committed to revolution and the overthrow of English rule in Ireland.[15]

When the Civil War broke out in 1861, these Irishmen rushed to the defense of the Union. Their efforts ultimately manifested in Connecti-

---

11. "One of the Documents" and "The Militia Disbandment," *Columbian Register*, October 6, 1855.

12. "The Militia Disbandment," *ibid.*

13. Thomas Cahill to Gov. William T. Minor, Cahill Collection.

14. Kee, *Green Flag*, 167–69.

15. For information on the Fenian movement see Ramon, *Provisional Dictator*; Walker, *Fenian Movement*; Snay, *Fenians Freedmen and Southern Whites*; O'Broin, *Fenian Fever*; Brady, "Fenians and the Faithful"; Lynch, "'Erin's Hope.'"

cut's only ethnic regiment, the Ninth Connecticut Volunteer Infantry. Recruiters imbued their unit with both Irish and American imagery, and the act of volunteering mended, for a time, the lingering nativist animosity and quelled questions of ethnic loyalty in the state, at least momentarily. This did not mean, however, that military service suddenly transformed civilians into well-disciplined soldiers, and Cahill's regiment suffered immensely from the misbehavior of a group he referred to as his "hard sort." Though there is no evidence that the delinquents in his unit were Irish, their behavior created animosity between the regiment and the local community in New Haven and revived angst surrounding ethnic stereotypes of disorder. So contentious was this relationship that it ultimately dictated the fate of Connecticut's Irish unit and had lasting repercussions on Cahill's experiences during the war.

The "exuberant, ragged, roistering volunteers [of that regiment] taxed the best efforts of New Haven's inadequate police force," noted one observer, and there was considerable relief when the unit was assigned to Gen. Benjamin Butler's New England Expeditionary Force and transferred to Camp Chase in Lowell, Massachusetts.[16] As Butler recalled, the regiment became part of his command because the unit, "owing to the somewhat exuberantly turbulent character of its recruits, could not be readily reduced to discipline at the hour of its recruitment, and was not in a condition to be properly sent away except under a fostering care."[17] Trouble seemed to follow the Irishmen wherever they went. Arriving in Lowell in early November, the men of the Ninth met a chilly reception. When news came that the rowdy Ninth was due to relocate to Camp Chase, the citizens rapidly organized an auxiliary police force to defend their community. Although the police brigade eventually disbanded without incident, its formation was nevertheless telling of the broader attitudes concerning these Irish volunteers. Making matters worse, Connecticut newspapers reported with dismay the behavior of the men who allegedly destroyed a considerable amount of property on the trip to Lowell. The *Connecticut Courant* noted that the Ninth "will be the men to meet our Southern brethren in the field. . . . They have some first rate officers and some first rate men . . . but many of them will have to be taught by B. Butler . . . that there is a vast difference between a sojer and

---

16. Niven, *Connecticut for the Union*, 67.

17. *War of the Rebellion: A Compilation of the Official Records of the Union and Confederate Armies*, series 3, vol. 1, 653 (hereafter cited as *Official Records*).

a soldier."[18] Such accusations weighed on Thomas for they ultimately reflected poorly upon his leadership abilities and appeared repeatedly as a major concern in his correspondence throughout the war.

In only a short time the men from Connecticut made their presence known in and around Camp Chase as they would cry, "Connecticut over the fence!" before jumping the wooden stockade surrounding the camp on their mission to flirt with local factory girls. After only fifteen days in Lowell, though, they, along with the Twenty-Sixth Massachusetts, moved to Boston, where they boarded the transport ship the *Constitution* for points unknown. Orders, opened aboard ship, made their destination Ship Island, little more than a sandbar approximately twelve miles off the coast of Biloxi, Mississippi. The island commanded the waterways that connected the Southern Gulf ports and was invaluable to the Union blockade during 1861 and 1862.[19] From this base Butler's men began to train for the eventual invasion of New Orleans.

December 1861 found Cahill and his men in a "a spot more desolate than Robinson Crusoe's."[20] Isolated from the cities, the regiment became a well-disciplined military unit as hours of hard work on the parade grounds began to pay off. As the winter progressed, Cahill became increasingly confident in the ability of his command. From a broader political perspective, the men from Connecticut found themselves in an interesting position. As one of the first Union regiments to reach the Gulf of Mexico, they were present when Brig. Gen. John Phelps issued his proclamation declaring the primary goal of the Union war effort to be emancipation and the pursuit of free labor. Thus Cahill's letters provide fascinating perspectives on this policy and the reaction of the men under his command. On a more personal level, his day-to-day interactions with enlisted men and fellow officers alike illustrate the challenges that the new colonel faced as he attempted to negotiate military bureaucracy—a source of increasing frustration as the war continued. Yet despite these personal struggles, Cahill and his men were part of a broader confluence of events far beyond their control.

As early as November 1861 the Lincoln administration, as well as officers in the army and navy, began to advocate for the seizure of New

18. "The Ninth Regiment," *Connecticut Courant* (Hartford), November 9, 1861.

19. Winters, *Civil War in Louisiana*, 28, 50.

20. Daniel O'Sullivan to "Friend," December 25, 1861, O'Sullivan and Hill Collection, private collection, held by Joseph Kelly, Toms River, N.J.

Orleans as "the simplest and most effective means of blockading it."[21] Although orders to assault the city reached the Gulf Fleet under Adm. David Farragut in January 1862, Gen. George McClellan initially opposed the move due to fears that the city's defenses, and in particular Forts Jackson and Saint Philip, which lay some seventy miles south of New Orleans and (theoretically) commanded the river approach, were too formidable. Ultimately, though, opinion shifted, and the Union command in the Gulf began its move on the Crescent City.[22] This would be one part of a three-pronged assault launched by Union forces against the Confederacy that spring. Almost directly north of Ship Island, Union forces moved into Tennessee and then northern Mississippi, an advance culminating in the dual victories at Shiloh and Corinth. In the east, McClellan's massive army moved via water to Fortress Monroe on the Yorktown Peninsula where, by early April, it was poised to attack Richmond.

For the men of the Ninth, these months of training were interspersed with brief moments of excitement. Most notable was the brief fight at Pass Christian, where Cahill and his men faced Confederate soldiers of the Third Mississippi. Charging the rebels' line "with an Irish 'Y-a-a-a-ah!,'" Cahill's men routed their enemy and became (allegedly) the first Union regiment to capture a Confederate battle flag.[23] Butler praised the soldiers of the Ninth for their "gallant courage and good conduct . . . [and] of their bravery on the field."[24] Preparations for the invasion of New Orleans proved anticlimatic as the navy charged upriver and took the Crescent City by surprise. The mutiny and subsequent surrender of the Confederate troops at Forts Jackson and Saint Philip saved the infantry from a desperate frontal assault.[25] It is difficult to imagine that the "invasion" of New Orleans was anything but a disappointment for Cahill and his men. While the regiment performed heroically at Pass Christian, the action of the navy on the Mississippi River made Butler's infantry rather inconsequential. When the Ninth Connecticut landed in New Orleans, as the second federal regiment to enter the city, they did so without firing a shot.

Placed on police duty, the regiment was transferred north of the city to Camp Parapet, where they defended New Orleans from potential Con-

---

21. Reid, *America's Civil War*, 93.

22. Ibid., 95–97.

23. Murray, *History of the Ninth Regiment*, 80–81.

24. Ibid., 84.

25. Pierson, *Mutiny at Fort Jackson*.

federate counterattacks. There, the regiment's numbers swelled as recruits from New Orleans and Texas poured into camp. Garrison duty
was by no means uneventful, and the summer months tried the spirits of
Cahill and his men. Moving north up the Mississippi River to Vicksburg,
the men were tasked with constructing a canal opposite the Confederate
Gibraltar in order to reroute the river away from the fortified heights of
the city. Grant's Canal, as the project would later be called, was an un-
mitigated disaster from the start, and by late July nearly all of the men
of the Ninth had fallen ill. Retiring south in early August, the regiment
rallied and fought bravely at Baton Rouge, where Cahill took command
of Union forces after Gen. Thomas Williams was struck down by rebel
fire. Under Cahill's command, the Union forces routed the Confederates
under Gen. John C. Breckenridge. On the fields outside of Baton Rouge
the Irishmen of the Ninth Connecticut lived up to the fighting spirit of
their race and earned renown in their hometowns.

"Victory at Baton Rouge," the *Hartford Daily Courant* announced on August 19 in an exaggerated account of a relatively small engagement.[26] Cahill's troops did, however, rout the Confederate attackers, despite being
outnumbered nearly two to one.[27] The rebels "got their fill of it there
though sick as we were," Sgt. Thomas Knablin wrote to his wife a month
after the battle. "Out of a Company of 90 men all we could muster was
about 40. It was so with every Regiment and Company that was at Vicks-
burge[.] In fact the whole of them were little better than sick men."[28] "We
have always been in the advance," Cahill noted in a letter to his sister,
"but I rather expected that as it deems to be expected by the people of
every thing that has the name of being Irish in the fighting line; well we
have not suffered more than Others and we have a good name, wherever
we are known at home or here."[29] It was the second time his regiment
performed well under fire, and Cahill's leadership made him enthusiastic
about the responsibilities and prospects for advancement, at least for a

---

26. Only 5,100 men were engaged at Baton Rouge. Winters, *Civil War in Louisiana*,
123. In comparison, at Fair Oaks, Virginia, on May 31, 1862, nearly 84,000 men were
engaged. At Gaines's Mill, a month later, 85,000 men fought as Lee attempted to push
McClellan away from Richmond. Stoker, *Grand Design*, 140–56.

27. "Victory at Baton Rouge," *Hartford Daily Courant*, August 19, 1862.

28. Thomas Knablin to Mary Knablin, September 7, 1862. Thomas Knablin (Co D, 9th
Conn. Vol. Inf., Civil War), pension application no. 429,164, certificate no. 399,850, Case
of Files of Approved Pension Applications, 1861–1934, Civil War and Later Pension Files,
Department of Veteran Affairs, Record Group 15, National Archives, Washington, D.C.

29. Thomas Cahill to sister, October 20, 1862, Cahill Collection.

time. Yet for reasons unclear Cahill was passed over for promotion time and again.

After Baton Rouge the regiment resumed garrison duty in New Orleans. During the fall of 1862 Cahill witnessed, firsthand, the impact of the federal occupation on the Confederacy's largest city. His correspondence provides fascinating commentary on day-to-day operations in the South. His frustration over not receiving promotions contributed to a sense of honesty in his observations and commentary that might otherwise have been restrained out of a sense of duty. During this time, Cahill struggled with concern both over his family and the realities of the military service as he experienced it on a day-to-day basis. Of particular note during his time in the South was the corruption that accompanied occupation. Cahill's interactions with the dishonest and corrupt regime under Benjamin Butler contributed significantly to his general frustration over not being promoted. That undeserving men would be promoted over a proven and capable officer such as himself could only be further proof of the problematic political nature of a war that still seemed very far from over. While detached on provost duty in southern Louisiana in the winter of 1862–63, Cahill's men avoided both of Nathanial Banks's failed campaigns—the attempted capture of Galveston in January 1863 and the campaign against Port Hudson that spring. On January 19, after considerable effort, Cahill received an extended furlough and traveled home to New Haven.

Returning to Louisiana at the end of April, Cahill resumed command of the Second Brigade of Gen. Thomas W. Sherman's Division (Second Division, Nineteenth Corps under Nathanial Banks) and found his men spread throughout the countryside guarding New Orleans from potential rebel threats. Cahill's return ignited some animosity among his soldiers, who chafed under his strict discipline. Unruly behavior continued to plague the regiment, which suffered one of the highest numbers of general courts martial trials in the Union army during the war, but there was also considerable friction between Cahill and some of his company commanders, which contributed to a number of resignations during the first two years of the war. Combined, these issues isolated the colonel from his command and there was a notable lack of camaraderie and cohesiveness among the men in the regiment.

The summer of 1863 marked the high-water mark for the Confederacy as Robert E. Lee's Army of Northern Virginia advanced north into Pennsylvania only to be defeated at Gettysburg. The psychological impact of this victory was compounded by federal advances along the Mississippi

River, in particular the capture of Vicksburg and Port Hudson, which opened the river to the Union and effectively divided the Confederacy in half. As the rebels retreated on all fronts, Union forces took to the offensive in moves toward Richmond and Atlanta that would eventually take Connecticut's Irish regiment away from their relative comfort in and around New Orleans and cast them on the scarred battlefields of northern Virginia, where they would join in the final grand offensive against the Confederates in that region. The momentary joy of victory coincided with troubling news from home—the draft had arrived and New York City was in flames. Although New Haven experienced no violent protest, the draft caused much consternation among the Irish American community, though concern was undercut by stories of draft dodgers, who became symbols of scorn for those who had sacrificed since 1861.

In April 1864 the veterans of the Ninth Connecticut who chose to reenlist were granted furlough and returned to Connecticut. Those who decided to serve out their three-year term stayed in Louisiana.[30] Thomas had reservations about continuing his service past his three-year obligation, and his final letters bear the strain of three years in the military. The battalion that took to the field in Virginia in the summer of 1864 bore little resemblance to the regiment that had originally marched to war. Only 294 men remustered and they returned to the front in what became their most intense period of service. As Cahill's letters show, the colonel and many of the regiment's officers struggled with the decision to rejoin the regiment after the conclusion of their initial three years of service. Having upheld his contractual obligation to the federal government, Cahill simply wanted to go home. Despite the reservations, he led the re-formed regiment as it became part of a three-pronged campaign to cut off the Confederate capital. As Ulysses S. Grant moved on Richmond from the north in what would become the Overland Campaign, forces under Butler moved up the James River toward the Confederate rail hub at Petersburg. In the Shenandoah Valley, during the summer of 1864, Union forces under Philip Sheridan were tasked with driving rebel forces from the region and securing the last line of supply for Lee's army. Cahill and his men participated in two of these three movements. They served at Bermuda Hundred and Deep Bottom, Virginia, before being transferred to the Shenandoah Valley in late summer. There they fought at Winchester and Fisher's Hill, important Union victories that finally secured the valley and its vital base of supply. For those at home,

---

30. Murray, *History of the Ninth Regiment*, 180.

the uncertainty that accompanied the campaign, especially when news reached home of violent clashes in the valley, was difficult to bear. "I have little courage to write [for] we are not certain if you are alive," Margaret noted in September in a letter that she tersely concluded with two words: "Come home."[31] Thomas obliged her request. Frustrated with his military experience, Thomas resigned his commission and turned over command of his regiment to Lt. Col. John G. Healy on October 12, 1864.

Thomas quickly transitioned to peace, rebuilding his construction business, which flourished in the years immediately after the war. His success was short lived, for the colonel of Connecticut's Irish brigade died on August 31, 1869, at the age of forty-two. Margaret, his confidant and closest friend, followed her husband a year later, on July 25, 1870. Ellen, who had been so very important to Margaret during the war, took the younger children and raised them as her own. The younger Thomas, a doctor, played the most active role among his siblings in promoting and preserving the memory and legacy of his father and the Ninth Connecticut. He was part of the 1903 committee that returned the battle flag to the veterans of the Third Mississippi and helped Thomas Hamilton Murray complete the *History of the Ninth Regiment Connecticut Volunteer Infantry*. Edward, the little boy who so desperately sought to emulate his father, was responsible for preserving this letter collection, which passed to his son, Thomas, and then to Charles Sibley, Thomas Cahill's great-grandson, who so graciously provided access to this invaluable collection.

The experiences of Thomas and Margaret Cahill during the three years between November 1861 and October 1864 were not necessarily unique. Historians have often written of the jarring impact that Civil War service had on family and relationships, and it is clear from the Cahill letters that others in their circle of friends, including many whose names appear below struggled with similar emotional, social, and economic issues that came with military service. Few letter collections, however, offer the extensive and detailed perspective of the home front found in the letters written to Thomas by Margaret and by others in New Haven during his absence. As a contribution to the historiography of the Northern home front, such perspectives enhance contemporary understanding of ways in which nineteenth-century Americans were daily impacted by the Civil War.

For their part, Thomas's letters, which make up the bulk of the collection, provide important insight into the war. The Union may not have won the war without the victories in the west, and those men who

---

31. Margaret to Thomas Cahill, September 24, 1864.

occupied vast tracts of enemy territory played a vital if often overlooked role in the Union war effort. That they did not march gallantly into the slaughter at Fredericksburg or hold the line at Little Round Top does not negate or lessen the service and sacrifice of these men during the war. In fact, it could be argued that the captivation with narratives that focus on the brave soldier boy makes the letters of Thomas Cahill all the more important because they force the historical community to make sense of the multitude of ways in which Union soldiers experienced the war. Certainly, when called on, the men of the Ninth Connecticut performed heroically under fire. That such experiences were the exception rather than the norm for Cahill and his men should only add value to the contribution of his correspondence from Louisiana, for it expands upon the day-to-day life of men tasked with occupying and controlling enemy territory for an extended period.

Margaret's story, though, is equally compelling. Over the course of the war the colonel's wife offered keen insight to the situation on the ground in New Haven and kept Thomas well informed about the political and social issues on the home front. In Margaret's letters, the war takes a new and very personal perspective. Women, of course, played a vital role in the war effort as their loyalty and support served as a stabilizing force on the Northern home front. Often, public portrayals of female patriotism underscore the bonds between soldier and civilian and the willing sacrifice of those at home for the Union cause. Margaret's letters, however, paint a decidedly different picture. There is no evidence that she was involved in the type of war work that many of her peers committed themselves to. She did not organize sewing circles and made no mention of any participation in events sponsored by the Sanitary Commission or other charities. When she did engage in charitable work, it was in a personal way—as a conduit through whom those at home could contact their loved ones in the Ninth Connecticut. For the most part, though, Margaret's letters speak to the frank reality of life for those who stayed behind during the war. Hardly the patriotic officer's wife, Margaret was, at the most, a tentative supporter of the war effort, and her letters attest to the struggles that emerged in her husband's absence.[32]

In constant fear over her husband's well-being, Margaret's letters provide a window into life on the Connecticut home front. Although the

---

32. For work on women and the home front see Silber, *Daughters of the Union*; Richard, *Busy Hands*; Giesberg, *Army at Home*; Attie, *Patriotic Toil* ; Ramold, *Across the Divide*; Clinton and Silber, *Divided Houses*.

Cahills were rather well-off, Margaret struggled throughout the war as she was forced, by necessity, to transition out of the traditional gendered role prescribed by nineteenth-century society. With the departure of the Ninth, Margaret took on increasingly important roles including dealing with outstanding bills, handling difficult renters, paying the mortgage, and collecting interest on war bonds. While she grew increasingly confident in her abilities, she nevertheless lamented the absence of Thomas. The birth of her third child, also named Thomas, on July 13, 1862, only compounded the struggles at home. Certainly, the daily task of childrearing was trying, but for Margaret this was compounded by the fact that her children served as a constant reminder of their father's absence, and she begged her husband on numerous occasions to return. It was only her pride, she wrote, that kept her from letting others in New Haven know the true extent of her suffering over his absence.[33]

Alongside familial duties, Margaret also served as a liaison between soldiers and their families, in essence serving as the "colonel" of her own regiment composed of those families left at home when their husbands, fathers, and sons marched south to defend the Union. But in the fall of 1863, after considerable discussion, Margaret, her three children, and Ellen, left their post, traveling south to join Thomas in New Orleans. Her decision was driven by a number of factors, in particular the daily trials and tribulations that came with her dual roles as mother and newly minted head of the household, and speak to the struggles faced by thousands of women in the North during the war. As they stand, Margaret's letters are frank confessions of the difficulties of life at home during the war. Although the vast majority of these letters speak to Thomas's experiences and concerns, those from Margaret provide blunt commentary on the home front, illuminating the realities of her war. Dealing with bills, tenants, mortgages, bonds, and the social expectations of a colonel's wife, Margaret stepped into her husband's shoes—albeit hesitantly.

What makes Margaret's letters even more striking is that she was far from "average" during this period. The wife of a colonel and financially well-off, Margaret fits the mold of the group typically studied by historians of the Northern experience—middle- to upper-class women actively engaged in war work. Because this group typically left written accounts of their activities and played the most visible role at home during the war, they have become the focus of many historians of the Northern ex-

33. Margaret to Thomas, July 24, 1862.

perience, who see this support at home (in direct contrast to the reticent nationalism in the Confederacy) as one of the key factors in Northern victory. Yet her hesitant patriotism, a timid and tentative support of the war effort that was informed by the very real emotional, physical, and economic hardships that accompanied military service, helps give voice to those on the Northern home front who suffered immensely, yet silently, over the course of the war and whose experiences have largely been lost among the celebration of Northern unity and Union victory.

As it stands, this collection is one of the, if not the, most extensive letter collections written by an Irish American soldier. Finally, and perhaps equally important, though, many of the letters that Margaret wrote to Thomas were saved. These letters from home are the only substantial collection written by an Irish American woman on the Northern home front known to exist. Margaret herself was not an immigrant, and thus her experiences are removed, generationally, from those of Irish immigrant women.[34] But, as the wife of a leader of New Haven's Irish American community, Margaret's letters shed significant light upon the experiences of a middle-class family of Irish descent in one of America's growing cities. The correspondence between Thomas and Margaret Cahill tell an excellent story. Their trials and tribulations in each other's absence make them very relatable figures, and their experiences help expound the realities of Civil War service for many couples divided by conflict. Their war was a personal struggle dictated by the difficulties that military service imposed on young families. Their letters help us understand the ethnic soldier in the Civil War and provide insight to the true impact of the war upon Americans—regardless of their ethnic heritage.

---

34. For work on Irish American women see Diner, *Erin's Daughters in America*; Nolan, *Ourselves Alone*; Lynch-Brennan, *Irish Bridget*; Lee and Casey, *Making the Irish American*; Erie, *Rainbow's End*.

Editorial Method

The Cahill correspondence is remarkably readable though the letters contain spelling errors typical of Civil War correspondence. Margaret's letters have slightly more spelling errors than Thomas's, but none are so egregious as to significantly detract from the content of the letters or distract any potential readers. It is interesting to see that her spelling improves significantly over the course of the war. That said, I have chosen to not make any corrections to the spelling in the correspondence. In the rare instance where the word is confusing, I have inserted the correct word in brackets. Where words are unreadable, typically due to the condition of the letters, I have noted the reason in brackets. I have also chosen to not insert "[*sic*]" within the documents as this would become tedious and would disrupt the flow of the letters to a degree that would ultimately detract from their readability. However, neither Margaret nor Thomas used punctuation in any consistent way, and they rarely separated their thoughts into readable paragraphs. Because some of these letters read in a Faulknerian manner, I chose to incorporate paragraph breaks and punctuation in an effort to delineate thoughts and ideas as they occur in order to clarify these for the reader. With the exception of these issues, the letters were transcribed in full and as accurately as possible.

Footnotes introduce historical figures, important members of the regiment, and significant events that help clarify the narrative. In most cases, soldiers were identified from the original muster and descriptive rolls of the Ninth Connecticut, and I provide rank and company for reference. I have avoided footnotes where Thomas explains who the person was. Furthermore, there are times where both Thomas and Margaret discuss people whom they know in New Haven. While there are a few important and recurring characters in the correspondence, many are unidentifiable. Although they are connected to the family, they have little historical relevance and, thus, I chose to not footnote those men and women. Nor did I footnote individuals who appear only once in the entirety of the collection.

I have attempted to provide, in as concise a manner as possible, the place of the Ninth Connecticut within the major military campaigns, but due to the space available I am unable to give as extensive and detailed a military analysis of these events as they warrant. I urge readers to explore the secondary material that I have suggested. Finally, I have chosen not to footnote naval vessels. Simply, the task of identifying civilian transports (of which most of the vessels named in this correspondence are) adds little if anything to the narrative and provides unnecessary notes for the reader to comb through. The one exception that I must point out here, though, is that the *Constitution* that Margaret and Thomas write so often of is not the famous warship but, rather, a civilian steam transport that was pressed into federal service.

I have had the privilege of getting to know the Cahills over the past six years while I transcribed and edited these letters. Very few others have read their correspondence; at the time of writing this, readers number in the single digits. The letters below represent only a selection of the total correspondence. The remainder are available in digital format, housed at California State University, San Bernardino, and are available to interested parties. My goal here was to preserve, as accurately as possible, the experiences of Thomas and Margaret so that the reader may see their lives in much the same way that they saw them during the Civil War over 150 years ago.

CHAPTER 1

Organization

Thomas to Margaret

Camp Chase Lowell Nov 7th 1861

My Dear Wife

We arrived safely at this camp on Tuesday Morning at 10 o clock. we had an awfull time with the Hard Cases on the manny of the Cars had no Lights in them and when they Commenced to hammer one another they could not tell where the blows came from; they smashed the glass in the car windows; and raised the mischief generally: we went through Meriden Hartford and Springfield without stopping and from Springfield to Worcester and to a place 17 miles from here Called Groton Junction where we arrived at 1½ o clock A.M. and remained at that place until 8 o clock on Tuesday morning when we Left for Lowell arriving at 9½ Am we were met at the Cars by Col E. F. Jones[1] of the 26th Mass Regt and after escorting us through the city delivered us into camp pretty well tired out:

and now with reference to Life at this Camp E. F. Jones of the 26th Mass is in Command of the Post and stands on his *Dig.* he is a very strict Disciplinarian and inflicts a verry severe punishment on the Hard Cases. The camp is surrounded by a High Board fence and there is but one gate so that when they get outside it is next for impossible to get in without coming in at that Gate and if they have no Pass or have over staid their Pass they are clapped into the Stocks or on a 32 Pound Bll and Chain clapped on them and nothing is allowed to Prisoners in the Guard House are not allowed

---

1. Col. Edward F. Jones, Twenty-Sixth Massachusetts and colonel of the Sixth Massachusetts (ninety-days) Regiment, would later serve as lieutenant governor of New York from 1886 to 1891. Bowen, *Massachusetts at War*, 944–45; "A Leading Figure in the Civil War: Gen. Edward F. Jones , Who Died in Binghamton Thursday, Aged 85," *Saturday Globe* (Utica, N.Y.), August 18, 1913.

anything to Eat but Bread and Water. I tell you it makes some of the hard Cases open their Eyes when they See the way Prisoners are punished here.

Our Baggage Came on to day and we had it on the Camp at 1 2 o clock m and I am writing this letter on my Patent Desk sitting on your mattress: I shall sleep on the camp to night. I have slept at a Hotel Last night with Dr. Galagher Major Frye.[2] The Dr and Harrall[3] are trying to find a place to Board their wives near the Camp; I do not know How they will succeed. If they find a Place near the camp I wish you would come on and see us. we are not any farther from the center of the city than our New Haven Camp was from our House But it is along walk to under take to get meals at the hotel and Herritty[4] has not got his arrangements to feed the field and Line mess: we are badly off at present for Victuals the Line Officers feed with their men: but they say that the grub is not as good as it was in New Haven.

General Butler gave the Line officers a terrible going over this morning and unless I am verry much mistaken he will train some of them ere Long. he told them among other things that once duty commenced He drank no Liquor and they should not besides a great many other things not at all pleasant.

Kiss Mary[5] and Eddie[6] for me. I am afraid it will be impossible for me to get home as I expected this old Butler and his Commd at this Post are such strict Disciplinearians that I dislike verry much to ask anny Leave of absence so soon after coming here and doubt very much whether I would get it if I did. if I can arrange to have you Come on here I will. Harrall wanted his wife to come on with you. she would stop at New Haven and arrange to stop over night at Springfield. it is getting Late and I am cold sitting in the tent. Seargent Lawler[7] has just arrived from New Haven with Eleven men and tells me he has something in his trunk for me from you when he gets it up to Camp and says he Left you all well and that you are going to New York with Mrs Gallagher no more at present.

from your Loving husband
Thos W. Cahill

---

2. Charles A. Gallagher, regimental surgeon and close friend to Cahill. Maj. Frederick Frye, a New York lawyer by trade, was a captain in the Third Connecticut (ninety-days) Regiment before joining the Ninth Connecticut. Murray, *History of the Ninth Regiment*, 333.

3. Quartermaster William Harrall, of Bridgeport. His name is spelled in a number of different manners throughout this collection. Ibid., 86, 333.

4. Herritty, who appears throughout the correspondence, was a businessman and served as a sutler to the Ninth Connecticut.

5. Cahill's eldest daughter; she was three when Thomas left home.

6. Cahill's second born; he was almost two when the war began.

7. Sgt. John Lawler, Company D.

Margaret to Thomas
Nov 10th 1861

My Dear Husband

I recd your letter on Friday afternoon, I would have answered it at once but not withstanding all you Said about not coming home I could not give you up until the Last Train arrived this Morning. I felt very uneasy about you. I feared you might be suffering with cold and then Such a Storm as we had Last night—but thanks to your Band Leader (I do not know his name) I feel very different now. he called within the Last hour and gave me very satisfactory news about you.

He told me you had a Stove in your Marque and two windows, how very Stilishe I am very glad you have a stove. I hope you will not Spare the fuel.

I went to New York on Wednesday Morning. I came home on Friday. I bought you some nice blankets and a very Sash. I hope you will Like it. and a pair of gloves and a pair of Box Spurs. those I will bring to Mr Murphy[8] and if he cannot put them in those Boots you left to be mended I will have him Make you a new pail—Mr Widmen[9] Paid me $25,50 cts last night-

Now about the OM Society.[10] I wish I knew what to do. Smith came here while I was in New York and Said the Insurance had runout. I saw Mr Geory last night he said James Cannon told him he had made it all right. What does he mean?

I went to the Bank yesterday. they told me I would Lose three Months interest—that would be too gratifing to their Candidate for Treasurer J. Harry if you can hold on with Safty until January or So—I have just heard that Mrs Galagher and Harralls Wife were going to Lowell in the morning that they have a very nice Place to go too in a private family. this I *heard*. they have not let me know any of their arrangements up to now.

5 oClock P.M Sunday

I will do nothing towards going until I hear from you again—the Children are not very well. they were quite sick Last week. I asked them what

---

8. Murphy was a shoemaker in New Haven.

9. The Cahill's renter. His name may actually have been William E. Wightman.

10. This likely refers to the O'Mahony Society of New Haven. John O'Mahony, a veteran of the 1848 Young Ireland uprising, traveled to the United States in 1858, where he was tasked by the head of the Fenian movement (known as the Irish Republican Brotherhood in Ireland) with organizing Irish Americans who were devoted to the cause of Irish nationalism. Miller, *Emigrants and Exiles*, 335–36.

I should say to Papa they said, tell him to come home. I hope I will hear from you tomorrow. I will send your Shirts and all the other things with Mr Band Leader on Wednesday. I will go to the Post Office with this now so that you may get tomorrow.

from your Affectionate Wife

M. E. Cahill

P.S you did not make any mention about your Cold I hope it is Leaving you M.C.

Thomas to Margaret

On Board Steamship Constitution[11]
Harbor of Portland State of Maine
Nov 22 1861. 8 O clock AM

My Dear Wife

I avail myself of the ships coming to anchor to enable me to drop you a few Lines simply to anounce myself the Dr and all hands able to eat a hearty breakfast after one of the sickest nights Ever put in by Mortal men. I did not believe save the ships crew that there was a dozen men aboard ship that were not sea sick. we had a verry rough Passage from Boston which port we left at 1 oclock P.M. yesterday arriving at this Port at 1 o clock this morning. I do hope we shall not have annother attack. the Dr held out Bravely Laughing at all hands and prescribing all sorts of ridiculous remedies but he had to come down at last. the Poor Chaplain was terrible sick But all right this morning: he goes ashore this morning to communicate with the Bishop of Portland[12] with reference to the Maine Regt.

I have not left the ship since I saw you. I have had a Busy time stealing Every opportunity to run our Camp Equipage and private Baggage on Board. the 26th Regt had such an Everlasting low of Equipage and Baggage that when I looked out on the dock I made up my mind that we stood a poor chance of getting our stuff on Board unless by strategy. so I set my men at work running our stuff on Board at Every Possible chance and finally succeeded in getting Everything that was brought to the dock

---

11. This does not refer to the famous USS *Constitution*, "Old Ironsides," but to a civilian steam transport.

12. Bishop David W. Bacon, the Diocese of Portland's first bishop. Byrne, *History of the Catholic Church*, 541.

on Board. not so the 26th they Left a Large quantity behind and Col
Jones was Like a crazy man. the rest of the material will be forwarded by
a sailing vessel which will sail in a verry few days. Quarter Master Harrall
I shall leave behind at Boston to see the rest of our Equipment being obtained and forwarded. you can write to him and send that check or note
payable to his order for me direct to Lieut W. H. Harrall Quarter Master
9th Regt C.V. and he will get gold for it and bring it on to me that is if
you have not forwarded it to the address of Capt Proctor.

there is another gentleman on Genl. Butlers Staff you might communicate in the absence of Capt Proctor in case he should be absent that
is Capt Haggerty. it would be well for you to Look up the List of officers
of genl Butlers staff. it was published shortly after we went to camp. it
will give you the titles of the officers and if you fail to hear from one
you can try another. I will write you again at the first opportunity. I have
not yet ascertained our destination as we sail under sealed orders. we
take the Maine regt on Board here. I do not think of anything more at
present and must hurry up as the Quartermaster is waiting to take this
letter. I wish you would answer Father Harts[13] Letter for me. I will take
any opportunity I may meet at sea to write you. try and make yourself
as comfortable as possible. give my love to all enquiring friends Kiss the
Babies for me.

I remain your loving husband
Thos W. Cahill

Thomas to Margaret

On Board the Steam Ship Constitution Sunday Nov 24th
6 O'Clock P.M.

My Dear Wife
I take the opportunity of the Steamers arriving to Fortress Monroe[14]
where we expect to be tomorrow afternoon to drop you a few lines. We
left Portland at midnight on Friday and are now about 300 miles due
south of New Haven and perhaps 50 odd miles from Land with a south
west course for Fortress Monroe. we have had a head wind all last night
and to day I Eat the first hearty meal since we started at noon to day. ditto

13. Father Matthew Hart, parish priest of Saint Patrick's Church, New Haven, and close
friend to the Cahills.
14. Fortress Monroe stood at the tip of the Yorktown Peninsula in Virginia.

with the chaplain who ocupies a state room with myself and the doctor: the doctor has not been sick at all: but the chaplain was able to eat his dinner and I hope to be able to eat my supper and shall stop writing untill after supper and enjoyed it hugely if it stays down all night.

have no means of ascertaining our destination yet we go into Fortress Monroe for orders and to take on Board our Brigadier now Col Phelps[15] of Vermont formerly a Col in the U.S. army. I think this sets pretty hard on Col Jones our present commander whom we supposed was to be in Command. I cannot say that I care as he has not impressed me verry favorably and he is certainly not verry popular. I think he feels this severely as he has been acting Brigadier all through the war having always 2 or 3 regiments under his command:

there are several Ladies on Board Mrs Col Jones Mrs Lieut Col Farr[16] Mrs Major Lawtill[17] Mrs Major Frye now what they are going to do the Lord knows, I forgot there is also Mrs Doctor Hooken. they will most likely have to trudge back alone. pleasant aint it, if we should be placed permanently in garrison it might be all right but at present. I think them decidedly in the way. we have also 2 or three reporters on Board one for the N Y herald one for the Times the *Captains Clerk* and another. so you will probably have a graphic account of our voyage between them. they will probably continue with us so you will have lots of news.

I wish you would pack up all the Back numbers of the times and some Local papers and send them on: If any men want to join us tell them to go the Assistant Quarter Master Foster in Sheffields Building and he will send them on to the Depot at Camp Chase where we Left one company to recruit for the Regt under Capt Nelson.[18] I directed him to send home the N Haven Flags as we have received our magnificent state colors. I must finish this scrawle as the motion of the vessel while I write is verry disagreeable. Adress my Love to all Kiss the Babies for me.

I take hold again as I hate to send you any waste paper. I hardly know what to say. we have splendid Living on Board the Boat thus far for the officers; Both Regts Mess together. I forgot to tell you that after going to Portland we did not take the Maine Regt on board. I do not know the

---

15. Col. John W. Phelps of the First Vermont Infantry, a West Point graduate and captain in the U.S. Army, became colonel of the First Vermont in May 1861 and was promoted to brigadier general soon after. Hargrove, *Black Union Soldiers in the Civil War*, 62; Oakes, *Freedom National*, 220–23.

16. Lt. Col. (later Maj.) Evarts W. Farr was with the Eleventh New Hampshire.

17. No one with this name served in the Union army during the Civil War.

18. Capt. John H. Nelson, Company K.

official reason but myself and Lieut Col Farr of the 26th were deputed to Examine the further capacity of the Ship for carrying another regt and we made up our minds that we had not room for another regt and so reported. I do not know whether we take anny more troops at Monroe or not. we might take 3 or four hundred but thats all possible. I feel ashamed of the Equipment of our troops along side of the Mass men. the contrast is too bad and is a shame to the state. I made requisitions on the Genl Govt before I Left Boston and hope we have a good supply one of these days.

Again good Bye

Shall write you by every appt

Thos W. Cahill

N.B. If Johny Reillys[19] [mother] calls to hear about him he is well. he sleeps in my state room and is all right. the same is true of all the men and officers saving of course Sea Sickness. the most of the officers are sea sick some of them severely but no danger gravely. OBrien[20] and D Carroll[21] all down at once Leaving the Co without a commissioned officer.

The above was written expecting to be at anchor at Fortress Monroe Early this Monday morning where we are at this 10½ o clock PM at anchor about nine miles from the mouth of the chesapeak. these vagabond secesh having put out the lights along shore. we are laying off waiting for Daylight. The Dr and Myself are laughing over the wry faces of the Lady Passengers when the Purser of the ship informed them that they must be paid for as Cabin Passengers at the Rate for Bound alone of 2 dollars per day. I tell you the Major and Lady are sour enough over it:

this is a fine night and all hands are enjoying themseleves finely and all well without an exception. we do not know yet what our destination is and I will keep this open to the last minute to Learn all I can and let you know after all. perhaps you will Learn before we do where we are going we may possibly go ashore here and wait for more troops to come on to

---

19. He was likely referring to the parents of Pvt. John Riley, Company A.

20. First Lt. (later Capt.) Lawrence O'Brien, Company B, was a twenty-two-year-old mason from County Tipperary. The Cahills and the O'Briens were family friends, and Thomas and Lawrence served together in the Emmet Guards, one of New Haven's two Irish militia companies in the years before the war. Papers of Lawrence O'Brien, held in the private collection of Jeffery Cook, Trumbull, Conn.; database of Fenian Militia Units compiled from the weekly column titled "Military Matters," which appeared in the newspaper the *Phoenix* (Brooklyn, N.Y.) between 1858 and 1860; Murray, *History of the Ninth Regiment*, 346–47.

21. Second Lt. Daniel Carroll, Company B.

us send me what information you can cut it in small pieces about the military of our state particularly the 12th Regt CV which we expect to join us.

I forgot to say to you I want the Old Heller[22] to send me ½ a Large and small Buttons to S Button Letter T. One of Coat Buttons come of last night. I have just signed an allotment Bill Leaving 120 dollars to be drawn by you this.

6½ o clock A.M. Tue No 26

We are just turning the ships Bows to shore after laying at anchor all night. it is a Lovely morning. I wish you would send on my Fatigue Coat. I begin to feel the need of one. am sorry did not leave my Flannel Collars on and Tell Heller that the buttons are coming off the Trays of my great coat. I am not certain but I had better have more than ½ dozen buttons perhaps 2 dozen. I have but a few minutes as we are in sight of the Fort and the Letters are going ashore. so good by and god bless you Kiss the Babies and my Love to All Enquiring Friends.

　　Your Loving Husband
　　Thos W. Cahill

Thomas to Margaret

At Sea off Savannah on Board Transport Ship Constitution
November 29, 1861

My Dear Wife

I commence this Letter in the hope that we may by some chance Speak some passing vessel; although since leaving Portland it is a singular fact that we have not run near Enough to a vessel to Speak her and although in the direct tract of the coast and to India trade and of a naval expedition to Port Royal[23] we have not seen a Blockading vessel;

on the all important Subject of our destination. the seals were broken on the 2d day out from Monroe and our destination is Ship Island fifty miles from New Orleans. our object to seize and hold possession of the Island and fortify it. this will take a long time. I scarcly think we can do anything on the Main Land; not the least for a Long time. this Island has been partly fortified by the government and at the breaking out of the

----

22. It is possible this refers to Jacob Heller, a New Haven clothier.
23. Port Royal, S.C.

Rebellion the Rebels attacked the place and drove out the artisans and Laborers and burned down the Quarters and houses. the Island is said to be from 7 to 12 miles in length and from ¼ of a mile to a mile in width.

I think the men will get a long nicely this winter as they will be at their usual work digging and delving. if the Poor fellows on the sewer were out I think they would have a good winters work, and Safe Quarters as the fleet cover the island with their guns and it is so narrow that the Rebels can get no foothold once we get possession. this is not verry glorious occupation but reasonably safe;

we are now enjoying July weather and shall have it still warmer as we run into the hot waters of the gulf stream on the coast of Florida. We shall probably double the capes tomorrow, I like our new general verry much and am Exceedingly Satisfied with the change though the other Col is not. I do not know what we are to do with our heavy clothing thought we shall need them nights but I wish I had a light blue flannel Blouse for the day time with shoulder straps; though if you have ordered the one from Heller done mind as that will be enough;

Send me the little Pamphlet Book on surveying "Weales Series" in the Book Case. I am sorry Patrick Maher[24] did not come out as the peculiar work before us would be Exactly in his Line and I think give him a chance for Promotion. I dont Know as there are anny masons among the Mass Regt although we Expect a strong force of masons and Laborers and Carpenters with Ready Made Houses from Boston. we are now ascertaining the number of masons and Carpenters in our Regt so that if necessary we may use them: we have nine stowe aways on board Little shavers from 9 to 13 years they have given me a deal of annoyance as the Mass Col is continually calling them my troops I suppose they will be sent home.

We are now 3 oClock PM Sunday Nov 30, 30 miles south of Carysfort Reef light house. the shores of Florida appear magnificent as seen from the ship it appears nearly one immensely Lusciousnious and Magnificent forest: what a country for such the Inhabitants. on the left we have the distant Reefs of the W Indies. the Water is as a Mill Pond we shall double the Florida Capes to night and Expect to Reach our destination on Tuesday. the perspiration is pouring out of Every one of us. I write with all the Cabin doors and windows open. I have been obliged to throw off my Drawers and retreat to one of my flannel shirts;

---

24. Patrick Maher was a friend of the Cahills and served with Thomas before the war in the Emmet Guards. He gained a commission as major in the Twenty-Fourth Connecticut. Murray, *History of the Ninth Regiment*, 23.

We see Lots of Queer Looking fish of Every description and Birds I must go on deck to look at a Light said to be seen forward: The Light seen is Sombrero Key Light; and we are running down to Key West: it is a Lovely day on Deck the dolphins Flying fish and sword fish are playing about the ship in great style. every few moments some monster of the Deep pokes his nose out of the water and Looking at us pokes down again: we are now nearly 2 weeks on Board ship and since we got over our sea sickness we are verry Busy making out our returns and it would seem as though we never would get through all the writing we have to do. it is a never ending job of Book Keeping.

I am going to try to find a matter Enough to fill this Letter for you though I really do not know what to write about but I will keep it open and work a little from time to time as this vessel will probably be the one to take back the Letter: so good bye for this time:

9 o Clock P.M. Monday Dec 2d.

I snatched a few moments to say we are about opposite Pensacola and some 300 miles from Ship Island where we expect to arrive tomorrow night. Such a job as I had to day the Genl called upon me to account for 16 or 18 young Ragged vagabonds that have been hanging around us in New Haven and Ever since and I have been 3 days trying to get our Captain to pick them up and wee finally mustered 16 of them. I had to take 2 of them and the Dr 2 more of them as servants. 1 to the chaplain 1 to the Lt Col 1 to the Major 1 to L O Brien 1 to the Adt 2 for Drummers and the Rest for Drummers. I took one Thos McGreen whose mother Lives in Wallace St. the other John Dunn is from Danbury. I do not know what I shall do for clothes for them and they are all filth and Rags but in as much as I must have something to answer to the name of servants on the Pay Roll perhaps it is just as well as I certainly shall not pay them much. I forgot to say that the general took 2 of them himself, I do not know what our chaplin will do for a Bed he has nothing to lay on;

This is a warm sultry Evening. Good Bye Kiss the Babies for me and I will keep the Rest for a Description of tomorrow and with the help of God of our Landing. did you answer Father Harts Letter for me? give my respects to the gentlemen of the city. tell Johnny Rileys mother and friends that he is well and hearty as is Every Body Else thank God on Board.

2 oClock PM Dec 3

have just sighted Ship Island. all Excitement on Board: the Weather has changed to a delightful coolness: we shall have to hurry up now to get ready to Disembark the reporters from the Herald are busy taking notes; there appears to be men of war Laying off the Island.

4 OClock PM.

Dropped anchor off East End of Ship Island. the men of war are the gun Boats R R Cuylen and Massachusetts. they have had a busy time Lately. they have some 150 to 200 thousand dollars worth of Molasses, Sugar, and turpintine filed upon the Beach. they have 2 Steam Boars 2 Schooners and several small craft also Laid up here prizes. there is a sort of a Fort on this End of the Island and a Light House. the Keepers house is the only one on the Island. there is a no wood on this End but the other is apparently well wooded. I will have time enough to write you of the geography of the Island and will try to describe our Surrounding tomorrow. Major Frye I have detailed with Lieut O Brien and fifty men to go on shore at 6 o clock in the morning to pitch tents so good by for to night.

10 O 'Clock P M Thursday Dec 5th.

after 2 days hard Labor have got our camp so that the men are under Canvass but such a spot was never seen for a camp. just imagine a collection of snow drifts from five to twenty feet high a perfectly white fine sand that would make the fortune of Michael Healy[25] being precisely such as he peddles; we had a terrible job of getting our stuff up from the Landing place as it had to be carried upon the mens shoulders through the fine sand a good half mile and was verry hard work: we must now go to work to Level down the Snow Drifts so as to be able to move around in our company Street: I am afraid the white sand may effect our eyesight from the glare of the sun in hot weather, the End of the Island we are on is a barren Sand Spit but the west End is covered with Wood and there is said to be plenty of Raccoon and wild hogs so called. there is 40 or 50 head of Cattle left here by the secesh. Capt McCarten[26] returned from a foraging Expedition there this afternoon and reports finding plenty of oysters in a lagoon he thinks hundreds of Bushels. I think I will ascertain the truth of this to morrow if not to night. I send you some tickets taken on Board a Rebel Steamer which has performed good service in landing us from the Big Ship.

---

25. This was likely forty-five-year-old Michael Healy of the Fifth Ward of New Haven, who worked as a trench man in that city.

26. Capt. Michael McCarten, Company C.

I have just heard that our commanding genl Phelps has been issuing some infernal nonsense in a proclamation he has posted up on Board the ship.[27] I have not see it yet but Father Mullen is down on it and I think I shall be if my opinion is asked on it—it as said to be A La Fremont-[28] The naval officers on this station say that he will not be allowed to publish it:

I do not find our clothes much too heavy. not as much as I expected. it is delightful weather now I wish you would send me pair of green glasses merely as a precaution. I wish I knew how Barney and the horses are getting along. I am afraid they will have a Long voyage. the Maine Regt having not yet arrived: Let me know all about everything that is going on at home. it is getting verry Late and I am verry tired so good night and God Bless you and the Babies Kiss them for me.

   your affectionate husband
   Thos W Cahill

PS Tell Patrick Maher I Expect several Long letters from him.

Margaret to Thomas

Undated [likely early December 1861]

My Dear Husband

I met with Wm Sperry the Council Member he enquired for you very kindly and said he would write to you soon.

Our friend P. Maher is in a pick of trouble trying to find sympathy. he thinks he was not well treated by you that he could be street commissioner if you choose to use any influence for him. him and myself had a pretty sharp talk on the matter. I will not repeat it to you now it is too *small* but you would be suprised to hear all the nonsense has been put into words since you left us.

---

27. An outspoken abolitionist, Gen. John Phelps issued one of the first emancipation proclamations of the war from Ship Island in the winter of 1861–62, calling for "FREE LABOR AND WORKINGMEN'S RIGHTS." Such language was at odds with the early war policy of the Lincoln administration regarding the "Union War" and created considerable animosity among the troops and at home. *Official Records*, series 1, vol. 17, 18–20.

28. Rev. Daniel Mullen, first chaplain of the Ninth Connecticut. Gen. John C. Frémont had issued an emancipation proclamation on August 31, 1861, before President Lincoln repudiated it. Frémont's proclamation asserted that "the property, real and personal, of all persons in the State of Missouri who shall take up arms against the United States, or who shall be directly proven to have taken an active part with their enemies in the field, shall be confiscated to the public use, and their slaves, if any they have, are hereby declared free men." McPherson, *Battle Cry of Freedom*, 352–54.

his Father Died about two weeks ago every thing dont seem to be just right. P.M. goes to Mr French to school. he is studying Engineering. his wife and Baby is well I believe. I went to see Jonny Rileys mother. she was very well and glad to hear from him. she thought it strange he did not write to any of them. she came tonight with some stockings to send him and some tobacco. it will be welcome no doubt.

I am sorry I forgot to send a big nedle but I will make up for it by sending him a whole dozen. tell him we do not forget him—

I bought you some glasses today. I hope you will like them. the dull colored glass is highly recommended. I will send you a pair of goggles. I think them a grand invention. I am having you a very nice fatigue cap made if it will only fit.

all the New Haven Banks have suspended special payments. they issue U.S. Notes

altogether. I am sorry I did not have some gold but it is too late now.

Good night My dear Husband it is 11 O Clock P.M. God Bless you and send you safe home to us. it is our constant Prayer, even little Eddys.

Thomas to Margaret

Ship Island Dec 7th 1861

My Dear Wife

I have just this moment Learned 2 o Clock PM that the Constitution Leaves at 4 O Clock PM. So I write to say that we are all well to date; it is exceedingly warm here the men are in their shirt sleeves and bare footed. I have just Distributed the muskets and Equipments to the men.

I am afraid that General Phelps proclamation will make trouble here. I have not seen it but understand that the naval officers denounce it bitterly. have heard some of them myself. Father Mullen is also very bitter against it and says he will denounce it as Containing Sentiments anti Catholic. it is also said that the Massachusetts Regt are very much opposed to it. some of them are threatening to resign. as for myself shall be Cautious in my movements but certainly shall not Endorse Either Abolition or Infidelity on sectarianism. I is a *Little Singular* to say the least of it: That he should have issued such a Proclamation with out Consulting Col Jones or Myself.

Mrs Frye goes home with this and promises to call and see you. the steamer returns in 2 weeks. I hope you are all well. I think of all at home when I have time to think at all. If Mrs Gallagher should want anything in the way of money Please let her have it. the Dr says he would not ask for it and does not know as she wants any; I have allotted you 120 dollars of my Pay and I believe he has done the same. say to her that he is well:

While I write there is a naval engagement going on within sight of the Island. the Little Propellor New London from New London CT seems to have taken a prize from the Rebels and seems to be fighting 3 more of them at the same time. this little craft has taken all the Prizes here and she is only a small craft. the De Soto is Laying off the Deep Water to Cover her and she runs in Gallantly to the shore and if she is not whipped she will bring them off. I think of nothing now to say to you. Do your best and I will do try with Gods blessing to do the same. Kiss the Babies for Me.

    Yours Truly
    Thos W Cahill

Thomas to Margaret

Ship Island, Mississippi Sound
Christmas Day [December 25, 1861]

My Dear Wife

I take up my pen to day as a memorial to the day. we had an Early mass at Six o Clock and another at 10½: Just at this time I received an invitation from Flag Officer McKean[29] to go on Board the Niagara. We Embarked on a Small Propellor Tug which arrived here from Philadelphia for the Quarter Masters department. the Field and Staff of the two Regiments were present and received with all honors. this ship had just arrived here from Pensacola where she had taken an active part in the recent Bombardment;[30]

I must confess that I had rather a poor opinion of the Artillerry Practice of the rebels when I found that they had only hit this monster of a ship in two places during a fire of more than 24 hours continuance with open deck on which were working between 5 and 6 hundred men. the shot that struck did not penetrate her side and not a man was injured:

---

29. Flag Officer William W. McKean, commander of Gulf Blockading Squadron, 1861–62. *Official Records*, series 1, vol. 4, 16.

30. This two-day bombardment of Pensacola, occurring on November 9–10, 1861, was part of Confederate efforts to take the federal stronghold Fort Pickens, which commanded the mouth of Pensacola Bay. Tucker, *Civil War Naval Encyclopedia*, 1:231–32.

It is a lovely day and if we were among green hills and meadows instead of Barren Sand Banks it would be considered splendid weather for
Early September at home. we feel Rather lonesome however thinking of
friends at home wondering what they are saying about us and whether
any one is left in New Haven: We had rather a good dinner to day considering our circumstances. we draw our provisions from the Field and
Staff mess from the Commissary of the Brigade as provided by the Regulations at their Cast at the place of purchase so that we Live at a fair rate
of cost for the prime necessarys. Prime Pork at 10.50 per bl Hams at 9
ct per pound Sugar 9 cts Coffee 17 Flour 6/50 and all articles of food
furnished the soldier for Rations at Lower rates than you can purchase
them at Retail in New Haven.

Of Course we have no delicacies or Luxuries except some 15 lbs of
Dried Apples. We can get Preserved Meats and Poultry and manny other
Luxuries Put up in Cans from the Brigade Suttler: at an extragant Price
but I am glad to say that our mess are all of them up to this time apparently as anxious to save their pay as myself so that we get along verry well
on our Camp Fare and are all in excellent health and heavier in flesh
than when we Landed: The men are also in the most Excellent health and
spirits. indeed they have improved so much that I can scarcely recognize
a great many of them as being the hard looking and worse acting cases of
Camp Welch: they have possitely not had a glass of rum since they came
on the Island and it will be next to impossible for them to get a Drop
while they remain here; only imagine a month of perfect sobriety among
this crowd and no prisoner in the guard house no insubordination and
no trouble only to Eat their rations and the most splendid weather.

A Prefect Paradise of a sand Spit is it not but it must be a mighty hot
spot in the summer time and I hope you have sent me the Fatigue Coat
as my Dress Coat is getting the worse for the wear and I shall need some
new fatigue Pants and a Dress Pants. we have not heard anything from
Harrall yet and the King Fisher has been lying here two weeks and over
when we might have had our Letters and our Materials for the men had
it been put on board of her as he should have done.

No more this time.

from your loving husband
T. W. Cahill

Margaret to Thomas

December 26th, 1861

My Dear Husband

Will you Say? Why did you not write to me on Christmass Day: Well to tell you the plain truth I was not able. I felt so nervous and lonely I could not—I meant too but failed in the undertaking—I hope you Spent a merry Christmass or a happy one at least and all the poor creatures who were away from their houses.

I finished my last letter to you telling you I would try to Send your Coat with all possible haste. I learned through the Daily Papers that the rest of Gen Butlers expedition was to leave Boston on Thursday next and Mr William Donnes came to the house on Wednesday evening and said if we sent you things by express he thought they reach Boston in time but that seemed almost impossible to me. I could not trust this by express so I went to Chappel Street in the morning bought a small valiese and Packed in all I could make it hold and started off for Boston. I reached the great city at 9 O Clock P.M. just imagine me in a strange place at that hour of the night. but I did not feel at all uneasy about myself. if I could only accomplish the object in view all right—very fortunately I had no trouble in finding a hack and told the Driver to take me to the Revere House.

it must have been near or quite 10 o Clock when he got there for the outer doors were closed but I gained admittance—asked for a room and Supper—obtained both and was treated with great kindness or imagined I was—after Supper I went to the Hotel office to asertain if any of the Genls Staff were Staying there and my quickest means of Shiping your valuables. my first question was answered very satisfactory to me. the Clerk says there is Mayjor Strong standing by that Desk I will send to him (but that rascle I heard from him before the words died on *his* lips. I had introduced myself to Mayjor S. he told me I had been misinformed about them going out so soon that they were likly to remain in Boston for some time to come but he said they were sending out transports vessels every day and that he would send on your valiese the first opertunity. he heard at that time the Constitution had arrived at Port Royal and that was your destination. he told me that too was false. he laughed and said you were going to a far better place but did not name it. it seemed very cruel to me to think I was speaking to a person who knew where you were at that time but could not tell me. but I suppose he could not or he would. but how are you going to open the valiese? I have the key.

I let Patrick Maher read your last letter. he said he would write so you would get a letter when the Constitution went Back to Ship Island. James Wrin said he would write to you. I hope they will for my letter will not be the most interesting. the Children are very well now. Mary has just recovered from the Measles. She got along nicly and we think her out of danger now. Eddy is growing fin[e]ly. he is a Lovely Boy. he talks very plain. he would keep you Laughing from Morning until night he makes such odd speeches. I wish you could hear him pray for you and after his meals before he leaves the table he says Thank God for my good dinner God Bless My Dear Father and send him safe home to me, and Jack[31] too, he made me feel very sad the other day he dressed himself up in *style of course* two or three shawls twils pieces of new flanell and various other garments. he came to me and Said good bye Mamy I going down South to the war to My Father—I could write all day and not tell you half of his funny tricks. he is standing beside me now with a piece of mourning calico on his shoulders he says he is going to Church. Mary enjoys herself with him. any thing she wants and is afraid to get herself all she has to do is to tell Eddie. shes sure to get it if its within his reach.

Larry Cooney spent Christmass evening with us. he Looks fine. Sent his Best wishes to you—Mr Connors[32] Came to see us before Christmass. he brought me two Bushels Potatoes 1 Bushel Aples two nice fat chickens dont you think he was kind—he went to Hulls and Bought me one half of a small *pig* and Salted it down for me so you may feel easy about our Rashions. I wish I knew all about yours—Send me all the information you can about Sending out things to you—I can find out very little here—I heard yesterday that the 12th Regt were not going out for 4 weeks Longer—I hope you have read all I sent you ere this and my letters too. if you need more Stockings or any thing else let me know in your next letter—I called on Father Smith[33] a week ago to have him remember the 9th and particularly yourself in the Mass on Christmass Day. he told me to send his kind regards to you and Father Mullen—Father Sheridan[34] too said his second Mass on that Same Day for you—I was not able to go see

---

31. Jack was Thomas's horse.

32. Richard Connors did not serve in the Ninth Connecticut, but he appears time and again over the course of this correspondence. It is clear that he was a family friend of the Cahills and lived in New Haven.

33. Rev. John Smith of St. John's Church in New Haven. *Sadliers' Catholic Dictionary and Ordo*, 113.

34. Sheridan was the Pastor at Wallingford, Conn. Rockey, *History of New Haven Country, CT*, 1:407.

Father Obrien[35] but he enquired of Michael Fahy[36] about you and Said he would like one of your Photographs. I sent him one by M.Fahy I wish when you have time you would write to Michael. he has come very often to hear from you or mention him in your next letter to me—I have not answered F. Harts letter but I will try too. Mother Bernard[37] had a letter from him latly his health is not much improved I should judge from the tone of his writing—the weather here is about as usual at this Season— to day is bitter Cold the ground is covered with Ice and Snow. the poor Street Commissioner Caught it in this mornings paper his name is Brix I suppose you know him—

The letter carrier brought you a Large Book from Washington. I believe it had J. English on the cover listed your name and address. its title is Military Commission to Europe in 1855–1856– Report of Mayor-Major Alfred Mordecai of the Ordnance Department. do you wish it sent on to you—I would like to coppy this letter but I fear I cannot I have so much pain in my arms it is difficult for me to write at all I must adopt your plan write a little at a time I have suffered considerable with Rehumatism Since the hard frost came—What you Cant read guess at. I think you will be able to come soon what I mean. I wish you had those green glasses. I hope you will try for our Sakes to take good care of yourself. Nelson sent those Colors home to me. if you only know what an excitement they created. the Morning Courrier Published "The Colors of the 9th were Sent home and directed to the Col's Wife" that was enough. Before night they had it round the street that your Sword and all your Papers had come that you had resigned—was dead—and finely that the 9th was no more. such a time as he had with the poor woman—I will now conclude with repeating your Babies Pray in God Bless and send you Safe home to us.

 your loving wife
 M. E. Cahill

p.s. the Children were very much pleased with those [word unreadable] you sent them.

---

35. Father E. J. O'Brien, pastor of St. Mary's Church in New Haven. *Collections of the New Haven Colony Historical Society*, 21; Rockey, *History of New Haven Country*, 319.

36. It is likely that Michael Fahy is a relative of Pvt. John Fahey, Company H.

37. Most likely a nun in the order of the Sisters of Mercy, who ran the parochial school at St. Patrick's Parish, *Sadliers' Catholic Directory and Ordo*, 203.

Thomas to Margaret

Ship Island Dec 30, 1861

My Dear Wife:

I have just mailed 2 letters to you by the Rhode Island and I learn at this Late hour 9 o Cl PM that she may not sail until noon to morrow so I drop you a few more Lines. you will now if this letter gets on Board have 3 sets of Letters by her of different dates. The first when she stopped here on her way to Texas one I put in to day and this one takes its Chance:

4 Negroes came on to the Island from the main land last night. they reported that the people over there are driving all the negroes into the swamps many miles from the shore and that they are in great trouble manny being in favor of laying down their arms. This afternoon the Steamer Water Witch came in towing a French War Vessel she had run into and knocked her Engines all to pieces so she to tow her in and she will have to be towed to Key West or Havana for repairs, no news of Harrall yet, but I hear that there are two square rigged vessels standing in towards the Land and it may be him at last. I hope so for I am anxious to hear from home, we have a rumor here that England has declared war against us and is Coming down upon us: This is the most confounded place to learn anny news in though if I had papers I would have no time to read them. but we are anxious to hear from home.

our men are some of them suffering for want of shoes and under clothes. those infernal Quartermasters of Connecticut. I only wish it may come in my way to take a burn at them some time, we have a lot of new Knapsacks and Haversacks plenty of woolen and Rubber Blankets and pantaloons but a scarcity of shoes Drawers undershirts and Dress Coats and over coats though I have recd the Bill of Lading for them and Expect them with Harrall if he ever Comes. I begin to think I do not care so the goods comes whether he does or not though perhaps he is not to blame. Johnny wants you to tell his mother that he is well and happy. I have another little sharer named Tom McGuire of Wallace.

Our men are beginning to look like soldiers since we got our new muskets and I am really impressed myself at their decided improvement. I am working hard to get ahead of the 26th and have the Concert to think we Can. the men begin to think so too. we can average more balls in the target than them now as the main guard gives every morning after guard mounting you must apologize for me to my numerous friends particularly to Patrick Maher and William Geunz for not writing as I cannot possibly find time to do so. it is now going on twelve o clock and to morrow we are to have a grand review inspection and be mustered for reporting to Washington for payment. it certainly seems as if I never would get through all the work. no one can conceive the amount of reading writing and talking it takes to handle a regiment like ours. the company officers here working like beavers the last week may out their muster rolls in hopes to be able to get them off by the Rhode Island but she cannot wait for them. Good by and God bless you. granting you a happy new year. Kiss the Babies for me.

    Your Loving Husband
    Thos W. Cahill

CHAPTER 2

"A Prefect Paradise of a sand Spit"

January–February 1862

Thomas to Margaret

Ship Island
Jan 7th 1862

My Dear Wife

another mail I hear Leaves here tomorrow for the north. a navy mail
I suppose: We have had a mail here with a few letters and papers to the
19th of December from New Haven and the latest I have had was Nov
25th nearly a month behind; this mail Came by one of the new gunboats
from New York. these mails are sent to the Naval Lyceum which I believe
is at the Navy Yard Brooklyn. this mail was noticed in the Courier of N.
Haven on the Morning of the 18th Dec. I wish you would look out for
these occasional mails as they frequently furnish the most certain and
rapid means of Communication with the Gulf. there are to be 20 or thirty
of them the gun boats sent down here:

We have the N York Herald of Dec 19th containing a severe but in my
opinion well deserved Editorial on our Brigadier Genls Proclamation:
I do not know when anything has occurred which has caused me more
annoyance than the issuing of that proclamation and it came near getting us into difficulty too as Father Mullen took him Sharply to task for
it in a well written letter: A few days after receiving which he sent for me
and we had a beautiful rehearsal over it. he threatened to Court Martial
Father Mullen which was more than he could do as it turned out; but him
and I had it up and down for 2 hours and that was the End of it: what
papers we have seen sustains the views expressed by the Army and Navy
officers here towards it: it is pronounced a most senseless and bigotted
production: in other respects the Old Man is very gentlemanly and has
been very obliging and kind to us instructing the officers in the manner

of making out the multitiudinous reports which the regulations Call for and which are a confounded tourment not to use a harsher word: but he is I am afraid a good deal of an old "Cromwellian" as his figure and speech indicates. I think he is somewhat of a monomaniac.

The news of the tremendous row being picked up in England about the Trent affair[1] causes no small share of anxiety here as we should be verry much exposed here in Case of a war and would be liable to have our supplies cut off which would leave us in a bad fix for Provisions: If I had thought of this in time I would not have sent you the little native pig. I am afraid he will hardly be able to stand the cold climate and a sea voyage. I sent him in Care of Tom Fitzgbbon[2] in the Kingfisher. on the 5th Fitzgibbon came on in hopes to fill a vacancy which he thought might occur or that he might be appointed Commissary. no vacancy has occured yet and a Commissioned Commissary is not allowed so he was disapointed in his office seeking and is now going home to see if the governor will Employ him to recruit for the regt.

We are badly in need of recruits but I do not see how he could do much towards getting them. it is all right though if he gets a chance to Pick a bit Herritty has finally got his trunk out here horses and all right but he has no stock of anny account and there is almost a tobacco famine here now. the health of the regt is verry good. there are only 6 in the hospital and 12 treated in their Quarters. none of them serious. the 26th regt however Lost a man yesterday. he died of Typhoid fever: and is being buried while I write. Father Mullen is attending the funeral and I am afraid will get back, wet as the rain has been pouring down heavey for the last half hour and they have gone up the Island some ways. the 26th seem to have twice the amount of sick that we have: this cannot be attributed to the Care or kindness bestowed upon us as there is probably fifty men in the regt without a shoe to their feet or an overcoat or an undershirt. but the Lord and good constitutions stands by us and we get along bravely. the men are in good spirits and dont trouble themselves about annything. give my Respects to all friends and Kiss the Babies for Me:

Your Loving Husband
Thos W. Cahill

---

1. The Trent Affair occurred on November 8, 1861, when the federal warship USS *San Jacinto* stopped the English vessel *Trent* and removed Confederate foreign diplomats James Mason and John Sidwel. Jones, *Union in Peril*, 80–83.

2. First Lt. Thomas Fitzbgibbon, Company G.

Thomas to Margaret

Ship Island Jan 7th 1862

My Dear Wife

You see that although you have hardly done the fair thing by me in the way of Correspondence that I am in the way of spoiling a good many sheets of paper on my part. Dr Galagher is even worse off than myself as he has not received a Letter since he left: so that the single one I received left me one better than him: I was verry glad you sent me the Postage Stamps as we have none here and I wish you would put some in Everry letter and send letters Enough to keep me supplied: We Expect the steamer Constitution here within a week and if I do not have plenty of letters by her somebody will probably hear from me about it so look out and keep your pen in use.

There is a complete dearth of news here and literally nothing to write about. Father Mullen returned from the funeral beforementioned without being verry wet. he had gotten through the services and was giving them a pretty smart sermon from Issais [Isaiah] when he had to shorten it a bit. he was Mounted and had a smart ride home: he is a gay little man and attends well to his duties and only to that Except when he diverges a little to have a shot at the Brigadier, but he considers that as strictly within his sphere of duty as a soldier of the *Church Millitant* and I do not believe it will be best for the Brigadier to tackle him: Certainly he had better keep his tongue and pen off him: I like him Exceedingly and though we waited long we certainly lost nothing by waiting and certainly if I had the privilege do not know how I could make a better selection. his health which has hiterto been verry poor has since he has come among us been most Excellent notwithstanding rough fare and poor accomadations. he is laboring with marked Effect among us and he does work up and down among the tents checking the men and talking with them at all times. he was greatly scandalized by some of the Hard Cases when he first came here but he has cured all that and thinks they are a fine set of fellows now. I hardly think there was another Clergyman in the states that had a harder Congregation than himself when he took hold but he is a mighty plucky little man and wont back down for trifles and he does talk to them in a Right scholarly and really Eloquent manner in plain tense terms and clear language. he is certainly a model Chaplain and I begin to think he will make it a model regt and I tell you I begin to feel quite proud of the disposed Ninth. If we had another hundred men I would like it much; the men are improving rapidly. I am sorry to say that I cannot say as much for the officers. I am obliged to pitch into them pretty sharply Everry day and have only just commenced. good bye. my Love to all Kiss the Babies for me.

Good night
T. W.Cahill

Thomas to Margaret
Ship Island: Jan 18th 1862

My Dear Wife.

I once more take up my pen. not that I have anny in particular to say: Only that I am Sick and tired of Waiting to hear from home. I feel in better spirrits this Evening however than usual from the fact that the Sloop of War Portsmouth Came into Harbor on Friday and on Board of her was a Son of J. C. Hayden Late Chief of Police in New Haven. he Came on Shore this Afternoon and gave me a register of Dec 3 and 5 and a Courier of Dec 10 and the Captain of the ship sent the General a Herald of Dec 24, 25th and 29th. these I borrowed from him and just returned them

(9 0 Clock P.M.)

My tent has been full all Evening. Dr G Father Mullen the Lieut C[3] and Major took turns Reading them aloud: it was a Rich treat to us All: but that there was nothing in them from New Haven and the the Copies of N H Papers Contained nothing of Interest to us save a list of officers of Cont Regt.

I was verry Glad for one however that there Seems to be Everry chance of the war with England blowing over, not that I would object to having a slap at her on a fair footing but just at present she would have the Country at a tremendous disadvantage and a war with her would place us (down here) in a bad fix as it would inevatibly cut us off from our supplies and we would stand a chance of falling either into the hands of Dixie or John Bull: I have not received a scrap of inteligence from you since Nov 25th and the Dr has not had a single word at all. we have been Expecting the Constitution for 2 Weeks and not a sign of her yet. the Dr

---

3. Lt. John Carroll, Company F.

has the blues terribly and I do not feel all pleasant: It is certainly horrible that with all the ships that are arriving we do not get a single Letter. Manny a Curse both loud and deep is showered upon the heads of those having Charge of our affairs at Boston for not sending our mails down: the Gun Boat Connecticut is hourly Expected but we dare not hope for annything from her in the way of letters:

I hope you have written 2 or 3 dozen so that when they do Come it will make up: if not wobe [woe be] to you as I know well you are a mighty poor correspondent.

the health of our regiment Continues Remarkably good with the Exception of a few old Stagers. There is one Michael Fagan[4] of Bridgeport that we dont Expect to Live and Lackey McPortlnd[5] is rather doubtfull though doing better. we shall probably send home some 8 or 10 old men.

I signed 86 pair of shoes from the Brigade sutler and 216 woolen shirts or Blouses which helped us out. the men are in Excellent Conduct and spirits and improving Rapidly in their drill. they do not look or act much like the men of Camp Welch. the Old General is quite Complimentary in his notices of us lately and he certainly was not prepossesd in our favor at his first view of us as we appeared to a great disadvantage along side of such splendidly Equipped Regiments as the 26th Mass.

This is a mighty dull place for News. We have no Excitements worth notice save the false allarms about the arrival of the Constitution. for my Part I am verry much allarmed about her. our harbour Contains a great manny naval ships and Gun Boats and I do not believe the stories told about vessels running the Blockade. I cannot conceive it possible. some of our own war vessels however are in a bad condition with their machinery. four of the new Gun Boats built at Philadelphia have broken down at this station. Dr Galager and the Quartermaster and the Quartermaster Seargent started away in a flat bottomed boat to take a sail up the Island about 10 O Clock in the Morning and when they tried to get back in the afternoon the tide took them into the currents and they drifted clear over to the other side. they were out all night and got back about 10 o clock next morning being gone 24 hours causing us great anxiety.

I must hurry up this as I must go on a Post Council of Administration in the morning. I write this in the hope of its going in naval store ship "Supply" which is said to Leave for New York in the morning. it may not

---

4. Pvt. Michael Fagen, Company D.
5. Pvt. Lawrence McPortland, Company C.

go for a week yet. we never have the last notice of when they are going or coming. good night. god bless you and the Babies and all at home.

your affectionate husband

Thos W Cahill

Col 9th Regt C.V.

Margaret to Thomas

Jan 23rd 1862

My dear Husband

We have recd news from you at last. I began to think we would have to wait three or four weeks longer for that great old Monster the Constitution to come back to Boston She sailed from there a few days ago and then we were not certain about her destination. If news papers Report be correct, the Public know nothing about where she is going but myself for one of the many hope that some good mind will Send her Spedily to Ship Island.

I think it very likely that your coats and all the things I sent you are on board of her although Major Strong[6] assured me in Boston that he would take charge of your valise and send it to you by the first vessel that sailed. He is one of Gen Butlers Staff.

My dear husband I recd your 3rd letter on Monday Morning and your 4th today Jan 23rd. if you only knew how glad we are to hear from you. you would be well paid for your kindness for writing so many nice long letters to. do write often and tell us how you Look. you speak of every one but yourself not. but we like to hear from all but most particularly about yourself. I understand there is some odd letters come from the 9th by this mail and some very nice ones too. I recd L OBriens. he mentioned too about your sending me a little pig. I hope the little fellow will like the children. well be delighted to see any thing from their Father and something living too it will be grand. I expect we will have the Mayor and common council to see it. L Obrien says that some of your officers are finding some fault with you because you do not tolorate their New Haven Conduct. but he is delighted with your treatment towards them—

---

6. Maj. Gen. George Crocket Strong, who was a Vermont native, served on George B. McClellan's staff before he was transferred to Butler's command and appointed assistant adjutant general of volunteers. Warner, *Generals in Blue*, 483.

I ordered your fatigue and dress pants and your cap and straw hat. they will be ready to send by Saturday or Monday. I will try to fill a box and I hope it will reach you before spring. I called on the Mayor on Monday to tell him I had news. he wished to read your letters I left them with him. he said he would write to you as soon as he found out where to send them. it may seem strange to you but it is true that we cannot learn anything reliable about the mails going from from hear or Boston. I continualy enquire but cannot find out anything to Satisfy me. I hope we will soon have regular mail and then you will get news by the bushel—My Respects to all who may enquire for Me.

yours truly.

M. E. Cahill

Mary has heard that you sent her a little pig and such a time as she is having about it. she says the head and tail shall be Eddys and the rest of it hers. She says you must send her a cow and a horse but a goat will be all Ill ask.

The 13th Regt has not left here yet. Sam McDonnall has enlisted it[n] it. the 14th is going to be quartered in National Hall Olive St. the Select Men here have Commenced to Draft for the State Militia and to furnish men to fill all the Regts ordered for action. Since we have not heard from Father Hart lately he was well when we wrote. I have not answered his letter yet. I do wish you would try and send me a letter to send to him. a few lines and I will finish it—Father Sheridan is well. he comes to see us and to hear from you. I am glad to hear Father Mullen is so well liked. My kind regards to all.

My Love to you.

M. E. Cahill

Thomas to Margaret

Ship Island Mississippi
February 3d 1862

My Dear Wife

almost in despair of Ever hearing from you and our little ones. I again take up pen with the reflection that if I am desperate for not hearing from you it may not be a good reason why you should not hear from me. not a letter yet though vessel after vessel arrives with scattering letters from the others and for privates but not a sylable for me neither from friends nor officials have I heard a sylable. my health continues Excellent the weather is magnificient and while I write a severe thunder storm is raging. summer is coming and last week I rode up the Island and heard the Mocking Birds singing most delicously:

three of our officers have left here within a few days. one of them in a rather disgracefull manner. his name if T. C. Lawler[7] he is a barber a most miserable fellow. Lieut Shaw[8] has been half way sick for some time and was never Calculated for the place. the other was a Cousin of the Lieut Col who got mad at his Captain Coates and thought the old man was not going to get out of his way as fast as he wished. he was sorry before he left but I tell you I do not give these gentlemen a great deal of time to fuss around:

I have written to Patrick Maher about these vacancies so that if he wished to take advantage of it. I have also written to the governor and Adjutant General mentioning also Michael Faheys[9] name but have not *written to him* of it. *tell him* if he cares anything about it I think there will be lots of vacancies. at least it will not be the generals fault if there is not, the truth is they are not fitted for the place by their previous lives.

Lieut O Brien gets along nicely. he has been a little under the weather for a day or two but is out to day. he had a slight cold. Tell Richard Connor that Walt Maloney[10] is behaving splendidly. he is without Exception of the quitest men in the Regt. I tell you this place is the salvation of these men:

I dont think we will have anny fighting out here. we certainly will not unless we have a large number of troops. I think the government intended this move as a *ruse* to draw them down but they do not appear to bite so I think they will be calling us home or Else leave us to garrison this island. for this we are too many for an attack too few. that between the two I do not know what we can do Except to eat our rations which is all we do. we are suffering for clothes but the weather is getting warm and if they do not send us some we can go naked as there is no Ladies on the Island without doing any great harm and they cannot ask us to fight without Clothes. so long as we are well fed we need not care and

---

7. First Lt. Thomas C. Lawler, Company H, was discharged in February 1862. Murray, *History of the Ninth Regiment*, 343.

8. Second Lt. John C. Shaw, Company C, was discharged in February 1862.

9. Likely Michael Fahey, a twenty-six-year-old marble cutter living in the Fifth Ward of New Haven.

10. Pvt. Walter Malony, Company A.

we have three large ovens going on now as a fort Bakery who sends out 2,000 Rations of Fresh Bread Every other day. So we fare pretty well on this service.

I have a piece of that Cake you brought to Lowell and nibble a piece now and then to Keep you in mind and I show it to the Dr just to make his mouth water but Johnny guards it with a Jealous Eye. it is just as fresh as the day you brought it. I do not have a bag of letters from you. when they do come not a word. do you hear from me again? you must watch the papers and see the vessels leaving for Key West and the gulf as well as Boston. tell Patrick Mahon and M Fahey that I Expect to hear from them. tell Every Body I know they must write verry often and not Expect anny letters from me. good night god bless you all. Kiss the Babies for me.

Your Loving Husband
Thos W. Cahill

Margaret to Thomas

New Haven Feb 12th

My dear Husband

Isnt too bad I spent nearly all the morning writing a letter to you. I sent it by Boston. Ellen has just returned from the Post Office. I sent you Mondays and Tuesdays Times by the Same Mail—When I took up to days Times the first thing caught my eye was an advertisement of a Mail going from N. York for Port Royal and the Gulf tomorrow 13th in by the Philadelphia. Now I am so pleased to think you will get one letter and some Papers by her and perhaps this too with todays Times. I will make haste and I hope you will not Laugh at the writing. it is now over a week since I mailed the letter and Papers to N. York. I hope this will be in time for the mail so that you may know we are all well the children are very well.

Mary thinks it time for you to come home. Eddy thinks you are coming. when he hears the noise of the *cars* he always runs to see you. they never forget you. they ask of God Morning and Night to Send their Dear Father Safe home to them. Eddy Speaks very plain and says his prayers beautiful after his meals. he Thanks God for and asks Holy Mary to watch over his Father and bring him home soon. I hope their wish will be granted. Mr Thos Fitzgibbon is in Bridgeport and is going to recruit there for the 9th. I know it is thought he would do well here. I sent you all the news I could about him this morning—he called to see me—he had a letter from you for me—he promised to come again. I hope he will and take you some things from me when he returns. he promised he would. he looked very well I was so glad to see him, the pig has not arrived yet—my regards to all Love to yourself.

    Margaret E. Cahill

P.S. Remember me to Father Mullin. tell him I delivered his letter to Father Smith. he is well he was glad to hear from him—Good bye God Bless you.

4 oclock P.M.
    write often and long

Thomas to Margaret

Ship Island
Feb 26th 1862

My Dear Wife
    since my last letter to you by the Constitution and by the Saxon the Naval mail Steamer "Rhode Island" has arrived bringing your welcome letter of Jan 20th. "by the way" how did you happen to address it in Care of Quarter Master Tompkins brother. it was owing to this direction or not I cannot say but it Came safely to hand;

    I admire your idea of sending letters by both Boston and New York Though if there be anny truth to the reports that reach us of the large number of troops destined for this point they must Certainly send a great manny vessls down here from the Port of Boston: and they must come pretty close together:

    I cannot understand what the War Department intends to do with us all down here on these barren sand banks: I mean with a force of 15,000 men there is not room on this Island for more than 5,000 and Even then they should put some of them on the East End where the mosquitoes are. I wont say what you recollect the story about the Old man and his ash Cart when the boys pulled out his End board and he did not swear because he could not do *the subject justice* so by these horrible little tormentors: on the west end of the Island where we are Encamped the Island is not more than ¼ of a mile wide and on the south Beach the surf breaks with a tremendous roar and the full force of the wind from the Gulf in the night time. this sounds like thunder: and notwithstanding this and the clean strong air the mosquitoes are plentifull and how they bite:

    I suppose I need not say annything in my letters with refference to affairs here as we have the Celebrated "Puffer" reporter for the New York

"Herald" out here so that you will have the small amount of material the place affords dished up in the highest style of art. what an appropriate name for a newspaper Correspondent yet he says it is his proper natural name; by the way I have a terrible dislike to the whole fraternity of newspaper reporters. I think they Expect Every body to pay Court to them and they intrude themselves Everywhere and I presume write in accordance with the manner in which they are personally recevd.

we have had a verry busy time for the last week with a couple of United States Paymasters who have come down here to pay off the troops *they say* but it would seem to me that their mission was to torment us and make all the trouble they possibly can. they come down here with a Couple of Volumes of Printed Orders that none of the officers from the Commanding General down have Ever seen or heard of: and there is not an Officer on the Island they have not bothered: I got along with one of them verry well untill yesterday when they sent me a note saying that some of my Companies had not men Enough in them to Entitle them to a Captain and 2nd Lieut and that they would discharge them after the 28th.

now it has been verry Evident to my mind that our State has treated us verry shabbily from the first with reference to our Equipment and recruitment but the Cool insolence of these fellows is positively refreshing; if they Escape being thrown into the Gulf Stream which runs temptingly near us it will be wonderfull; but the manner we have been treated is a disgrace to the State of Connecticut. I see by the papers that our state authorities are going on raising regiment after regiment without paying anny attention to filling up those already in the field and I am left out here away from all means of ascertaining what is going on in the outside world and liable to be imposed upon by Every puppy with a shoulder strap who may Chance to stray down here to loaf around a few months at the Expense of the Government. but I am strongly inclined to think it would be as well for them to keep out of my way: they have not attempted annything personal to myself, yet and if they do I may give them something to think about. it would be doing the Country good service to drown some of their vagabond officers: who are fattening on the carcass of the Body Politic:

It does my heart good to hear our Brigadier General give them his Oppinion of them. it positively makes me love the "Old Mountaineer" to hear him pour out his invictines. he is probably the most stern old soldier in the service of the United States a sincere honest man who does his duty most thoroughly by the government. I am sorry that he issued that "Proclamation" and am glad that I made him no trouble about as he is probably at this time the best friend I have. in fact it is the current talk among the other regiments that he holds us up as an Example to them and that he has taken us Completely under his wing: although there is something overstrained in this yet he has Certainly shown us manny marks of approbation.

just while I am writing the paymaster sends me word that he will pay my regiment off first and on sunday next this being Thursday so I must quit writing to you for which I am sorry. but I have a big job before me to muster for payment. we it is said will be the first paid off and this paymaster has none of Our allotment Rolls out here with him and will pay off in full and we must send our money on by Adams Express. Kiss the babies for me.

Your loving husband
Thos W. Cahill

CHAPTER 3

"It was awfully sublime"

March–May 1862

Thomas to Margaret

Ship Island Mississippi
March 2d 1862

My Dear Wife

I once more take up the Line of Comminication with Home distant Home. what Ideas the word brings up: well all is well with us at this time and tomorrow. that long looked for Pay Day will arrive "Glad Tidings of Great Joy." The last week has been one of the great Efforts to me. I have had charge of the mustering of my Own Regiment for the muster for Payment of the 28th of February: On the muster of 30th December they were mustered by Brigd Genl Phelps and of Course all the papers were made out strictly according to his *directions* and under his *personal supervision* and the *duplicate copies required by regulations* were by *him* forwarded to Washington: these were sent by the "Rhode Island" about the 8th of January and the Paymasters left Washington about the first of February but they brought none of the Muster Rolls prepared with Such labor and came with them so that we were obliged to go through all the labor prior to the 31st of December and when we had got through with that; the Paymasters and Genl got into a Clash about the form in which the December Rolls were made out: and after wasting some days in a bootless discussion it was finally agreed that I should muster the Regts myself, for the 28th of February: and have the rolls made out to suit them: and as States above I have just finished this labor: and to morrow "God Willing."

March 3d.

the men will be Paid and in the Agregatate the Regiment will be a verry large sum. I cannot name the precise amount as I have not yet seen the footings of the Pay Rolls; but I think it will reach forty thousand dollars as there is 5 months pay due the men: now then Comes the next serious trouble. these Paymasters have not brought down their *Allotment Rolls which were made out and forwarded to Wm Charnley* both from Camp Chase and from Fortress Monroe, the only Roll they have with them is the one with the names of Capt Garveys Company B it being the *one Wm Charnly spoke of in his letter to me* as having the *names* and the *mens signatures* all in the *same handwriting.* and therefore in his Opinion and also in mine incorrect:

now then these Paymasters are going on to pay these men *without reffer-ence* to these *allotment Rolls: that* is they will *pay the men all that is Coming to them* and it is perfectly discretionary with the men what they do with their money when they get it. fortunately Adams Express Co have opened an Office here in the nick of time and those that Choose can forward their money to their families or friends or for deposit; but what I fear is the distance may render them Careless about sending it home and that they may waste it here. however we must hope that their better feelings may predominate;

I shall do my best to make them send it home And *Father Mullen* made a verry Eloquent and feeling Address to them at my request this morning which I think will have a good Effect. I am verry anxious to have them send their money and send it home: I cannot understand what has be-come of the Allotment Rolls. nothing particularly worthy of mention has occurred here since my last:

The 12th Maine and the Eastern B.S. Regt[1] with the Cavalry Compa-nies have not yet recovered from the Effects of their long Confinement on board Ship: I dont Know what they would have done with themselves if they had to go through with the same amount of hardship and labor which we did on our own arrival on this sand Bank: instead of having Every thing prepared for their Convenience after our three months la-bors: they have a great many sick. the 12th Maine report "193" one hun-dred and ninty three sick Every day since they Landed and this was a much talked of hardy Regt. The boast of the State of Maine as being the tallest the best looking and the hardiest and the most salin most Robust regiment which has left the New England states; I have learned to value such boastings at their just value and when I look over the files of Papers

---

1. The Thirtieth Massachusetts Volunteer Infantry, commonly referred to the Eastern Bay State Regiment, was organized by Benjamin Butler on December 31, 1861. Civil War Soldiers and Sailors System, National Park Service, Washington, D.C.

from home and read the tremendous blowing of horns which is being made over some of the regiments about to leave: I am forced to smile at how little they know about what they are talking about and these are all splendidly Equipped regiments while our men have suffered all sorts of privations for Clothing not a yard of which has yet arrived and we have a sick List of only "21" twenty one, and only nine in Hospital and none of them serious Cases: well nerily if man has frowned upon us the Lord has favored us and if we had a Clothing and 200 recruits I should feel inclined to boast a little myself.

Monday March 2d 1862 4 P.M.

The promised payment wasnt made to day. the weather yesterday morning was so warm as to be quite oppressive to me while going through the inspections of the Regiment but during the afternoon and evening came up one of those thunder storms of this climate and it poured down a solid mass of water untill the near morning when the wind came out from the north and has blown a gale all day and it has been the Coldest day of the season. so the paymasters did not get to work. but if the wind goes down they will commence to morrow and I hope we will be all ready with the *remittances* when the "Rhode Island" touches here on her way up the Coast with the return mail when the money will go home in a lump; the Express charges are for sums of 15,00 and under 25 cts 15 to 30 dolairs 50 cts 30 to 50 dollars 75 cts 50 to 75 dolls 1,00 75 to 100,00 1,25 100 to 150 1,50, 150 to 200 $2,00 for larger sums 1 per cent, these are the Express Charges if it be desired to *insure the money* against sea risks. they Charge one per cent additional this Costs something being Equal to about 2½ per cent on the small amounts but the men seem to be verry well satisfied and I have strong hopes that a large amount of money will be send home as there seem to be a verry generous feeling in the Camp.

Margaret to Thomas

New Haven March 3rd

My dear Husband

if I could only hear this morning that you recd any of my letters I could write with a good will and cheerful Heart but the thought comes up he will never receive this letter and what is the use of my writing. but then on the other hand you say keep writing all the time some of them must reach *me* and so I will and have done so. I Sent my last letter by Col

Denning[2] of the 12th Regt and a Box also a valise full of News Papers and your Commission. Col Denning took charge of it he said he reached Ship Island alive he would see you and give it you. he said too that he was going to bring you home and if he told me true Im sure I will think he is the *Bravest man alive* besides being one of the kindest. I found very kind overwhelmed as he was with care and toil on the eve of his departure from here yet he seemed so willing to serve you in any way I would suggest—and Major Peck also I found him very kind. he said he would take as good care as possible of the valise containing your Papers. I wish you would thank them Both kindly for me—

oh dear I felt wretchid that night to see so many men leaving their homes and friends and for such a long time too. it seems so long since you went away and if I could only—

I met the Governor that same evening or he came to see me rather. I hired a carriage to take me with your Box to the Steam Boat Dock. I would not Lose sight of it for anything until I saw it Safe on Board but I was disappointed in this. although Mr Peck one of the owners was with me and used his influence to get on Board but it was no use. the Soldiers on Guard seemed to think us of Small consequence at that time. in fact I felt the cold steel from their bayonet touch my body and not in a very gentle moment then. it was then and not till then I retired to the carriage and Mr Peck went in search of the Col. he came in a short time was soon followed by the Governor and Mayor. the Governor and myself had quite a chat about you and the 9th. I asked how recruiting for the 9th was progressing. he said that Mr Fitzgibbon had commenced and a Mr Fairchild.[3] he seemed to think P. Maher would do nothing for the Regt. He thought he would he being Capt of the Emmetts. now he said he was anxious to send you some good men and would do his Best. he spoke very highly of you. he said you was a good Man. he felt proud of you and felt great interest in your welfare—

I think it was without exception the stormiest night that ever came. if you could onle see us, the Snow and Sleet was falling thick and fast and the wind howled most fearful but the Poor old man did not seem to mind it. he stood and talked with me until his hair and clothing was well Powdered with snow. Patrick Maher went to Boston as soon as he recd your letter. he said he might have gone a month ago as well as then as so he

2. Col. Henry C. Denning of Hartford.
3. Lt. Frederick M. Fairchild, Company K.

might but *I know what hindered him.* I will tell you when you come home if you could do hearing it. He said all the things for the 9th had gone from Boston 5 days before he arrived there. he could see nothing there to be sent but a Box for Major Frye and they told him that would be Shipped that day. so I am still in hopes that you will get all I send you—he got a Pass over the Road—

there is considerable excitement here about bringing in the Water to the City. I hope some person will write you and tell the particulars for I have got so full of Military that I can talk of nothing else, I believe they have commenced to do something about Spring *Election*—I am writing this letter in my Bedroom at the north window and just now there is a crowd of Politicians leaving the *Dukes* in very good Spirits. appearantly the *Duke heading* of Course. Mr O Brien wrote a few days ago and gave full particulars of the 5th Ward Politics—

I wish you would let me know which Papers you would prefer now that I can Send them by express. I have taken the New York Times and New Haven Courier since you left home. I have sent them all to you up to this date—Lieut Shaw[4] is home he called to see me and Mr Smith [illegible] man. he came to see me before he went home. he looked very tired I asked him if he had any money. he said he he had 28 cts when he arrived in Boston and he bought crackers and cheese for the boys. they would not give them one meals vietuals in Boston. they got here at 2 oclock in the morning. the men not allowed to remain in Boston any time they remained at the Station House. the remainder of the night I gave Mr Smith 2 Dollars I think. he needed it he said he was sorry to leave you and if he grew Strong he would go back.

tell Dr he must not feel troubled about his Wife. her health is good at Least I judge so from the tone of her letters. she writes me often and she has written letters enough to the Dr to keep him in reading for a week. tell him not to worry about her Money Matters. I will let her have part of mine while it Lasts and there is some left yet. I sent her $50.00 Last week I raised from the Conn Savings Bank and there is a small sum of yours there still so do not feel at all uneasy about me wasting money. if the Dr wants anything sent to him he might let me know for I think I could send it to him in less time than it would take to write Mrs Galagher, her letters come here and then we Send them to her to Philadelphia. so you see it takes some time. We expect her to Make us a visit soon.

---

4. Lt. John C. Shaw, Company C.

we have three little shells you sent us in L Obrien Box. they are very nice. send us more if you can. I like the smallest ones the most. I haven't near enough to Stirng on my Watch chain. I think some of changing my watch. I would rather have a patent Lever. I think they are better time Pieces. in your answer to this tell me what you think *about it* and how much more money you will allow me to give in exchange. We have the two little Pigs you sent home. Mr Fitzgibbon has not come to see about taking the one that belongs to him yet. I do not know his address in Bridgeport. Which of them is Mine! The dark one I hope.

I recd a note from Mrs Frye on Saturday. She wished me to write her at Brooklin so that she might let you know if we were well. She said that her Husband mentioned about your not Leaving for home in his letter. I thank them both sincerely but I think it is a horrible state of things when I have Written to you so often I will.

if you ever get this give My Compliments to Major Frye and thank him for me for his rememberance of you.

Shaw told us Father Mullen was Sick I trust he is better give him my kind regards and to all *your* friends.

God Bless You from your Wife
M.E.C.

The Babies as *you call them* are very well . . . they do not forget their dear *father*

Thomas to Margaret

Ship Island
March 5th 1862
11 O Clock P.M.

My Dear Wife
I suppose you will say you may thank Pay Day for receiving so manny Letters from me if you Ever do recieve them. but this is not strictly the fact as I have written you 8 pages Large size letter paper full by the Rhode Island at this trip besides those sent in the money Packages; of course in writing so much I must necessarily use manny repititions, if not of words, at least of Ideas. but the fact of my being in some doubt as to your having received manny of my letters leads me to keep the same thoughts in my mind and naturally to repeat, in your last letter of Jan 23 sent to Care of Quarter Master Tompkins (and by the way how Came you to think of sending it in that way).

you speak of the Hillhouse ladies and Mrs Skinner reading my letters. well by you it is much "aint" it. I dont think I have had so hearty a laugh in manny a day as when I came to that quick Caution of yours to *arrange* the *Private* part of my letters for your self. of Course I can have no recollection of the language I may have used in some of them but I take it for granted that you would be likely at least to read them yourself before you trusted them with them. if not I take it they must have had some *surprises*;

The idea of Ladies of such *cultivated sensibillities* poring over my manuscripts tickles my fancy tremendously. well who would have thought it, it seems but yesterday that I was their Cow boy to day at least their Equal. yet such is the nature of our institutions and hither to the *theory*. however; I will do them the justice to believe they do take an interest in our familys welfare and I feel thankfull to them for their kindness to you; and their *friendship* is worth having under any circumstances as they at least have no *selfish motives in it*; this war has at least reminded many of the foolish distinctions which were fast growing up in our home and citys and will teach us to know one *another better*. I trust then you will meet them halfway at least as I have no doubt your kindly instincts will lead you to do without anny hint for one;

but indeed if I knew who reading my letters it is likely I might have looked at them Closer before mailing them. I commenced this calculating to give you one short page and here I am on the 4th without touching on the subject I commenced on which is to tell you that John Carroll[5] has chosen you to act as his Banker for his private fund. the poor fellow is sending his wife 150 dollars for her support and to pay his debts and he wants you to see that the 150 on this draft is deposited to his credit in the Orange Street savings Bank and you to keep the Book for him as he says he will want it when he gets home as he will be too busy to work untill he is starved out and he is afraid to give his wife the handling of too much at once.

You can take the check to Stephen D. Pardee the treasurer[6] or whoever is treasurer if he is not and he will make it all right and no one will know annything about his private bill but you and me. and he will send you moore from time to time as he gets his pay: and then if his family actually needs more than he sends which is not likely. they will with anny Economy on their part as he will send them some Every time he is paid,

---

5. It is unclear whether this is a reference to Pvt. John Carroll of Company B or Lt. John Carroll of Company F and B.

6. Stephen Pardee served as county treasurer in the late 1850s and helped organize the New Haven Savings Bank. *New Haven City Directory of the Year 1860*, 104.

and he does want anny one to know about this it is sent under Cover to you. James Lawler wants to do the same thing for his wife that Barney Lynch[7] did for his through you these men owe small debts around and are afraid their families will not get it if in their names as it might be seized in the Express offices it is after 2 o clock. good night and god bless. Kiss the Babies for me.

   T. W. Cahill

Thomas to Margaret
Ship Island, March 5th 1862

My Dear Wife

   2 hours ago I was obliged to abruptly Close a letter of this date by the arrival of the "Rhode Island." Major Frye has gone aboard. was certain whether she will wait long Enough to give the officers a chance to remit their money and I commence this hoping for a favorable answer and shall write a few lines at a time as I get a chance. I am fairly driven to death making out papers signing certificates witnessing orders attending at the Pay table and trying to get the sutlers acounts adjusted and advising the men with reference to the method of sending home their remittences. I believe that they are sending home a good deal of money some of them more than they ought with a view to their own necesities.

   while I write intelligence comes to me that the Express folks will not send home anny money by the Rhode Island and I have sent 5 or 6 pages of letters by her. I am sorry I have not numbered my letters to you as I cannot tell whether you have recvd all I have sent or not. I have sent a great manny. Major Frye has numbered his and knows his wife has not received them all. there is a great deal of complaint at the manner in which letters are handled. letters came here which are to different places along the Coast and some even to regiments about Washington. we sent them back but they must be pretty old before the owners get them. if they Ever do.

   no material change has taken place in officers here since my last; A party of Officers from this Island and some reporters and such straglers went over to "Biloxi" Last Friday and walked about through the village. they say that the military and naval officers of the Party took a glass of

---

7 Wagoneer Bernard Lynch, Company A.

wine with the Mayor of "Biloxi." they report verry few persons there and
the negroes all sent into the interior. The party succeeded in Capturing
some New Orleans papers as late as the 23d February they [*page torn*]
the news of the Capture of Fort Donnelson and Fort Henry which was
received with great Enthusiam in our Camp.[8] they also brought away a
pair of scales belonging to the U.S. founder in the Post Office their.

there are as yet no signs of the arrival of the vessils with that "Box" you
have been making my mouth water about. I also Expect 195 Packages of
Clothing for our own regiment by the North America.

Two deserters Came over from the Enemy to day having made their Escape from Fort Pike.[9] they are on board the "Hartford." they report that
Fort Columbus[10] has been taken by our troops and that 14 Regiments
had been sent away from New Orleans to reinforce their northern Lines.
I think our fleet are getting ready for an attack on the Forts below New
Orleans. if they take them I suppose they will be Calling upon us to hold
them but it will be a heavy Job as the Forts are said to be well mounted
and are well built Casemated Forts built by the U.S. Government:[11]

Our line officers are just paid off and the Field and Staff will come next
beginning at the bottom of the List. I think I will send you what [*page
torn*] spare in Treasury notes. these notes bear interest and I suppose are
better than anny other Paper money. at anny rate they are as good as the
Country and when that goes down nothing is of much use. you can dispose of as much as you need for use and deposit the Rest. in either Case
perhaps you might Consult Mayor Welch.[12] act according to your best
judgement and do not trouble yourself unnecessarily about it. I do not
know that you could do better than to deposit it as you find them without Changing them into anny other Currency. I am doubtful whether

---

8. Union forces under Ulysses S. Grant captured Confederate Forts Henry and Donelson
in February 1862. These fortifications controlled the Tennessee and Cumberland Rivers,
and their capture gave the Union water access into Tennessee and directly led to the capture of Nashville. McPherson, *Battle Cry of Freedom*, 396–98; Stoker, *Grand Design*, 115–23.

9. Fort Pike guarded the main waterway connecting the Gulf of Mexico to Lake Pont-
chatrain.

10. This likely refers to the Union capture of Columbus, Ky., the Confederate "Gibraltar
of the West," in February 1862. Stoker, *Grand Design*, 120–23.

11. Forts Jackson and Saint Philip guarded a bend in the Mississippi River some seventy miles south of New Orleans. Confederate defenses rested on the ability of these forts
and their cannons to prevent the Union fleet from moving upriver to New Orleans. Each
mounted some seventy-five cannons and was garrisoned by more than six hundred men.
Pierson, *Mutiny at Fort Jackson*, 7.

12. Harmanus M. Welch served as the mayor of New Haven from 1860 to 1863.

anny money will go home by the Rhode Island and I begin to suspect the Agent means to go home with it himself and in that Case he will be likely to find some excuse for remaining untill the other regiments are paid off. If I find that to be his game I may if I get paid in time put them in Care of Acting Master Churchill of the Rhode Island and perhaps take an order on the U.S. Treasurer in New York which perhaps may require you to go to New York to get it Cashed. but there is no use of my Speculating untill I get the money. but I write this that you may all my ideas on the subject and it may assist you [page faded] what ever way it may come and this rambling may show you that I do not know How to do it myself and I know how scary you are about money matters.

I have another Letter on board the Rhode Island and you or nobody Else need Expect a letter from me again for some time for I am tired of scribbling. give my love and respects to all Enquiring friends. I am glad to learn that your old and my old friends from the "Avenue" think of you in my *absence*. assure them that I have not forgotten them and hope to return to thank them for their manny acts of Kindness in the Present and by gone times. Kiss the Babies for me.

your Loving husband
T. W. Cahill

Margaret to Thomas

New Haven March 10th 9 OClock P.M. [1862]

My Dear Husband
I mailed a letter to you Last Evening and commenced another to night so you see I did not intend you shall be at a loss for news from home I see by the New york paper of today at the Steamer Connecticut was to sail today you ought to get by her 2 or 3 letters from me, and a Bundle of Papers and a great many letters and Papers from other parties who have sent them in time for her Mail.

Michael Fahy called to see us last Evening he recd your letter I read it—I owe him 45 Dollars on the work you ordered done by him. I paid him 20 Dollars some time ago that would make his bill in all 65 Dollars. he did not Present his bill for payment although I think he may need his money but I was anxious to settle with him and asked him about it. I will pay him the first one when I get cash from you. I did not like to leave myself without some money not knowing what might happen and I want to give Mayor Welch 100 Dollars for your horse. Wm Rouland came here to collect it. the Mayor told me I need not Pay it until I could make it convenient to myself besides the above I owe small bills to the amount of about 40 Dollars and if that confounded old Widmer would only Pay me I could Pay all my house bills without touching your money that is coming. I hope you will tell me what to do with it if you want me to deposit it in what Bank.

Mr Flood was here this evening. he sends his best wishes to you. he says he missed you more than once since you left here, Mr OBrien says the 5th ward is gone to Rot since you left it. by the way Mr Flood told me tomorrow was going to be a great day. they are going to vote for Delegates to Nominate City officers. now if I have not spoken propper in a Political sense you will understand it. I presume little P. G. the F. M. seems to be quite busy in the *Brick Mansion.* I think they are Practicing *Elocution* to-night. I told Ellen I did not think I would do much work tomorrow but take *notes.* I am getting sleepy so good night God Bless you.

Sunday March 16th

My dear Husband

I expected to have this mailed long before this. you will see by the first date when I commence it. I thought I would have a great deal of news to send you about the 5th Ward Politics but I made very wrong calculations that time for I know little or nothing about it only *this* the *Duke* got a great whipping and that itself is gratifying knowing that he Lost a few glasses of _____ on the head of it. I think he will stand a poor chance for alderman and street commissioner this spring.

Margaret to Thomas

[undated fragment, but most likely March 16, 1862]

I recd a letter from you this week. a boy by the name of allen carried it to me. he said his brother would call and see me when Came up from N. York.

I am very glad My dear Husband to hear you speak of feeling so well. I am sorry I did not have your Clothes made more roomy but there must be some let out to your Pants—

I told the Mayor what you said about your Regt not being full and your want of time to write to the Governor about it. he said the Governor was in Washington and would be gone two weeks but he would write to him or when he came home he would make it his business to see him and talk to him about it. he was very glad to hear from you he said he hoped by this time you had his letter and I hope so too.

I ought to have had two or three letters and Papers on board the same steamer the Philadelphia—I saw some days ago she arrived at key West and send her mail to Ship Island and returned to New York where she arrived the beginning of last week.

there is a great many troops passing through here every day but we have want of finding out where they are coming from or where they are going to. our Electors have been notified from Washington to keep all such matters quiet or they will be dealt with accordingly.

the 14th[13] left here last week. there was no notice given of their departure in any of the N. Haven papers and the 13th[14] will soon be over in a very quiet manner too. perhaps it is not prudent for me to write about such Matters but I trust my letter will not give any person but yourself the information and if every person is as interested for the safty of the Union as you are there would soon be an end to its troubles and I hope there will as it is.

I suppose you will think of home tomorrow the 17th of March. the Emmetts will turn out with the Highburians. the Montgomeries[15] will not turn out. there will be service in St. Patricks Church at 11 oclock in the morning but just imagine the slush they will have to walk in. the Rain has been falling for the two days and Last night the Snow commencd to fall quite thick and fast and then it began to rain again to day and froze so hard that it was with the greatest difficulty I could walk to church and then I was obliged to call on Wm Cooney to help me.

There is a letter from Father Hart. he will not be home before July. he is quite strong. it seems very lonly here without him. I hope in God both you and him I will be home soon. when I think of how hard you both struggled to make this cold hearted Place what it is or was when you left it for in my opinion it is fast going to its original ___ it makes me feel very sad. I am almost tempted to exact a permission from you but no I will not perhaps it would be [illegible]—

---

13. The Fourteenth Connecticut Volunteer Infantry was mustered on August 23, 1862, and served with the Army of the Potomac from Antietam to Appomattox. See Hirst, *Boys from Rockville*.

14. The Thirteenth Connecticut Volunteer Infantry was mustered on January 7, 1862, and served in the Department of the Gulf. See Sprague, *History of the 13th Infantry Regiment*.

15. The Emmet Guards and Montgomery Guards were Irish militia units in New Haven. The Highburians refer to the Ancient Order of Hibernians, an Irish fraternal organization.

We are all well—your little Mary was 4 years old on Friday. how delighted she will be to see you.

tell the Dr I had a letter from his wife Last week. I hope he has recd some of her letters. give him my kind regards. I called to see Mrs Herity the other day tell her husband she is well and her children too.

I hope the 12th Regt has arrived at Ship Island. Col Denning has some *goodies* for you. there is a rumor here that they have been wrecked but I do not believe it. I hope not at all events I sent a Box with them and a Box of Papers. I think you will be pleased with the Col.

I spoke to the Mayor too about Capt Nelsons Capt[ainship]. he will speak to the governor about him. I believe I told you before that I was told in Hartford he never had a Commission from Connecticut.

I send your commission in Care of Col Denning, I will now close my dear Husband with wishing you a safe and speedy return home God Bless you.

from your affect Wife
M. E. Cahill

Thomas to Margaret

Ship Island Miss
March 22 1862

My Dear Wife

I thought it might be as well to commence another letter while waiting like "Micawber"[16] for something to liven up that might furnish something to help fill a letter. Since my last letter to you the date of which I have forgotten there has been a Extensive arrival of troops the 4th Wisconsin, 6th Michigan, 21st Indiana, 13th Maine under the celebrated Neal Dow of the Maine Law notoriety[17] the 14th Maine and the 8th New Hampshire and the 31st Mass.

the 38th Mass was one of those regiments which caused the dispute between Genl Butler and Gov Andrew of Mass. it Came out at the same time as the twelft Maine, with a full set of Officers from the Colonel down

---

16. This is a reference to Wilkins Micawber, a character in the Charles Dickens novel *David Copperfield*, who was an "eternal optimist who, despite evidence to the contrary, continues to have faith that 'something will turn up.'" *Oxford Dictionary of English*.

17. Neil Dow led the antebellum temperance movement. Ashworth, *Slavery, Capitalism, and Politics*, 2:498.

and was known as the 2d Eastern Bay State Regiment. it had been here about a month when out comes another set of Officers throughout, the first set being in possession refused to acknowledge the second. so their has been two sets of officers standing here for one regt but the first kept their places and went on drilling the second waited on Genl Phelps but he would have nothing to do with the matter: consoling them in his dry way by telling them they were verry good looking heads but did not seem to have anny bodies, when they found their bodies would be verry happy to recognise them, but had not been accostommed to such knotty questions: but as the man who tied the knot is here now perhaps he can untie or cut them the latter I think;

I mean Genl Butler who arrived here some three days since and has not yet been ashore, but who notified as yesterday of his having arrived and assumed Command: among the List of Staff Officers I find the name of the Col of the E. B. S Regt[18] as a Capt on his personal staff and it strikes me as sounding the fate of all the others to find them. Chief yet such an "Irish" promotion from a Col to a Capt among these Line officers is Capt John A Nelson and his first Lieut Finegus who played me that scurvy with reference to Co K.[19] I tell you he is sorry Enough for his shame in that transaction and would be glad to fall back on the despised Connecticut Commission. I do not know how much power the major General may have in the case or how far he may be disposed to back up Nelson. one thing is certain I shall not allow anny trifling with the Rights of the State of Conn or with Commissions.

While writing the above an order is said to be issued and from the source from which I hear it have no doubt. its Esentially correct that the Brigades are assigned to the several Commanders as follows First Brigade J. W. Phelps Comd Consists of the following Regts the 9th Conn the 8th New Hampshire The 7 and 8th Vermont The 12th and 13th Conn The 1st Vermont Battery The 2nd Vermont Battery 4th Mass Battery and Company of Reads Cavalry of these troops there is only part of the 8th New Hampshire yet arrived and none of the Vermont of the 3rd Conn we have only 2½ Regiments of this Brigade present:

---

18. The Thirtieth Massachusetts, Eastern Bay State Regiment.

19. Cahill left a Capt. John Nelson at Lowell to continue to recruit for the Ninth Connecticut. When Nelson arrived at Ship Island with Company K, he told Cahill he had volunteered his services and those of his men to a Massachusetts regiment. Cahill's note here about the "despised Connecticut Commission" is a sarcastic reference to Nelson's apparent preference for a commission from Massachusetts.

Sunday March 23rd

The General Came ashore at 12 o Clock pm and has Officially announced General Phelps Brigade as above. I do not consider this a fair distribution for our General as it throws all the raw troops on his hands, and gives the best Equipped and disciplined regiments to Brigadier Genl T. Williams[20] who has recently arrived here from Hatteras. his Brigade rolls consist of the 4th Wisconsin a splendid regt 6th Michigan and 21st Indiana. fair troops these three regts have been in service since April and may be called Old troops. and our old friends the 26th Mass. I am sorry to part Company with the 26th as there had grown up quite a fraternal feeling between the officers and men of the two regts;

I dont know anny thing of the antecedents of Genl Williams but there is a great difference in personal appearance between him and Genl Phelps. I am quite satisfied to be with the latter for all his rough Exterior and positive hatred of the "Peculiar Institution" and should have Expressed myself so had I been Consulted. We have another Acting Brigadier appointed here in the person of Col George F Shepley of the 12th Maine a verry Estimable gentleman and a Lawyer and Politician of some repute of Portland Maine: but I fancy the appointing powers. never Saw him undertake to carry his Battallion through the Evolutions of the Line or else they do not consider skill in the tactics necessary [Cahill marked the following lines "Confidential"] to the position; his regt lays along side of ours and we have been out together with General Phelps in Brigade Movements of the "3 Volume Seats" and I hardly think the old "Mountaineer" knew he was talking to an Embryo Brigadier from the way he laid it out to him. I know if he had occasion to treat me so you would have had one more Sore headed Col coming home to Conn directly;

but I certainly have to congratulate myself on having Escaped from some of the scenes I have witnessed between the Brigadier Genl and some of the Cols and I certainly do not blame the general and he will have his hands full again now as he must go to work to organise his Brigade over again. the 12th Conn had not at this date *been out on drill* with us but presume they will tomorrow. it will necessarily take some time to arrange these matters and to drill raw troops in to annything like shape and I am afraid that the 2nd Brigade will be sent away before us as they are in fighting trim.

---

20. Brig. Gen. Thomas R. Williams was a West Point graduate from Detroit, Michigan. A veteran of the Mexican-American War, he was appointed brigadier general of volunteers when the Civil War broke out in 1861. He was killed leading his troops during the Battle of Baton Rouge on August 5, 1862. Smith, *Gallant Dead*, 49–51.

and I Expect while I am writing that one of the most terrific Engagements between the navy and the Forts is going on between the Fleet and Forts Phillip and Jackson on the English Bend Mississippi River 30 miles below New Orleans. These are two verry heavy Forts said to mount near two hundred heavy guns of which 50 are trained to Cover one spot in the channel of the size of a ship, which would oblige a ship passing to stand the concussion of from 50 to 300 shots before passing. it scarsely seems possible to reduce such forts with wooden vessels yet the new Comodore Faragut[21] seems determined, he has sent all his heavy vessels in here to put them in fighting trim by stripping them of all their sails and yards. and they are sent ashore and piled up upon my Parade Ground so that it looks like a ship yard, and what monstrous big sticks they are though they look so small when in their place on board the great ships. you may imagine how the splendid ships look when stripped of their plumage:

it will Either be a great victory or a terrible defeat. it does not seem possible to go by those Forts without losing some of them. It is possible that some of the troops now on the Island may be sent down to the mouth of the Mississippi; I understand there is a small town or village at some of the great mouth called Pilot town from its being chiefly inhabited by Pilots which is Considered an advantageous position. it is said to be deserted as all the pilots have been ordered up to new Orleans by the Rebel Government. but there are all conjectures as nothing will be known as to our destination untill we get marching orders, and I do not anticipate receiving them untill we hear from the Fleet on the Mississippi.

Father Mullen is in trouble about a chapel tent as the storm has torn down the large tent loaned him by Dr Gallagher and we have no means of replacing it. is wonderful what an Effect this Climate has upon our tents, tents which were new when we came on the Island are verry nearly unfit for use. they are Completely mildewed and are rotting fast, I made a requisition on the government for new tents shortly after arriving and hope to hear from them soon, while writing I hear the fifes and drums of some newly arrived troops marching up from the dock. I cannot conceive where they can fit them for our End of the Island is fairly Crammed with men. Somebody will have to get out of the way soon if they do not stop sending troops here. we received the balance of the clothing which I made requisitions upon the state of Connecticut for before we left and

21. Adm. David Farragut, first admiral of the U.S. Navy. For discussion of Farragut's role in the Civil War see Symonds, *Lincoln and His Admirals*.

the Quartermaster finished issuing them yesterday. there is not Enough of them to give us a new outfit throughout as we have only about half as many Complete uniforms as we have men but it enabled me to Equip all those who had never been Equipped and by carefull management it has made a wonderfull improvement in the Comfort and appearance of the men.

The Clothing sent to us I am glad to be able to say is verry Creditable to the state. all the articles are Excellent of the various kinds and the Dress Coats fit Every man as if made for him by a fashionable Cutter. the greatest benefit of all however was the under shirts. I received 912 red flannel Shirts of which we were badly in need of some 490 pair shoes and a splendid lot of blue flannel blouses 960. these are magnificient being just the articles for the warm weather we may soon Expect and being actually more than we need. we could let Every man have them and they look as well as dress Coats in line: I am a little short of pantaloons but Expect to hear from the U.S. Government soon with reference to requisitions made on them in January:

I can begin to look around at the other regiments now without being ashamed of myself and My "Falstaffs" regiment.[22] and to crown all I received at the same time a new set of Caps made of blue felt Cloth with a leather visor. they are a queer looking thing but will keep the sun and rain off the men heads. when I saw them turn out in line it put me in mind of the Old Scotch tune "All the Blue bonnets are over the Border" and by the bye that sounds like our Cognomen of "Connecticut over the fence."

Monday March 24,

word has just passed down the lines that a mail leaves for the north at 2 O Clock so that I will hurry to a conclusion. nothing has reached us yet as to affairs on the River. there is a general expectation among us as to moving but nothing definite. I must try to write to his Excellency is possible before the mail Closes as am waiting for the Quarter Master to make our return of Clothing received and make an acknowledgement of it. I have received a letter from Patrick Maher dated Boston Feb 20th which although it has lain in the Harbor some days only Came to hand yesterday. he speaks of ascertaining that all packages for the troops at Ship

22. This refers to a Shakespeare character, Sir John Falstaff, whose "ragged regiment" appears in *Henry IV*, act 2.

Island were put on board Ship E. W. Farley. that vessel is in the Harbor but nothing has been delivered from her yet. I am waiting anxiously for that Box. have not seen it or heard of it yet, it is not worth while to send out much stuff to us here. it is so uncertain of being received, I suppose the Adams Express is all Right. at anny Rate a receipt is taken from them is all Right for the value of the Parcels, I am sorry that P.M. thinks the war will be over so soon that it would not be worth while to take hold, hope it will but Cannot see it that light yet. you at home may be in possesion of Knowledge we have not.

Capt Duffy[23] has sent in his resignation. do not know what action I shall take on it yet. do not like to let disaffected persons go home just as we may be going in to action. give my respects to all our friends. Kiss the Babies for Me.

Your husband
T. W. Cahill

Margaret to Thomas
New Haven March 27th 1862

My Dear Husband

I wrote you on the 25th. I heard the Steamer George Washington was going to Sail from Boston with some troops for 9th Regt and 13th. I endeavored as you will perceive when you open the enclosed to send a few lines to you saying that some of the money sent to the 9th had came to hand. they told me in the Post Office they had telegraphed to Boston but was answered she would Carry no mail. I will now send it by New York I went to see Mayor Welch Last evening. I spent a good part of it with "Strange turn of Matters isnt it" him. had recd your letter. he seemed to be in high Spirits at its contents. he was very much pleased at Mr Heritys[24] account to. he spent one long Evening with him. he gives us all great Satisfaction. I mentioned about U.S Bonds to the Mayor. he said if I cut off the first row of those coupons and presented [*page torn*] of the Banks I could get the interest on them. it comes due the 2st of April yours being dated 1st October. he said I could get Gold in New York but it would not be worth while to go down for so small a sum unless I had to go on other Business—

---

23. Capt. John Duffy, Company A.

24. Herity [Herritty], who appears throughout the correspondence, was a businessman and served as a sutler to the Ninth Connecticut.

I Paid the Mayor $100 Dollars for Poor Jack. he Paid the Money to Pierce Rouland himself. I did not know he Paid it until I got some last night. he gave me your *note*. He wrote it by the next Mail going South he said—

Father Smith called to me Yesterday. he told there was no need of my Making those Bonds Payable to any person but keep them safe I am going to deposit Johnys and Carrolls Money this Morning—I will write you soon. we are all well fine weather is coming give my regards to all friends Father Mullen in particular. I hope the Dr heard from his wife. you may expect a Box from here soon. I have had you a flanil suit [illegible]. it is a poor afair but I will send it. there is no better flanell to be found here.

from your Loving Wife.
Mrs T. W. Cahill

Margaret to Thomas

New Haven March 29th 1862

My Dear Husband

Mr Herity has just been to see me. he came from New York on Friday night. he tells me he has made an agreament with a house in New York to send on some things by the first transport that leave N. York Boston or Philadelphia so I will send some things to you with *his things*. but it seems to me to be the same old slow way of sending but it May be as quick as by Express. I presume they send all goods in their care by Transport vessels. he leaves here for Providence R.I. tonight to see his Daughter. he thinks he may leave anytime after Tuesday. he will go see the Governor on his way home. he promised to come and see me if anything Special takes Place—I recd an answer to a note I sent to Capt Churchill of the Rhode Island on his arrival in Port: saying he would with Pleasure take charge of any thing. I wished to send to you a Box or letters but Mr Herrity has persuaded me to send it with his goods and it will be much easier for me to do so, in Case I send by Capt Churchill My Box will have to go to Philadelphia and all I have to do in the other case is to send it up to Dawsons Dugless in State St.

Mr Herity is having you a saddle Cloth Made. he tells me to go Look at it tomorrow and have it Boxed carefully ready to send on his return—he has given me a very handsome Black Silk Dress Pattern. Please thank him for me. I will wear it on your return home. Please God for the first time.

Capt C said he might call to see me on his way down: he was at home when he wrote to me: if he had time but I hardly Expect him because of having a Business Man for a Husband. I know how presious his time is but I will send this I[n] his care. I know he would be glad to bring you some news from home. I almost despair of you getting that great Box I sent you in care of P. R. George. I feel very uneasy about it. your Cap and Hat a Box of White Gloves a Pair of Gausttath Gloves 3 Pairs glasses for the Eyes 2 Pairs Pants Collars—Hanckerchiefs—Stockings—Shirts—Books—Papers and some Eatables besides a quantity of clothing for those Boys and considerable for the Hospital. I hope you have it, how are your Boots holding out? let me know in time to send you some.

I went to see Mayor Welch. I Paid him $100.00 on the House. he Paid it to Raylaid & Pierce Last Jan. he told me to bring those U.S. Bonds down the next day. I did So and Mr Charnley was in his office. he said if I would go with Mr C—to the Bank he would give the interest due on the first now of the Coupons to April 1st. he did so. he gave me 18 Dollars 25cts. this amont you will remember was marked on them. I will hold them if God Spares My Life until you return. the Draft I cashed, out of it I Paid Mayor Welch $100.00 Michael Fahy $45 Heller $50. 50 of this he Loaned me in Jan the rest for the Clothes I had made and sent to you. I had $5 left but I owed some other bills so I raised some in the orange st Bank 100 dollars 75 and that made me all right. I Paid out of that $21 to Mernik for groceries, for the first time since you left home—$7.50 to Mr Geary for Dues and fines in the Society for the *coming year* $8 for Insurance on the House—$3_26cts to Rutehen for Month Feb—6/00 for one ton Coal. so you will see I have little on hand to begin with again—

More about your Money in Bank here, when I settled with the Montgomery Society there was something over 200 Dollars left, I took 50/00 out and sent to mrs Dr Galagher and will replace it when she sends it back. I expected to get in from Mr Channley out of her allotment Money but I suppose hers was sent by Express to Philadelphia. she sent me her order on Mr Channley but of course he could not Pay Money he had not recd. she did not understand this at the time—her order reads thus

Philadelphia Feb 18th 1862

Mr Scharnley will Please Pay to Mrs Thos Cahill or bearer *fifty dollars*, and charege the same to account of

Dr Charles A Galagher

Mr Winefred C Galagher

I have drawn all but 100 Dollars out of the orange st Savings Bank in small sums from time to time as I needed it—so there must be somewhere near 300 Dollars on deposit still. so that I think I have managed well but it is for you to think so and not me. I hope you will understand it as I have written it in a great hurry. I want to send this by Capt C—

Now about the House. Widmer owes me 5 months rent. he says he will Pay me about the middle of April half and perhaps all. I think he will leave at May. Im not sorry—Cook has Promised to let me have 50 Dollars in a week or two: and that I will have to give to Richard Connors: and the balance as soon as he can—the only money I recd since you left here is 6_50 for 1000 Brick from Med OB since—

I hope you will come home soon. I do not Love to keep accounts I have deposited Johnys money and Carrolls too. Carrolls wife is Making a time about not getting More Money. but if what I hear be true she does not desire to get any more than will bearly support her—I wish I could feel as young and gay as She does but not to be so fond of. I hope he will take care of his Money—Mrs Lawler recd her Money yesterday. it came to me—she is a very fine woman. tell her Husband she and family are well and Barney Lynch to remember me to him. his wife came to me and got her Money. they are all well—and poor Johny he sent me word. he took good care of you. I will not forget him. I sent him such a nice lot of Fiddle strings in that unfortunate Box and his Mother sent him stockings and tobacco. if he will only bring you home and that soon—I have made enquiries about that Boy you have. nobody seems to know anything about him.

April 1st

My dear Husband I am going to send your Box today in care Capt Churchill. I hope it will not be delayed in the Express offices. the "Rhode Island" sails on the 4 or 5th—I have sent you some home made Bread and some nice Cake and put it up in a tin Box so as to keep Moist. I thought the Box would be useful for your Papers it having a Lock on and if you have no particular use for it tell Johnny to send me some shells in it. I never got those you sent by the "King Fisher"—we are all well—you will find in the Box two straw Hats. one of them or both is for Father Muller, the canvas one is said to be water *proof*—I hope he is well and he's made up his mind to stay with the 9th until their return—

I have written to Mrs Galagher telling her the "Rhode Island" is in Philadelphia. if she wants to send anything to the Dr. Remember me to him and all friends.

you loving Wife

M. E. Cahill

I am going to send your *Babies* in the Box.

Thomas to Margaret

Ship Island March 29th 1862

My Dear Wife

since my last letter by the "St Jogo de Cuba" of March 23rd nothing of special interest has occured here: The U.S. Frigate "Iroquois" Came into the Harbour yesterday Evening from somewhere north Confirming the intelligence which had reached us about a week ago through New Orleans papers (Captured on a shcooner taken in Lake Borgne by our invincible little gunboat New London) to Effect of the Evacuation of Mannasses and the advance of the Army of the Potomac[25], as well as the terrible attack of the Merrimac on those old wooden hulks which served as the Coffins for so manny gallant fellows:[26] but I have not been able to gather with anny distinctness the particulars of the working of the Ericson Battery[27] or boat or whatever it was that came up so accidently and as it is said drove the monster away: Every thing that we receive by word of mouth here we feel under the necessity of taking with a verry large grain of allowance:

by the bye I received by the Western Empire which arrived here as you will see by the Endorsement on the letter a letter from James Lannin which appears to have been written to me while we were laying at Fortress Monroe last November: it would have been of no use had Ive learned it then as General Wool[28] who Commands there would not grant the slightest favor to anny one Connected with this Expedition: However on the receipt of the letter as I recollected that General Phelps had Com-

---

25. Gen. Joseph Johnston's Confederate army evacuated Manassas in early March. Two weeks later George McClellan moved the Union Army of the Potomac down the Chesapeake Bay to Fortress Monroe on the tip of the Yorktown Peninsula, which would mark the beginning of the failed Peninsula Campaign during the summer of 1862. Sears, *To the Gates of Richmond*.

26. The Battle of Hampton Roads began on March 8, 1862, when the Confederate ironclad CSS *Virginia* (often referred to by its previous name of *Merrimac*) emerged from the James River to attack the Union fleet anchored in the Chesapeake Bay. During the battle the *Virginia* sank the USS *Cumberland* and grounded the USS *Congress*, proving the superiority of ironclad ships over wooden-hulled vessels. Park, *Ironclad Down*, 177–94.

27. The USS *Monitor*, an ironclad with a single rotating battery containing two 11-inch smoothbore cannons, was conceived by Swedish immigrant John Ericsson. It arrived at Hampton Roads in time to battle the *Virginia* to a stalemate. Mindell, *Iron Coffin*, 40–44, 70–86.

28. Gen. John E. Wool, a veteran of the War of 1812 and the Mexican-American War, was one of four general officers in the U.S. Army when war broke out in 1861. In the fall of 1861 he was given command of Fortress Monroe. Warner, *Generals in Blue*, 573–74.

manded at Newport News previous to being Ordered to this Command:
I spoke to him as to the probability of Effecting the transfer, he said at
once that it could not be done as the matter lay altogether with General
Wool and although he had been so long in Command under him that
he would not grant him the slightest favour when he was leaving on the
Expedition. He had however to ask all the ins and outs of the Matter and
I told him I wanted him on account of his ability as a drummer, Aha says
the Old man. that accounts for the Excellent beats and Calls that regt
used to have. I wondered where they got him. it was almost the only good
thing about the Regt the Excellence of their Beats: so that it would not
seem possible to arrange the matter now.

I had proceeded so far when the Orderly Called me to Head Quarters
where I recd Orders to prepare 4 days Cooked Rations and prepare to
move. further Orders written by and by.

4 O Clock P.M.
Ordered to leave tomorrow between 8 A.M. and 1 O Clock P.M. our
own the 12th Conn 26th Mass 4th Wisconsin 21st Indiana 6th Michigan,
go under Command of a General Williams, General Phelps is not going
at this time. I must say that I am some what down hearted at this movement. I do not understand it and feel sorry that General Phelps is not
going. I have great confidence in his ability more so than anny others
here.

I must Conclude as Johnny is turning Every thing upside down in the
tent. so good bye. give my Love to all my friends. to Ellen. Kiss the Babies
for me and let them prattle their little prayers for me. I will write again as
soon as opportunity offers. do not know when this will go as I will leave
it here in the Post Office. I cannot give you anny directions where you
will direct Except usual to Ship Island or Elsewhere. Good bye God bless
you and all at home.

Your Loving husband
Thos W. Cahill

Thomas to Margaret

Ship Island April 2 1862

My dear Wife
I wrote you on Saturday rather a long letter. most of it I remember
Rightly. the letter part of it was rather blue as the Order to march took
me as it never should a soldier rather by surprise. but it is terribly tring to

a man to have so manny running to him asking questions that he has not information on for no one here knows annything about annything. we were ordered to Cook 4 days rations and we have three of them Eat now and have not started yet. I leave Johnny Reilly and Barney behind to look after my trunks and the horse. I have given Johnny fifteen dollars to hold as a reserve and I am half inclined to think that I will send home half the Clothes I have here. the weather is getting so warm here that there is no use keeping them. so I hope you will not send me anny more Clothing.

If we go into Action I shall wear the Armor vest you were so thoughtfull as to send me. if it will not stop a rifle or Musket Ball I think it would a pistol or a bayonet or sword thurst. at anny rate I will lug it for your sake though it will be awfull heavy of a hot day. I have stowed away all my fine Clothes and all our officers are dressed like the privates and we all carry knapsacks too with our blankets so the secesh wont know us from the privates and if they Catch us they wont get much in the way of fine clothes. I am sorry for poor Father Mullen with his Knapsack and blanket but he is so spirited he will not stay behind. I am afraid he will not stand it on the march but he says he will try:

at the supper table to night word came that the big box had arrived and was down at the dock. sent a detail down for it and got it about 9 O Clock and such a time as we had unpacking and overhauling it. every thing was all right with the Exception of one bottle of Pickles which was broken. all my things are all right and I will have them packed up and left here as we are ordered to move in the morning. it is unfortunate it should come at this time as we have no time to profit by the kindness of the donors. no time in fact Even to make this acknowledgement of its receipts as I write this on the morning of the 3d just as we Expect to go. Father Mullen will try to write but thank those who helped you fill it for me. tell Wm Herritty that 20 of those Boxes Gallagher wrote about have come over thus he had better not send anny more of it out here and I do not know where we are going: give me Love to all and do not send anny more things out here to us as we may never get them. give my Love to Ellen. Kiss the babies for me and god bless you all.

Your Loving husband
Thos W. Cahill

Thomas to Margaret

Ship Island
April 8th 1862

My Dear Wife

I have sent you 2 or 3 letters which I suppose you will get at the same time you do this at the time of writing.

I was a good deal worried about many things as you may probably gather from the tone of them, I was far from being satisfied but matters have changed for the better since, and I hope you will receive this before or as soon as them.

I send you my Rough Drafts of the report of our Expedition to the mainland. I have been sorry since I commenced that I attempted to Re write a report. I cannot say half I wish to say about men and things.

The rough ninth have been trooping around the Splendid summer residences of the southern aristocracy built upon the meanest of all foundations: the unwilling labor of the Black: and such beautiful places; Hillhouse Avenue is a beautifull place well "Pass Christian" has a street 5 miles in length 3 miles of which is fringed with Residences Equal in manny respects and though of a different Architecture full as well built the grounds well Kept and full of Tropical Plants such beautifull Cactus in flower such sweet flowering trees such Splendid Hedges of Evergreens and Roses Fragrant and of all Colours. O such a change from the bleak sands of Ship Island. but we were not sorry for a chance to lay our weared limbs on its white sands once more now.

I am not going to give you another report of the Military part of the Expedition. "Pass Christian" lays along the Mississippi Sound a beautifull site and is used by the wealthy Citizens of New Orleans as a superb Summer residence and watering place. "Biloxi" is also a pretty place but not of the stamp of Pass Christian. it has near as many houses and some of them are fine ones but two there at are 4th Class. You can gather all the particulars from my report I did by any means intend to write so much and I might have written twice as much but I have not time. you can understand from the print of this where I got the paper. I send you the Communication intended for Major Genl Lovell[29] and your Excellisimod

---

29. Maj. Gen. Mansfield Lovell was originally assigned to the defenses of New Orleans and subsequently blamed for the loss of the city. Hewitt and Bergeron, *Confederate Generals in the Western Theater*, 233.

will please note that it was taken from the table in his tent with the ink still on the pen by Liet Lawrence Obrien who gave it to me. O such a hurrah our boys kicked up and such a bonfire. it was burned when I turned in on board the "Lewis" at 1 O Clock in the Morning of that night when Miles and in the sounds it lit up the whole country and with such Clerity that the inhabitants of Pass Christian did not know it was done. when we came back and they thought we going to get Licked. I cannot write any more at present. good night. Kiss the Babies for Me.

Your Loving husband
Thos. W. Cahill

I am going to send home my spare things of all kinds as I cannot take care of them. do not send me any more as I have no room for them. T. W. Cahill

Thomas to Margaret

On Board Steamer "Matanzas"
Off Pass L' Outre Mouth of Mississippi River
April 29th 1862

My Dear Wife

I can scarce find language to describe to you the startling Events of the last 14 days. We Embarked at Ship Island on Tuesday April the 15th on the Steamer "Matanzas" with a section of "Everists Battery"[30] and one Company of the 20th Mass and left the same Evening having in tow the ship "E. W. Farley" with the 12th Conn on board, and arrived at the South West Pass Early next morning: we have Genl Phelps on board. our Fleet Steam Frigates and Gunboats had gone up the River as also the Mortar Fleet: after some delay we also steamed up and passing the Steamer Mississippi with Genl Butler on Board at the Head of the Passes, west directly up to the Rear of the Fleet in the bend of the River near Forts Jackson and St. Philip and Came to an Anchor. 22 Mortar boats were making an incessant discharge upon the Forts throwing thirteen inch shells over 200 lbs weight and 27 lbs power at Each discharge.

---

30. The Sixth Massachusetts Volunteer Light Artillery was organized at Camp Chase in the fall of 1861. Massachusetts Adjutant General's Office, *Massachusetts Soldiers, Sailors, and Marines.*

you may read from the reporters pens a description, I can only say it was awfully sublime we remained in this position on day and night when we were ordered down the River to anchor near the Mississippi "Steamer not the Frigate of that name" and from there were sent down to the South west Pass leaving the Farley at the Head of the Pass, to Endeavor to get the ship "Great Republic" with Brigd General Williams and 3 Regiments over the Bar; spent 2 days or more in this fruitless and dangerous attempt and were obliged to give it up. during this time the bombardment Continued with little or no perceptible Effect upon the Forts:

in addition to the Forts the Rebels had Constructed a sort of a Chain Bridge across the River supported by vessels anchored on the River. these Chains were interlaced under and over these vessels so as to pressent a verry formidable obtstruction to our vessels going up the River to the attack on the Forts: the Chains must be cut and a gallant choir of Volunteer sailors went up in small boats and drove off the guards and in the face of the Fire from both Forts and 2 batteries on either end of the Chains with Cold Chisels and hammers cut away part of the Chains and the next nights renewed the attempt and Cut the whole thing to pieces. this in the face of Forts Batteries and Six or Eight Rebel gunboats one large Floating Battery Carrying 16 guns and a wonderfull Iron Ram.[31] was there Ever anything like it in the Annals of Warfare and not a man hurt it. Exceeds in Cool daring and success full accomplishement anything I Ever read of.

The next night the Fleet steamed up the River. the Flag Ship Hartford Comodore Faragut leading the van: The Awfull Iron Ram Started for the Fleet. the Frigate Mississippi was her mark. that noble ship Kept straight on her course. the Ram got frightened and swerved to the Right. the Mississippi struck her on the fore quarter and the Hartford an after quarter and rolled the Monster over on her back; at the same time pouring Each a broadside into her. flames burst from all her ports she rolled Over drifted against the banks of the River and went down a mass of flame with all on board.

The Fleets steamed by the Forts leaving 2 Rebel gunboats behind them as unworthy their notice. the floating Battery also before spoked off which was formerly a dry dock. Our Vessels verry little injured during remarkable passage and steamed up the River scattering the Rebels like

31. This likely refers to the CSS *Louisiana*, a Confederate ironclad moored alongside Fort St. Philip. Pierson, *Mutiny at Fort Jackson*, 16.

Chaff before them up to the "English Turn"[32] where they had 2 heavy land batteries raking the River mounting a large number of heavy guns. here had Collected a large Concourse of Orleaneans to witness the whipping the Yankees were to get: Slam bang went the noble Frigates Broadsides in to their batteries and down went their mud walls. The noble Tars out with their small boats go ashore and spike them Guns and away went the Crowd of spectators through the swamps well satisfied the Yankees were not whipped.

These were the last of their Batteries and the Fleet without stopping went up to New Orleans and it now lies helpless under their guns. You will observe that the Fleet had not reduced the Forts but had run by them: leaving part of the Enemys gun boats behind as well as the dry dock Battery. What was now to be done. the Forts must be reduced or taken at the point of the bayonet. We could not get at them from the River and by Examining a good map you will observe that the Gulf of Mexico sets up verry near the River of the Back of Fort Phillip and is Generally Called "Bay Rondo."

Genl Butler thought we might come in Rear of Fort Phillip and if we Could find footing we must Carry it by Assault. a truly desperate undertaking: so we left the south west Pass and taking the terrible hulk of the "Great Republic" with her 3,000 troops in tow started on our mission. with so heavy a tow we necessarilly made slow progress and the Mississippi arrived one day before us and was landing the 26th Mass. Gen Butler Came along side and ordering us to Cook three days Rations and prepare to disembark as soon as he Could get off the 31st Mass.

we worked hard all day and night and the next Morning myself and Officers were on the Quarter Deck with Our Glasses watching the movements about the forts where were a great smoke and while intently watching a huge magnificent column of white smoke rised with flashes of fire arose from their vicinity. it resembled Engravings I have seen of the sudden Eruptions of "Vesuvius." it was a wonderful sight arising in a perpendicular Coloumn about a ¼ of a Mile high and when spreading out like a huge umbrella.

This occurred on the morning of the 28th. on the Morning of this day 29th we received intelligence of the surrender of Forts Jackson and

---

32. An S-shaped turn in the Mississippi's seventy miles about the river's mouth of New Orleans. Milburn, *Pioneers, Preachers and People*, 152–55.

St. Philip and Orders to again take the Great Republic in tow and sail for the South West Pass and await Orders. this was pleasant news for us as the attempt to Storm the Forts if determinedly defended would be a desperate undertaking as as they are said to mount 300 Guns and we know by deserters they have 900 men and are surrounded by a deep wide ditch full of Alligators who are said to be fed there;

We are now 2 O'Clock P.M within 20 miles of the South West Pass and I hope we may receive Orders to proceed up the River and to report to Genl Phelps from whose Command we have been I hope *temporaly* detached. I suppose he is in Command at the Forts: We do not hear verry Encouraging accounts of the Union feeling at "New Orleans." it is said that the vagabonds of the City set fire to all the vessels at the wharves which were loaded with Cotton and destroyed them Calling out to the Officers of the Fleet to go and take their fine cargoes: the Comodore sent a Flag of truce ashore for the Mayor and at the same time the boats Crew set the American Ensign on the wharfs. while the Officer was gone for the Mayor the Rabble insulted the flag and finally tore it down and at the same time fired upon the flag ship killing a sailor on board. the Comodore instantly turned his pivot gun upon them and it is said killed 25 of them at one discharge that quited them, I suppose the troops will be ordered up to the City to take possession and preserve order.

I am sorry now that I sent home my Dress Coat and scabbard but I did not want to risk so much valuable Baggage at the Commencement of the Campaign. I am more sorry for the scabbard than anything Else as I suppose I can get a Coat in New Orleans, and for that matter a scabbard too. you need not send me any thing untill matters get more settled and I have some definite idea of where we are going to be. I am hurrying up this letter in hopes to get it on board the Frigate "Colorado" which lies off S.W. Pass being too much draft to go over the Bar and they will put it on the Rhode Island on her return. it is said that there is a schooner in the River with a mail from Ship Island. I do not see how it came out unless it is some of the Old Winter Mails as I have not heard of the Arrival of the Rhode Island although Expected for some days past. we are all well and in the best of spirits not withstanding our long stay on ship board without naming anny. all are well. the weather is delightfull. give my respects to all enquiring friends and Kiss the Babies for me. God bless. and Ellen.

Your Loving husband
Thos W. Cahill

Thomas to Margaret

On Board Steamer Matanzas off the Dock at New Orleans
May 2nd 1862

My Dear Wife

we have within the Last hour Come up from the "Passes" to help to hold this immense City. it seems Completely at our Mercy. I heard there was a mail on board a Gun Boat for the 9th. sent for it and here I have 6 letters from the last of Feb to the 29th March. I am almost Wild between the Conquest of the City and the little *ones picture*. why did you not send your own.

Capt Churchhill brought me the letter your sent by him. it was all we got as yet by the Rhode island as the letter mails for us at Ship Island. she was lying near us now and I write this in great haste and hear she goes to night. Everything has to be thought of and acted upon here like big hurry

we have not been assigned quarters as yet ashore Except to Land every hour. the 12th Conn is ashore and 21st Indiana. I hope we may get Comfortable quarters as we are verry much fatigued by our long confinement on Ship Board. the Fleet lays off the City threatening it with its guns. there is said to be a great manny Roughs who are disposed to make trouble but they can do nothing as they are Completely over powered.

with reference to Business Matters of yours I am well pleased with your arrangement of them. I think there can be need of your assigning them to annybody (Mayor Welch will understand that).

I am glad you sent to Mrs Gallagher. the Dr was well pleased. I hope this affair will be over soon. as things look now it seems likely although the secesh papers are said to have announced a Defeat of our forces under Gen Buel[33] at Corinth or Shilo. we do not know what to believe and we can hardly realise our great victory.

do not give yourself any uneasiness about me. their men have Evidently got in the way of running away when we came in behind the Fort Philip (by the Coast as I mentioned in a great big letter 16 pages I have left on the Colorado for the Rhode Island and which you will get as soon as this).

---

33. Union general Don Carlos Buell, an 1841 graduate of West Point and a Mexican-American War veteran, was given command of the Army of the Ohio. He fought at the Battle of Shiloh on April 7 and during the siege of Corinth in April and May 1862. Both were Union victories. Warner, *Generals in Blue*, 51–52; Green, *Campaigns of the Civil War*, 29–33; Reid, *America's Civil War*, 143.

The Rebels in the Forts mutinied and [illegible] their officers and Came up to the 26th Regt which was the first to Land and surrendered themselves. They were all let go without their arms. I cannot write any more at Present. god bless you all.

your loving husband
Thos. W Cahill

Thomas to Margaret

Reading Cotton Press
New Orleans May 4th 1862

My Dear Wife,

as you see by this heading we are in the Great City of New Orleans, and are quartered in a large Cotton Press, the Owner is a strong secesh, and I am ocupying his Office as Head Quarters. it is a Delightfully Cool place. you do not know how Odd it seems to live in a house after so much tent life. The officers get their meals on board the Matanzas which vessel will probably take on our Mails: as the Rhode Island lays high upon the Bank of the Mississippi where she ran aground. it will take some time to get her off. I am sorry for it as it may take some time to get our letters home. I have a letter on board of her for you written in pencil acknowledging the delightfull receipt of 6 letters of yours during the month of March and about the first of April. you speak of business and money matters. I must congratulate you and myself on the business tact which my absence has developed in you, you seem however in great anxitiety lest your management may not be satisfactory. I have repeatedly urged you to give yourself no anxiety on that account as I am well satisfied with all you have done:

With reference to Father Mullen. he is one of the best men that Ever lived but he is altogether too delicate and sensitive for rough life he is obliged to lead with us and it seems like a direct interposition of Divine providence that he has been Enabled to hold out so long. I scarsely dare to hope that he will be able to hold out against the heats of the summer, but trust it may so far as our personal intercourse is concerned. it is and always has been of the most pleasant nature: yet nothing but his earnest devotion to the Cause and Divine help could have sustained him for so long. the Revd Bishop should if possible have sent a more Robust man. still I think his health is no worse than when he joined but rather better. if he leaves us it will be for his healths sake but I should regret it exceedingly.

Just as I commenced writing this I received the Box by the Rhode Island. but it makes me feel bad to say the Cake is all spoiled. it is too bad but I am afraid it was too fresh. it is badly moulded. I will try to save the Bow Wow for dear little Eddy if I possibly can. it makes me feel awful homesick to see the dear little faces you sent me in the letter and Box and I wonder you did not send your own and Ellens. I sigh and pray for the happy day when I may honorably see you all again. I shall certainly seize the first opportunity to do so.

I hear Col Denning is working hard for a chance to get home. he is in no ways fitted for such a life. I think it doubtfull if he succeeds though he has a great political influence but every Officer is needed here at present and it looks bad to see anny one trying to get away.

The papers you sent by the same box are verry acceptable to self and officers as they were tolerably new. if we could have had them during the terrible 18 days we were on board the Matanzuas but better late than never, I have not said much as yet as to our position here. in fact I hardly think it necessary as the reporters will undoubtedly say Enough to satisfy all on the the subject but take their words with a grain of allowance.

Your Loving husband

T. W. Cahill

I Continue writing as I find a chance. I Expect to go up the River to occupy some position between the River and Ponchantrain in with the 12th Conn. I believe it is not far from here; I do not like our being in the City with our men. they are altogether too much Exposed to the influence of Liquor of the worst description and I believe it to be drugged at that, I have had a good deal of trouble from this cause and last night a good many of them ran the guard and one Mark O'Neil[34] of Bridgeport got stabbed and I hardly think will live.

The people here though Completely Conquered are far from friendly and it is not by anny means safe to be out late at night unless with a guard strong Enough to Command respect. I will try to send you some papers from here or Extracts which will perhaps be better than to send whole papers. you will notice they are verry bitter. it was a terrible surprise to them when our frigates were seen coming up the river. their best officers pronounced forts Phillip and Jackson with the fortifications at English Turn as impregnable to all the navies in the world. indeed they were not alone in this particular as the English War steamer a 50 gun ship the

---

34. Pvt. Mark O'Neil, Company D.

"Liffey" which has been lying at the S. W. Pass for a long time sent up
their first Lieutenant to New Orleans at the time the Fleet first moved
against the City to make some arrangements for the safety of British Subjects in Case the Fleet succeeded in forcing the Forts. That Officer returned from the City and reported that there was no necessity of making
anny arrangements for the protection of foreign citizens there was no
Chance for anny vessels getting to the City.

I was on board the "Colorado" on the afternoon of the day that The
Flag Officer of the Liffey Came on board to congratulate our Fleet on
their brilliant succeess. he said it the greatest naval feat of the age and
the above facts The Officer of the French Man of War Milan were of the
same opinion with reference to the Defenses.

Father Mullen waited upon the Archbishop imediately his arrival.
he will probably send an account home which you will probably hear
through Father Smith. by the way give him and Father O Brien and Sheridan my respects and you do not say anny thing in your letters about
Father Hart. have you not heard from him?

We have had one grand Parade through the streets of New Orleans
with a full Band and Colours flying by order of the Major Genl. We gave
them all the Irish lines we had and yankee Doodle Dixie the star spangled
banner and the Red White and blue. our state Flag takes the Irish here
all down with its Harp and Motto. they stand around my window all day
looking at it it has a verry good Effect. Genl Phelps ordered out to play Every Evening and it has a verry good Effect. we are said
to be in the worst part of the City but it is verry quiet not a word of noise
or insolence and the people dance to the music on the side walks while
I write. they are dancing under my windows to [illegible] so I Comfort
myself that while they dance they are doing nothing worse. if it were not
for the Rum I would like to stay here,

we are going about 4 or 5 miles up the River to a place called Carrollton[35] where the Rebels have been fortifying with 500 men since last
August. the intrenchments are 2 miles long running from the river to the
swamps of Lake Ponchantrain. the Rebels deserted it on our arrival and
we go up to take possession and hold. Genl Phelps has been up to see
it and says it is a splendid Zig Zag work with a ditch 20 feet wide in the
whole length of its front and as it runs from river to lake on impassible

35. This fortified position, eight miles above New Orleans, originally was intended to
guard the upper river approaches to New Orleans. Winters, *Civil War in Louisiana*, 26, 98;
Official Records, series 1, vol. 1, 582.

swamps it will be Easily held against a strong force. and we are to have the sloop of war Portsmouth on the River in our Front. the Whole of the first Brigade will Come up as soon as we get vessels to bring them from Ship Island. I heard I have a shipload of stuff for the Regiment at Ship Island being the return I suppose to a requisition for Clothing and Camp Equipage which I made on the US Government last January. Our Regt will be in great trim when we get our new stuff.

Our men find lots of Old acquaintances here. I think if we were to stay here another week we would have the biggest half of the Irish here with us. you would laugh heartily here to night to see our Officers dancing with Orleans girls up and down the side walks. I can see Capt Johnny Healy[36] leading off the set and the hearty laugh of the Crowd shows how they Enjoy it. well it is a queer War. anny how it is getting late and I must Close. the Dr does not hear from his wife Yet only through you. God bless you all at home. Kiss the babies for me.

Your loving husband

T. W. Cahill

Thomas to Margaret

Camp Parrapet, Carrollton LA May 26th 1862

My Dear Wife.

It seems a long time since I heard from you by mail. I answered the last letters by Capt Churchhill from New Orleans when I informed you that we were to move up the River which we did to our present Camp where we are at present pleasantly located. at least we have green fields of Corn and sugar Cane and white Clover all about. there is woods near our Camp and the sight of the green fields and trees is a great relief to our Eyes after the glare of the white sand on Ship Island:

This is a delightfull Country in some respects: The Magnolia Tree is now in full flower filling the air with its delightfull perfume. I rode down to the Lake Shore where the Shell road runs out from New Orleans. a fashionable watering place for the wealthy people of the City. there is a beautifull garden attached to the large Hotel there in which I saw a Centurry Plant nearly ready to blossom. the owner a Litchfield Countryman

---

36. Capt. John G. Healy, Company G.

says its flower stem grows at the rate of 6 inches per day and that it will soon blossom it is not about 19 feet high about six inches in diameter:

I also see plenty of Bannana trees about in the gardens and anny quantity of Orange trees with their dark green beautiful leaves and fruit. The woods however have a verry dreary appearance as the trees are Completely Enveloped with the Long grey Louisiana Moss the same we use for beds and Cushions only that the light grey bark is rotted off before it is sent to market. so far I have no great fault to find with the Climate as yet on the Countrary rather like it. as you know I prefer Warm Weather to Cold anny time. neither do I think it bears verry hard on the men as yet true we cannot drill as we did in the winter 4 or 5 hours a day now about two: but I looked out for that and made them work when I could: The great drawbacks are want of drinking water and by far too much rum and mosquitos: I hardly know which iritates me the most while I write. the Last pest are in a perfect cloud about my Ears and it is dreadfull hard work to write a letter.

I am taking in a large number of recruits and they are verry stalwart men much Larger than the overage of our men: They are natives of Ireland Germany and some from Northern and Western States. They represent themselves as having suffered terribly during the Last year and seem glad to Come among us. our regt has such a tremendous name here some how or other that they walk out here about 8 miles to join us. While I write I heard 6 have Come into Camp. Luckily I have just recived a supply of Clothing Complete for 694 Men which Enables me to Equip them with all but Blankets and acoutrements. Our horses were brought on by Barney from Ship Island on the 24th. they were in good Condition. my horse feels fortunate. Barney is well as is all your acquaintances. Lieut Daniel Carroll[37] is going home soon. he has resigned. he could not agree with Capt G.[38]

I have not left the Camp save on the abovementioned to the Lake Shore since we came here and probably should not then only that I had sent Capt John G. Healy down there with his Company to guard a Cannal where schooners run out from the City to the Lake Ponchantrain. these vessels and their Crew and passengers must have passports with Enumerates the amount and description of baggage they are allowed to

---

37. Second Lt. Daniel Carroll, Company B.
38. Capt. Patrick Garvey, Company B.

Carry. these passes and luggage have all to be examined and it is really an verry Critical and nice business. Johnny is doing splendidly at it and giving Every satisfaction to Everybody more particularly myself. I have him trained anny how. he will make a splendid Officer if he Continues as he has so far.

I see by 2 or three Copies of New Haven Papers of the 8th and 10th of May that you have the News of our Pass Christian affair—Wm Herrity arrived out here in good health and spirits. he has taken a store in New Orleans. his goods have not yet arrived. I think he will find a ready market.

I intend to promote John McCusker[39] to a 2nd Lieutncy vise Carroll. I think Capt G will soon go home. I must Conclude this letter as the mosquitos are bothering the life out me. I can scarsely see the paper with them. I suppose you have full descriptions of our doings and of our Location in all the papers. we are ourselves the 12th Conn 8th New Hampshire 7th Vermont behind a Long fortification 10,744 feet long 12 feet high with a ditch 20 feet wide built in a Zig Zag format is a strong position.

We Expect the paymasteres here very soon. I have some thoughts of sending home what I can spare in sugar but it will depend on the price when I get my money. I have not paid annything for horse feed yet and do not know what the Bill may be for that. Fitzgibbon and Fairchild reported yesterday with their handfull of men. it was hardly worthwhile bringing them out here. George Kenedy Called to see me yesterday. he is discharged and going home. Dr Galager has not had a letter in a long time and you have not mentioned his wife in your last letters. he is almost discouraged if Dr Herz[40] is on Ship Island yet attending an Hospital our wounded man John Leonard[41] with some others will be sent home soon. I shall send home all the sick and delicate men now as I am getting men who are acclimate. I saw one John McElroy[42] a friend of Presons[43] here. he looks well as also James Sisk.[44] give my respects to all Enquiring friends. write me if you have heard annything from Father Hart. remember me to the Kind sisters mother Bernard and Sister Lucy. I will try to

---

39. Sgt. John McCusker, Company B.

40. Unknown Union surgeon at Ship Island.

41. Pvt. John A. Leonard, Company A.

42. There are no John McElroys in the muster and descriptive rolls of the Ninth Connecticut. This may refer to a local resident.

43. Possibly Pvt. Phillip Person, Company D.

44. There are no men by the name of Sisk in the muster and descriptive rolls of the Ninth Connecticut, and no James Sisk served in the Civil War from the state of Connecticut. This may refer to a local resident.

write you by Every mail but I hate to send by sailing vessels. My love to
Ellen. Kiss the Babies for me and good night you all.

Your Loving husband

Thos W Cahill

Margaret to Thomas

New Haven May 30th [1862]
2 OClock PM

My dear Husband

I have just recd your Letters of the 13 and 14 from Camp Paraphet. I
need not tell you I was delighted to hear from you—that you know—but
if I say I do not hear from you half often Enough—do not think me too
selfish—you know I had no Idea when you levt home that you would be
done so Long. but enough of this what I was going to say will do neither
of us any good under present circumstances. I will trust altogether in
Gods Mercy and hope for your return very soon—take all possible care
of yourself and be caucious about what you Eat and where you eat and
where you get it. I fear very much you are not in midtst of friends—

we are all well. the children are very well and growing fin[e]ly. you will
think so when I tell you that I have to give one Dollar for Eddys shoes and
the same for Marys yesterday. they are making great calculations on the
good time they will have when their dear Papa comes homes. if they carry
out their [illegible] strictly there will not be much of you left.

I can tell you they try my courage very much when they talk it all over
by themselves and then come to me as it were to confirm it saying "Mama
wont we Hug Papa and kiss him too when he comes home." Mary thinks
she will have no wish ungratified. She can buy all the Dolls and every
thing else she needs in that line when you come home. her demands will
be many so be prepared. I can put her off very easily leaving it all for you
do to—

I do not know for certain if you will get this letter. it is advertised that
the first steamer leaves N. York for N. Orleans tomorrow. perhaps you will
get this before you can get letter by the "Rhode Island." she will sail from
Boston on the 10 of June. I will send all your Papers by her and a long
letter if able. if not Ellen will. Yes My dear Husband our dear good friend
Ellen who will soon have the whole care of your house and children for a
time, a short time I hope but what would I do without her now—we owe
her much gratitude but you are not invisible to that—

I went to New York in April. took Eddy with me. I cannot say I enjoyed Myself. the weather was very unpleasant the most of the time. we both took head Colds from which we are just recovering. tell the Dr I spent one night with his wife and Baby in Philadelphia. I presume he has the Glad tidings ere this if not tell him his little Daughter is a beautiful healthy Baby was two weeks old when I visit. Looks like *a Baby*. his wife was well and strong. far beyond my Expectations but she recd no money from him at the time I saw her later part of April.

I went to see Mr Schannley about it. he could nothing for her without the Drs Receipt from the Experss Agent. if he has sent the Money home and there has been any foul play he had better sent the receipt to his wife or whoever he chooses that she may get it sometime of course. he must know she needs it although I think she has every comfort she needs. her people are very kind and attentive to her but it makes her feel uneasy to think the Dr has sent his Money home and she has not to get it. I wish he had sent it to New Haven. it would have been all right. I have not heard of a single case but hers where the money was delayed—

Give Father Mullin my best wishes. tell him I recd his letter. I feel very gratful for his kind acknowledgements and will write soon. Father Smith has spent the Last hour and a half with us. he read all your last letters. was delighted with them. sends his kind regards to you—I have much more to say but fear you will not get this it is so late I hope you will—

there was a letter from Father Hart last week. his health is improved some but not enough to Come home for some time yet—do not feel uneasy about us. everything is going on well Thank God—I recd those papers by Express they were recd by the Gov too—Mr McCartan came to see us twice. Father Sheridan says if he has a wife who would play him such a trick he would give her one good pounding and then do no more for her.

Your Wife
M. E. Cahill

CHAPTER 4

"You may well call this a horrible war"

June–August 1862

Thomas to Margaret

On Board Steamer McClellan
Mississippi River June 1st 1862

My Dear Wife

as you may judge from the heading we are again on the move. This time to Baton Rouge to join 4 other Regts under Brigd Genl Williams: I will write you from there as soon as possible, you may remember the member of the Band who came to get a leave of absence to go to look for his brother by the name of Allen[1] from Fair Haven. he has suceeded in coaxing a furlough from Genl Phelps and is going to try Genl Butler. he may possibly succed. I wish I could:

I am in hopes this change of locality may be for the best. our Camp Parapet was surrounded by water from a crevasse four miles below us. The land is higher at Baton Rouge than there and it considered healthy. you may recollect your brother was there some time. I do not Know whether ours will be a permanent home or not: It is too bad about their pay as the Paymaster was in the City ready to pay us off for the April muster and had one set of our papers with him. He will have to follow us up now I suppose and he will pay off the troops in the City first probably.

I have Enlisted near 200 men in New Orleans. they fine looking men much better looking than the average of our men. I am not at all pleasant with the looks of the Country along this River. there are some fine looking plantations and houses but the land is too flat, it seems well cultivated. there is no Evidence that desperate destruction of property we read so much about: the people seem intolerably passive standing in

---

1. Regimental band member Oliver Allen.

small groups staring at us as we sail by: I can see manny females in apparent mouring which is suggestive of friends lost, still it may be mere fancy as some ladies affect that style of dress.

We are now at 10 PM at anchor waiting to go up at daylight: The Naval officer who is taking us up. a Mr Goodwin. he is from the Flag Ship Hartford and his description of the Passage of the Forts is highly terriffic and if I were not aware of the facts would sound like a tale of fiction. Do you remember one Gray who was with Theabald in Nicurauga and of whom he used to tell such stories? he is now in our regt[2] and I Expect I may see the other Every day. I can recognise his red head among a thousand. all our friends are well but the Dr. Gets no word from home. I hardly Expect to hear from verry regularly now unless the governments puts on more boats and I do not know what Communications will be kept up with Baton Rouge: Keep on writing however as you have done and I will get them some time and they are always good when they Come. I hope Father Hart is home and well. if so remember me to him and ask him to write me: give my respects to all Enquiring friends. Kiss the Babies for me God Bless you and the little dears. give my love to Ellen and I remain your Loving husband.

T. W. Cahill

Thomas to Margaret

U.S. Arsenal
Baton Rouge LA
June 4th 1862

My Dear Wife

I write you by the return of the McLellan to N Orleans. I have nothing to say save that we are all well and Comfortably quartered in the Property of the U States. there is a magnificient shade here and the Buildings are Clean and high between Joints Conseqeuntly airy. the Gov Buildings here are verry fine and the Rebels left them in a hurry and did not have time to injure them much. I do not at the present see what we were tumbled up here in such a hurry for and Can see nothing in particular to be done. So far however the Change is delightfull.

this is a verry nice place resembling New Haven very Much particularly in its fine shade trees, at first I considered the move as only temporary,

---

2. Pvt. Patrick Gray, Company K.

but seeing Genl Williams it looks like a more permanent affair as he has ordered up all my tents and Camp Equipage: I am afraid it may bother me about the mens pay somewhat it may not have. Even as the Paymaster may Come up here as there is so many men here. we have here Nims[3] and Everests Batteries[4] and 2 gun boats. The Large vessels of the Fleet have been up the River as far as Vicksburgh but are now at N Orleans.

The People here are said to be quite and Civile and are beginning to Come back from the run they made into the Country. some of them were scared nearly to death and say they ran as far as they could untill the water from the Mississippi river which has flooded the whole Country stopped them from running anny farther, we are on the Hill here and I say let the water Come down, it may be the Easiest way of settling the Chivalry and Cooling their blood and is cheaper than ball and powder and not half as troublesome to us. I do not know how I shall like my new Genl. liked the old one well Enough but he had too many Contrabands. his camp was full of them. do not know how this one is but have not seen anny of much consequence at the present.

Must bring this to a Close in time for steamer. Kiss the babies for me and love to Ellen. Regards to all friends.

Your Loving husband

Thos W Cahill

Margaret to Thomas

New Haven June 9th

My dear Husband

I hurried off a Box to you this Morning filled with papers and hoping it would go by the Steamer Rhode Island. but they sent me word from the Express office that she would carry nothing but letters so I must content myself with writing a few lines—your Papers will go by way of New York. they will reach you Sometime—we are all well at home but we feel more anxious about you every day. I do wish we could hear from you. more frequent Business is very dull here. everyone is complaining of the "Hard times." I believe there is nothing doing in the way of Building or improvements in the City—there is a great many sick and wounded

3. Second Battery Massachusetts Light Artillery, commanded by Capt. Ormand F. Nims. Witcomb, *History of the Second Massachusetts Battery*.

4. Sixth Battery Massachusetts Light Artillery, commanded by Capt. Charles Everett. *Official Army Register*, part 1, 142.

Soldiers from Gen McClellan's Army in the City. they tell me there is no Conn. Men among them. I hope the Poor Suffering Strangers will be well Cared for Oh! when will this frightful War be ended.

the House is very Still and Lonely. Niolsmen[5] moved out about two weeks ago. I have not put out a Bill because I dread to rent the rooms to Strangers. While you are away Tenants has got to be so important in their feelings—there is nothing talked of among them I believe but about going away with rent and Hamering the owners at that. I have had no trouble of this kind at all. I *am without the rent* since you left home but he makes very fair promises and I hope to get part of it at least. the House is very much abused but I am trying hard to have it Look a little like old times and it will soon I hope. I had Coyle send me a man to do some White Washing and I had the front Door done over and the front stoop painted. it Looked very hard. I had one coat of White Paint put on the Bed rooms and the Walls whitened upon the whole. we Look Smug and Clean. I had James Green to dig the Garden and Plant the most of it with Potatoes. the rest of it I planted myself with some Beans—Cabbage—and some *Flowers* of *course*. all our little Pear trees Bolssomed this Spring. three of them will Bear a number of fruit and our little Cherry tree is full of green cherrys and goosberry's are just fit for *Pies*. and you so far away that I cannot send you some—

well this is a query. would I read a letter from Mrs Galagher this Morning. She and Baby is well. She has recd the Dr's Money—Father Obrien wished to be remembered to and Father Smith and Sheridan. he did not Expect Father Hart before fall. I hope you will be here to Welcome him—how is Father Mullen? I hear he is going to have a nice Chappel Tent Sent him from here. Give him my Love—and all friends—Good bye My dear Husband. God Bless you and Send you home soon to us. this is your little Babies Prayer three or four times a day—

From your Loving Wife
Margaret E. Cahill

---

5. One of the Cahill's tenants, though they have been lost to the historical record.

Thomas to Margaret

On Board Steamer Diana
June 23d 1862

My Dear Wife

your very brief but acceptable letter of the 28th of May came to hand at Baton Rouge La on the 10th of June: We left camp Parapet on the 31st of May for Baton Rouge: and left Baton Rouge en Route for Vicksburg on the 19th of June and at 8 P.M. of this date *tied up* at a small village Called St. Josephs to give the Cooks a chance to go ashore to cook for the men: We landed yesterday at a place called Ellis Cliffs 10 miles below Natchez to take a Battery on said Cliffs which had been firing upon our boats going up and down the river: but the Enemy fled before we arrived: So we had our march for nothing. it looked like a formidable position.

It is very tedious this steaming up this terrible long crooked river. you can get a very good idea of this river and the positions on it from copy of Frank Lislies[6] of May 10th if you have procure one:

I write to you this without the slightest idea of how I can get it to you or when I shall hear from home again: I see you are anxious about my coming home and I can gather from another ambiguous word or two in your letter why you should be so: But God is good my Dear and we can only trust in him: I can only say that you are not a whit more anxious that myself; I would have been away before now if I could have made an honourable retreat. Other folks can go but I am given to understand that I cannot be spared and we must not Either of us give way to despondency as the Lord has laid out the work for us he will support us in it:

My health thanks to Divine providence continues Extremely good: as does that of the officers and men Indeed Extremely. so we have great reason to be thankful for the blessing of such good health for yourself and the little ones at home and ours here: With the exception of a few left at Baton Rouge to be discharged the health of our regiment is re-markably good.

---

6. Frank Leslie's *Illustrated Newspaper* was published by English-born Leslie, an engraver and newspaperman in London before moving to the United States in the late 1840s. His *Illustrated Newspaper* first appeared in 1856 and had a circulation of more than 150,000 in 1860. When the war broke out, Leslie committed that his newspaper would be dedicated to depicting scenes of the war for public consumption in the North. Forbes, *Thirty Years After*, xi.

I might fill up a great deal of paper in attempting to describe the sights along this wonderful river but have such little hopes of getting this letter off that I feel discouraged about writing: there are some remarkably fine sights but the general features are dreary in the Extreme as there has been terrible floods here which on most cases has Completely ruined the Crops and drowned a great many Cattle: The Planters or somebody Else have destroyed nearly all the Cotton on hand and have not planted any more this season. the land is all planted in Corn and that has been in a great measure destroyed by the floods in the Lowlands and the want of rain in the high: Sugar has not been so generally destroyed as Cotton. I saw thirteen Bales of Cotton in one place to day as we came up the River apparently thrown over board and floated ashore.

These people are perfectly wild in their insanity and I have my doubts as to the Length of time it will take to restore them to the little sense they Ever had.

Dates of the 28th of May are the latest we have seen and we have heard some very bad news through secesh sources of McClellans reverses at Richmond. we do not credit them but they annoy us as the suspense is very great. We hope the river may be open to Cairo soon and that we may hear from Davis fleet soon. at present we are all in the dark as to what has been done or is doing above. You speak in your letter of Ellens writing. I have not received her letter. Kiss the Babies for Me and I pray for your welfare. give my love to Ellen and say I will not forget her kindness.

your loving husband
Thos. W. Cahill

Thomas to Margaret

On Board Transport Steamer Diana off Vicksburg June 24th
10 O Clock P.M.

My Dear wife

Major Frye has returned from his tour of duty as Field Officer of the day and reports that Commodore Davis Fleet is within 2 miles of us in a direct line but so Crooked is the River that by water it is 7 or 8 miles or perhaps 12 miles to them. The Bomb Boats have been at work at Vicksburg since yesterday morning and only Ceased at 9 O Clock P M to day. the Brooklyn is Cruising up and down in front of the City firing an occasional gun but ellicits no reply. I think their batteries are silenced but can tell better in the morning: the other large vessels of the Gulf Fleet are lying within hurling distance of us: and there are several of Com Davis Fleet within 10 miles of us near the Yazoo River where it is said they are cutting away a Raft placed there to prevent them from going up:

You will ask what are we doing well at present. we are detailing 200 men per day to Cut a new Channel for the Miss River in order to turn it away from Vicksburg and to leave her all alone on her Bluffs which she has so impudently attempted to use to ban our progress up the Mississippi. this is a great scheme if it will work as it promises and it may be another Evidence that we Cannot be stopped when we want to go ahead. I do not know whether it will be continued if the City surrenders, we have had 2 Severe marches since we came up the River. one at Ellis Cliffs and another at Grand Gulf. in neither place did the rebels wait for us [page torn]. we had a terrible hot march at the latter place for nothing.

I do not know how to tell you to direct your next letter. I may be up or down the River but suppose you wrote two or more and send by way of the West. the Papers will tell you how to me at Vicksburg New Orleans or Elsewhere and those by the Gulf of New Orleans or Elsewhere. I have no more time to write. am comfortable and well living on board the steamer. the men only Commenced work to day and seem to like it. will try to make you a sketch of the proposed work. Kiss the Babies for me. my Love to Ellen. hope to get a letter from you by the next boat from N Orleans. this letter goes at day break and all letters must be out in 20 minutes. will run over the rule to make you a sketch.

 God bless you
 Your aff husband
 Thos W Cahill

Thomas to Margaret

On Board Steamer Diana
Mississippi River Near Vicksburgh June 30th 1862

My Dear Wife

I wrote you a few days ago and sent my letter by one of the western Fleet; it is said that they will have regular Communications Every few days by way of Cairo and Memphis, so I send you a few lines; we have made no perceptible progress since my last: I say we I mean the Fleet for not much is Expected from the small land force here at this time unless the stupendious attempt we are making to turn the River out of its usual Channel amounts to more than it seems at present to promise: we are still digging with about 700 soldiers and 4 to 5 hundred negroes: and will let the water on in a few days but as the river is falling rapidly I have not much faith in the scheme. *never did* but that is not my business. we work as we are told and do as well as we can and I suppose you had as life here of our digging as fighting.

The Rebels are showing considerable fight here with their Batteries and the Position is naturally verry strong. the most of the Fleet have gone past the Batteries with out much loss; the Bomb Boats Continue below and fire occasionily. the Buildings in the City must have suffered severely as have some of the Batteries. we are lying on the Right Bank of the River Coming down the Position I marked for you on the little sketch I sent you. it is said the Commodore has sent word to General Halleck[7] who is said to be at Memphis to Bring down a heavy land force to take the City in the Rear. It is said the Rebels have 20,000 men here: and we may have to starve them out by shutting them up. if they are so strong it is too good a position to take by storm. we have no late news and are in a fever of anxiety to hear from McClellan; as I am to hear from you am well as usual thank God as are all our friends here.

The weather is warm but do suffer more than we would at home this time. have no thermometer so cannot give you the measure of heat. Am satisfied with it however it is said that it will not be warmer. the mens health continues good Considering the heat and the work which makes them desire to shirk all they can and the Dr does not feel like being verry severe upon them neither do I. there is negroes Enough in the Country and I feel as though they ought to be taken for that work they are beginning to collect for that purpose.

If this Reaches you within a few days Direct your answer

Col Thos W. Cahill 9th Regt Conn Vols: Genl Williams Brigade: Genl Butlers Division Near Vicksburg, Via Cairo.

Kiss the Babies for me. give my love to Ellen and all friends.

Your Loving husband

Thos W. Cahill

---

7. Gen. Henry W. Halleck, a West Point graduate, gained popularity after Union successes in the western theater at Shiloh and Corinth in the spring and summer of 1862. After the fall of Corinth, Lincoln brought the general east to take command of the Union war effort as general in chief. Warner, *Generals in Blue*, 195–97. For a full account of Halleck's life and service see Marszalek, *Commander of All Lincoln's Armies*.

Thomas to Margaret

Opposite Vicksburg
July 5th 1862

My Dear Wife

½ an hour since I heard that the Tennessee would leave for New Orleans this Evening though it looks like taking the Back track on sending letters to send them by the old way of the Gulf. Yet I thought I would send you one that way although I have sent you 2 by the way of Cairo and Memphis by Com Davis Fleet. so I only send you this as a stray waif.

we are all well. so far the place not yet taken and no immediate sights of yet. the Enemy is pretty strong here. too strong for the weak detachments sent up from New Orleans. Com Faragut has sent to Memphis for more land forces some say 20,000. We have some of our men pretty Close to the Enemy on the other side of the River. they are thrown out at pickets.

we have not yet got the ditch cut through that is to turn the Mississippi River out of its Course. dont know when we shall however it is only negroes that will be at work on it soon as we are collecting them from all around here. some 800 or 1,000 of them at work on it now so will not want the soldiers to work on it soon. I only send this in case annything should happen that I should not get them in through by the way of the River. have not heard anny news as yet from Richmond nor from anny where Else. hope to hear from home in a few days as Com Davis the Dear good soul promises to send a boat up the River every 2 days and they will Come back mail both ways. so I Expect to hear while we lay at this place and Davis keeps the River open Every 3 or 4 days while we lay here. Shant write much at this time as I Expect it this will not get home for some time after letters by the River. good by. my Love to Ellen. Respects to all Enquiring friends. Kiss the Babies for Me.

    Your Loving husband
    Thos W Cahill

Thomas to Margaret

On Board Steamer Diana July 8th 1862

My Dear Wife

Your Welcome letter of the 9th of June by the Rhode Island came to hand yesterday: I was glad to hear that yourself and children were well as I drew different information with reference to yourself from the preceding letter. how came you to give me such a start. So Widmer has Cleared with the Rent. well it is what might be expected from the Black Rascal. it is just such Canting hounds as him that brought this trouble upon us. if such fellows had Confined themselves to cheating us our money it would be less matter. I think I would not trouble myself about renting the place though. it would be a help to get Enough to help pay the taxes but an Empty house is better than a bad tenant any day so let the rooms alone unless it suits you:

Tell Mrs Geary that I met a friend of hers of the name of Cunningham at Baton Rouge. his brother is a Clergyman in Batavia New York he is also a Brother I think of the young man who was staying with them for College before I left home:[8] he has a farm or Plantation as they Call them here about 7 or Eight miles from Baton Rouge. I franked a letter for him to his Brother in Batavia which was how I came to know him. the poor man was verry much frightened and did not know what to do between the two parties he has one son in the Rebel army did not know whether he was dead or alive—the other son who had been at College north has Escaped so far but was away somewhere I suppose to Escape the Conscription. You may well call this a horrible war. the most so the world has Ever seen. as God only knows when it will be Ended.

We are tormented here with Conflicting accounts of affairs before Richmond and with rumours of foreign intervention and know not what to believe: we expect a boat down from Memphis however Every hour and hope to learn something definite.

Your speaking of the gooseberry pies makes my mouth water but what is the use. we must take our destiny as the Lord Wills.

---

8. Rev. Thomas Cunningham of St. Joseph's Parish in Batavia, N.Y. Cahill's acquaintance was, most likely, Patrick Cunningham, a farmer, who in 1860 lived in the parish of East Baton Rouge and owned around $720 in property. Patrick's eldest two sons (Hampden and Thomas) were born in New York in 1842 and 1843. *Calendar of the Catholic Church,* Archives of the University of Notre Dame, Ind., 487; Eighth Census of the United States.

my health Continues good thank God. the men and some of the Officers are suffering from summer Complaints but none of them are seriously ill at present. we have lost three men since we left Carrollton. 2 of
them we left sick at Baton Rouge and one died here this morning: they all
belonged to Co I Capt Curtiss. they died from general debillity. Our men
have been working on the ditch or Cutoff which our wise Commander is
working at. but they have been scouring the plantations up and down the
River and have now about a thousand negroes and have discharged the
soldiers from the digging for which they and I am gratefull.

I have not yet ascertained what we came here for. the Navy have not yet
silenced the Batteries and fear they will not. We have not ¼ the necessary
strength to take the place: and the Comadore has sent to Memphis for
troops to attack by Land. some say 40,000 men. I presume this will depend materially on the state of affairs at Richmond. I sent you a sketch
of our position. since sending it we have moved up a little higher nearer
the position of the Bomb Boats on the west side of the River. Johnny put
on the Extra touches but the main part was copied from one by the En-
gineers Employed on the Expedition.

The Enemy are at their Old game of planting Batteries along the River
behind us as we come up. they have another at Grand Gulf and the Boat
that brought up the Mail by which I recd your last letter was struck 12
times in Coming up. I Expect we shall have some trouble from them yet
but hope for the best it is possible. we will go down the River again soon
if the western troops Come down from above. we can do nothing here
alone. I do not like this Brigade neither do I think they like me. The
Lieut Col tells me that he understands by his letters that Col Denning is
not Coming back here again. I suspected as much when he went away but
he was quite indignant when an officer in my presence hinted as much
to him. he said was no Wilson to do such a thing. perhaps not but I have
not heard of his Coming back here yet.

If I get near Genl Butler again I will make a desperate Effort to get
home on furlough but fear it will not be granted. if not I shall be almost
tempted to resign though I should hate to do that and wish to bring
the regiment home with me. but as you say I did not Expect to be gone
so long. but what can we do the war must Come to an End some time
though what the result will be the Lord only knows. one thing is Certain
our section is not the worst off. this End of the Confederacy is in a horrible Condition. I do not see what they are living on unless it is their spite.

Give my respects to all friends. I wrote a long rambling letter to Mayor
Welch before I left Carrollton. have had no answer. do not get any letters

from any body but you are the folks all dead. got 4 couriers of June 9th from Capt McCarten. thank him for me. give my love to Ellen. Kiss the babies as usual for me.

Your Loving husband
Thos W Cahill

Margaret to Thomas

New Haven July 10th

My Dear Husband

Your very welcome letter came to hand this morning. I need not tell you how delighted we were to hear from you. I also recd yours dated 23rd written on board the same Steamer. it was mailed in Cairo July 1st and I had it on the 5th. if I could only have had it on the 4th Oh Dear: What a day I spent. I can never forget it and only think of it, they were absurd enough here to Ring their Joy Bells and fire a *National Salute* when the very air was full of wailing on account of that terrible Battle before Richmond,[9] the celebration of the 4th took place in Bridgeport the Governor and all the *Great Connecticut Warriors* were there. I wish I had the Drafting of some of them in my hands—

I wish I could send you the papers regular. I sent you a Box full about 4 weeks ago. you do not speak of getting them. there has been but very few letters from the 9th lately. their friends are beginning to feel very uneasy but your last letters has given them great comfort in your answer to this. please mention B. Leynch James Lawler their wives are very much troubled about them and poor Carroll how is he getting along. his wife is a wretched Looking creature it is well he did not send all his money to her it would have all been gone Long ago. tell him I enquired for him—

I am a little uneasy about those U.S. Bonds of yours. there is considerable talk here about their becoming worthless if a Foreighin Power will have to interfere with us. of course every thing will go down. I wish I had

---

9. The Battle of Malvern Hill, which took place July 1, 1862, occurred on the final day of the Seven Days Battles, as the Union army withdrew from Richmond. Soldiers formed a line along Malvern Hill, an "elevated, open pleateau . . . just under a mile north of the James [River]." The Army of Northern Virginia launched an assault on those lines on July 1, 1862, suffering some 5,650 casualities to the Union's 3,007. Despite the Union victory, Gen. George McClellan, ordered the army's continued retreat, thus ending his Peninsula Campaign. Sears, *To the Gates of Richmond*, 308–36.

Gold in their stead. it would be too bad to have such hard earned Money become Worthless—I sent Ellen to see the Mayor about it and the Tax is on the Place. he sent me word not to feel uneasy about them but that they were not worth as much as they were when you sent them home. I think he said they would bring two or three Dollars less Premium.

July 11th.

when I left of writing yesterday I left this letter on the Book Case Desk and Somebody made an attempt to finish it. Mary says he was Eddy and he says Mary told him to do it. so you see they both had a hand in it and I will let it go.

My dear Husband I recd your last letter dated July 30 this morning. it is perfectly delightful to hear from you so often when I *must* make up my mind that I am going to see you home a soon as I expected. I know you will come as soon as you can. hope that will be soon—we have very hot weather here. it has completely used me up. I am lazy in every sense of the word but promise to do better—

My health is good as is that of the children very good and Ellens too. Father ORiely[10] was in Town last week. he called to see me twice. he feels very much *interested* in your welfare. he Says God will Protect you and bring you safe home. Mary asked him to Pray for her Papa. he told her he never forgot him that he Prayed for him in Europe and surly would not forget him here. he says we may Expect Father Hart home any day. I wish he was here now—

I must tell you about my success in gardening. I will begin with that nearest the House. the Grape vine never looked so fine or had so many grapes on and the little Cherry tree is full of fruit nice large Cherries the goosberries and currants is most tempting to Look at and we have any quantity of them. four of our pear trees is laden with fruit and the Peach tree at the foot of the garden is covered with nice healthy looking Peaches—I think we can dig our Potatoes next week. so you see we are getting on nicly—if we could only get you here to help us make use of them. the Pig is growing nicly too—James Feeny came to see us today. he has been home some time. he was Wounded in the Leg. it is reported John Sheffery is dead. I saw by the paper he was seriously wounded—

10. There were at least four priests with the surname O'Reilly who served the Catholic population of that city during this period. Shahan, *Catholic Historical Review*, 162–63.

advise me about those Bonds and write often as you can if only a few lines to let us know you are well—God Bless you and keep you from ill—Ellen is well Sends her Love. from your Loving Wife M. E. Cahill

You will say what Paper to write a letter on but when I tell you that your little Mary went to the store and bought it you will not think light of it. I know she goes to the store regular for me and goes to Mrs Murptly done. Eddy always stands on the front stoop and will not leave it until Sister Marry comes. it is getting dark I cannot see Longer.

    Good Night and God Bless you

    Yours M. E. Cahill

Thomas to Margaret

Near Vicksburg July 20th 1862

My Dear Wife

    your welcome letter of July 11th Came to hand today. how good it does seem to get a letter only eight days old and how it makes my mouth water to think of the Gooseberries Courants and of new potatotoes. Well never mind. I'll think more of them when I get home please God and it does one good to know that Eight days ago all was well at home:

    you ask what to do about those Bonds. I would not sell at present and we have not got a great deal of them to lose and those we have are the best there is;

    I do not know when we will get our pay and think not for some time and allotments Come into play at this payment. I do not know but you might draw some Gold on those allotment. speak to Mr Charbley about it.

    I see that since the disaster before Richmond.[11] Gold has advanced at a tremendous rate. I shall try to get all I can of the pay left in my hands in Gold. I do not know how I shall send what I shall have to spare home whether by the Paymaster or by the Express. if we are paid here I shall have to make use of the Paymaster who I think told me that he could arrange to pay to my order at home. if I cannot use the Express this would be my only Chance of getting it home.

    you do not mention having received My Box from ship Island which I sent to you on the ship "Undaunted" by Addams Express about the 15th

---

11. Cahill is referring McClellan's defeat at the Seven Days Battles outside Richmond. See Gallagher, *Richmond Campaign of 1862*; Burton, *Extraordinary Circumstances*; Sears, *To the Gates of Richmond.*

or 20th of April Last. it Contained my Dress Coat and Scabbard my Over
Coat and Epaulettes and a Considerable amount of under clothes. in fact
Every thing I could get into a strong Chest 20 inches deep 2 foot wide
and over three feet long: I paid Addams agent $5 freight on it and took a
Receipt for it which I suppose I have among my papers if I did not send
it on to you which I do not recollect about now:

I wear nothing but my dress uniform flannel shirts with or without
Collars mostly the latter no handkercheif. The Weather is verry hot here.
we have shifted our men off the steam boats to the Bank of the River
near the West End of the "Cut off" and are Covered by the Guns of the
Western Fleet. We did this for the sake of getting the men into the fresh
air. it is Cleared fields where we are now and pretty airy but the heat
of the sun is great. but I think it better than being in the woods on wet
ground:

The men are a good deal Debilitated from the heat but I do not apprehend a great amount of sickness: there are a good manny however that
I would discharge and send home if I could get the necesary papers for
this discharge but I Cannot procure them. there has been 4 deaths in the
Regt since we came up the River. one Lieut Fairchild of Co H who came
out about the middle of may. he belongs and is married in Bridgeport.
One Louis St V Hallauer[12] one of the first Class musicians of the Band.
he was married to one of the Simons sisters who have a shoe shop next
to the Attwaters in Grand St. one old man named Waldron of Co B[13]. one
named Robertson of Co I.[14]

The men are getting home sick as in fact we all are. the uncertainty
of our movements tends greatly to this End. we do not know how where
we are going to be from one day to another. all this tends to depress the
spirits and make the men uneasy which of course reacts upon the health.
now we are situated at present. we cannot tell when we are ordered to
move. in fact since I have been writing this I have recieved a verbal order
to move my sick back to the boat with a view to sending them to Baton
Rouge for a Change of air and we cannot tell the moment we may be all
sent off Somewhere. it is said Com Faragut has received Orders to leave
here. we came up here to assist him. the Fleet Cannot take Vicksburg and
it will take a powerfull land force to do it.

12. Louis St. V. Hallauer of New Haven.

13. Pvt. Thomas Waldron, Company B.

14. Pvt. Seth Robertson , Company I.

The Ram Arkansas also has broke loose and is giving both Fleets a great deal of trouble. I doubt if they Can take her. it will not do to leave her behind:

The tremendous Cut off that was to have done so much is about given up so that really things are in a worse shape than when we Came here: How it will End I do not know and as I am not responsible let them do as they like.

I will take care of my self and my Command as long as I can and then I will stop. I dislike to offer my resignation but feel that I cannot serve under such a man as we are under at present a great while and I shall take the first opportunity to Escape. but I must try to do so in an honourable manner. if I could only get my papers for discharges I would send home half the Regt before I leave myself: but then I really do not know what to turn my self to. there is no liklihood of their being any business to do for a long time after this infernal war and there must be a complete change in all the affairs of Life. if I could get along with such confounded _____ [as written in the original] as I am under now I would continue from seat of Policy as well as from Patriotic motives but this is all speculation. I cannot tell what may turn up. yet however you can understand that I feel like Coming home as soon as I can and I want to take Care of my friends and get them out with me or into better places if they stay in it.

you want me to mention Barney Lynch and James Lawler in my letters and John Carroll. you Can always understand that if I do not mention them particularly if it because they are all well. John McCusker is also well as is Lieut O'Brien. in fact all that we are acquainted with are well and have been. so I think you have no reason to find fault with the Length of this Letter and I have a good mind to stop here as you did in the middle of a page because it was getting dark and you had no Candles. I suppose so. miss Mary bugs the paper and Master Eddy trys his hand at writing. now I think Mary ought to write a letter as well as him. I wish I could get the Mocking Bird Jonny has Raised home. it is a splendid Bird. Kiss the little dears for me. give my Love to Ellen and my Respects to all Enquiring friends.

Thos W. Cahill

Margaret to Thomas

New Haven July 24th 1862

My Dear Husband

Our little Thomas Mathew is 11 Days-20 hours old at the commencement of this letter. I will try to have him weighed before I close it to
show you what a fine little fellow he is—the most hungry little Boarder
I ever had in my house and such a pair of Lungs you have never heard.
I know—Dr Ives wrote you a day or two after he was born and Ellen has
written twice since so I sincerely trust by this time you have all the news
of his coming—both the Doctors have been very kind to me and most
attentive. could not be more so if I was their own child. I have had a great
many sudden changes up to two days ago but with Gods help they have
all passed over and I am Mag again but only on *Conditions* and those are
that you must come home. now I have said *must* (but not in anger) and
that means a good deal. I cannot help it for my Heart is nearly broken.
I cannot hold out much longer and you must give me credit for being
patient a good while—you know I have too much feeling or pride or
whatever you may choose to call it to let any person know my real feelings
about your being absent—but I am not ashamed to tell you that it is the
greatest trials I ever had. although I have had many and sore ones too.
but none like this I think.

Friday Morn July 25th

My dear Husband I recd your letter written with pencil and dated July
16th this morning. and so you have and another narrow escape. well I
hope it will be the last. God is very good to us. try to get to New Orleans
and do not leave it while you again it has seemed to me that you were only
sent up the river to summer privations or to be slauthered by the Enemy.
if I can call the Natives by such a name. I am very much inclined to think
we have our greatest Enemys in our midst—if I keep in this strain much
longer you will wish I did not write at all. but come home on furlough at
least and a few days will open your Eyes to the real state of affairs.

I am very glad you spoke about P.G.[15] in your for I am tired trying to
Convince people he is a Model Man for I took him to be such. but do

---

15. Capt. Patrick Garvey, Company B.

not anoy yourself trying to keep him. let him come. he will be very little thought of here. L.OB.[16] must be a very pure minded young Man. he never Spoke of any difficulty only once when he said that Some of the officers could not go to rest at night until they had a good "Grovol"— some person has just called and who do you think it was Capt Palmer.[17] he is going to stay home 30 days. I was so pleased to him. he speaks with some sense. he was sorry he could not see you before he came. he could not stay but a few minutes but he told a great deal in that time he spoke of you in the highest terms. he says he never came across a Gentleman he thought more about. he promised to come see me again and take out anything I wanted to Send you—

now about our returned Capts. I have never heard of them Speaking ill of you. I don't think they did and if they were inclined to do so they would hardly done do so. I think they would get more knocks than smiles. Duffy is back to the old match. he sports his uniform yet says he is going back to the Regt. they tell me he is trying to get permission from the Gov to raise an other company for some of the Regts now getting up—

I will soon have to stop writing. I am getting tired. the children are well they are very much pleased with little Thomas. he is well and hardy too—the Mayor answered your letter to him on its receipt. he is Looking for another from you—We have to take Postage Stamps for change. if you want to change 1 Dollar bill you must buy the worth of it or 75 cts worth and take the rest in stamps—

I wish I knew what to do with those Bonds how to dispose of them to the best advantage. I am so anxious to have Father Hart come. he would tell me what do to but T Sheridan[18] is very kind to me. he comes every day to see us and hear from you. I spoke to him yesterday about my Money Matters. the poor Man. he came Early this morning and gave me 40 Dollars of his own to me to hold on to the Bonds until I heard from you—to want nothing of myself while he had it. indeed he has kept the life in me for the last 8 weeks. he sent me two bottles of B_ that and he alone kept me from sinking entirely—

---

16. Reference to Lawrence O'Brien.

17. Lt., later Capt., Charles S. Palmer of Stratford, Company I.

18. Lt. Terrence Sheridan, Company E, who was only twenty-two when he enlisted, was constantly in trouble. Among other things, he married a Southerner and was arrested for drunkenness and lewd behavior. It seems Sheridan's parents hoped that Thomas would look after the young lieutenant during his time in service.

I expect my Dr's bill will be no small sum. Oh I must stop. I stole a Mary on the nurse. She is as sleep and thinks I am the same. good bye God Bless and Protect you.

M. E. Cahill

Thomas to Margaret

On board the Steamer Diana Off Baton Rouge July 26, 62

My Dear Wife

You will see by the heading that We have again Changed our location. you should think that nothing strange by this time. Com Faraguts Fleet got Orders to leave Vicksburg to the Western Fleet and as our Orders were to accompany him we left when he did. at this moment I am not positive whether our Regt will remain at this place or go to Carrollton but I suppose we will remain here. Herrity has got up here and opened a store and is selling off fast. think I should prepare to remain here as I consider it is perhaps the healthiest But am somewhat afraid that infernal Ram "Arkansas" which Our two fleets allowed to slip in between them may give us something awful by bothering our transports.

I have Just received yours of June 17th in pencil in which you Complain of suffering from nurralgia. but as I have recd letters from you of July 12th by the Up River route I know that you were well this by the. I have just received a latter from Mrs Dr Gallagher Complaining of not hearing from the Dr. why? what in the World Can be the Matter with the Philadelphia Post Office. I know the Dr writes as regular as myself and that he has attended to his duties perhaps the most regularly of any man in the Regt. he does not hear from her at all. what Can be the matter. they are both in despair at not hearing from Each other. not 5 minutes ago I requested Major Frye who was writing home to request his wife to let you know of our arrival here. we are not an hour on the dock yet and I have not had Orders to land yet. I have no time to write. the Dr is on another boat which has not yet arrived. Expect him every moment. if this gets home write to Mrs G and assure her that all is well with the Dr. you said that his remmittence had been recd. he would not have known that were it not for you. it will not be possible for me to answer her letter by this mail if it leaves as soon as we Expect now [illegible] I can get this on board.

what does she mean by saying I am to have an other little stranger to welcome me home? Lord save us. why dont you tell me so yourself. you have not said a word about it or a slight hint in your April letters. I wish I could be home with you. I will try at any rate but hardly dare to hope for its success. all your acquaitices are tolerably well. John McCksker has been a weak turn before we left as had Father Mullen and Capt Healy and Bernard Lynch and James Lawler but the Change of air has brought them up God Bless you my Dear wife.

I wrote you 2 long letters by the Western route but I fear the last was destroyed by the Rebels. do not send anny more by that Route as I fear it will be Closed again. direct as before to New Orleans or Elsewhere do you best to read this as I have not taken 5 minutes to write it. god bless you all. my Love to Ellen. Kiss the babies for me whether 2 or 3 or more or less.

    your Loving husband
    T. W. Cahill

Margaret to Thomas

New Haven July 27th

My Dear Husband

I do hope you have heard from here ere this. you ought to have two or 3 letters from us by the last mail. nothing of interest has turned up since my last, we are all very well little. Thomas is growing fin[e]ly. I wish you could see the little fellow but you will soon. I know Father Hart has not come yet although we are tired watching him. we expect him in Every steamer. I hope he will come soon.

all our friends are well. Mr OBrien has just gone home. he spent most of the morning with me. he felt so pleased when I told him you mentioned his son in your letter. you know how he acts when he is well pleased about anything. I have heard for a long time that F McKeon sends home the most [unreadable] letters. they say he tells most fitiful stories about food and hardships of the severest kind. now what I wonder at is why dont he come home. what keeps him there suffering so so much? but like every-thing Else it may not be true. but then there must be something to it. I told a person Early last winter that if he did not stop sending home such letters or come home himself I would write to you and Genl Phelps and let you both know what a Baby he was. the old man his Father felt very indignant at it. he will never forgive me. he has not been to see me since I cannot say. I am sorry.

Now I am very much surprised that the (Dr) does not hear from his wife. I am certain the Mails leave Philadelphia as often and regular as they do New York and if they write to each then what can come of their letters. there seems to be something queer about it to me. I have told you often that she never lived in New Haven after the Dr went away and still I find Capt Palmer in search of her in New Haven. there is a good many kinds of people in this world I find.

I hope to get a letter from you tomorrow. I trust in God you are well. George Kenedy is home. Mag was in a terrible way about him he was so long coming home—Kale Eagan heard from Retin. he sent his Love to you. he has been quite unfortunate about getting work. he is in the Mines now and doing a little better. he wants an the Girls to Come to him in the Spring—is there nothing I can or something I mean that I can send to. I think anything I would send would get to you. I feel bad when you tell me not to send any more things but but I would like to get them soon after being sent, Well [illegible] hope to see you soon. God Bless you.

From your Loving Wife
M. E. Cahill

Thomas to Margaret

Baton Rouge August 16th 1862

My Dear Wife

Your Welcome letter of 24, 25 of July Reached me during the Excitement following our fight of August 5th.[19] I think it was on the 7th that I received the letter announcing the birth of little Thomas Matthew. So you see good luck Comes in Couples. to hear of the Birth of a son and win a Battle at about the same time is what is not often vouchsafed to Mortal Man: (I cannot say thus I was as much surprised by the news from home as I was to be Called so suddenly to the Command of the Army of

19. Battle of Baton Rouge, August 5, 1862. Gen. Earl Van Doran, then in command of Vicksburg, "believed that it was critical to hold the Mississippi at two points in order to facilitate the supply of Vicksburg and guarantee communications with the Trans-Mississippi." Wrecked by disease and with the promise of naval support from the Confederate ram *Arkansas*, on August 5 Gen. John C. Breckenridge launched what he believed would be a surprise attack on the Union troops at Baton Rouge. Union commanders, though, had been made aware of the advancing Confederates, and although the Confederates made considerable progress during their initial assault, federal gunboats eventually turned the tide, their withering fire forcing the rebels to withdraw from the town. Cahill took command of Union forces after Brig. Gen. Thomas R. Williams was killed by rebel fire. Stoker, *Grand Design*, 182; Winters, *Civil War in Louisiana*, 114–24; Smith, *Gallant Dead*, 49–51; Murray, *History of the Ninth Regiment*, 108–24.

Baton Rouge Even for the short time that I held the verry responsible position) Because a Certain lady in Philadelphia had intimated some thing of the kind in one of the verry few letters which succeeds in getting through:

I had written so far where your letter of the 27th Came in. well now there must have been a question prominent in your feelings between the 25th and 27th and to be able to write two long letters within two days gives me great Encouragement. how singular it is that all your letters Come to hand and nobody Else does. I have not recd any letters from El-len or the Dr that you speak of. yours are the only lucky ones. So My dear wife is anxious to have me come home. Oh dear what makes you talk so. it would do me a heap of good to See you all again. but how Could I part with you and all the Orders from Head Quarters are against the Chances of Getting a leave of absence. and as far as resignation I suppose A Man is a traitor that asks for it at present. I shall try however for your sake. I have worked hard to keep in with the General and have done him some ser-vice since I have been here so I will make bold and ask for a *Leave* for as long as I can get and this for your sake and the babies and my own as well.

Father Mullen is going to New Orleans to day he has been verry unwell and is just able to move about. I hope Genl Butler will let him go home as his health is verry poor. he is not strong Enough for such work, I suppose you will have all the news of the Battle of the 5th so I need not write you about it. The Enemy are threatening another attack. I do not believe they will do it again. We have Entrenched ourselves in the arsenal Grounds and are ready for them if they do.

You speak of being short of Money. you had better draw a note and get it Cashed on a Bank. Dr Ives or any one will tell you how to do it. I did not like to send you what pay I got untill I got the 4 months pay on the 1st of July. but if I do not get off I will do so the 1st opportunity. I have recd the 1st two months pay with the Exception of the allotment I have with me because I did not like to run short. bye the bye could you not raise some on the Credit of the allotment in September or October? it is one hundred and 20 or 25 per month.

I am in a hurry to get this to the steamer so good bye and God bless you all. till I can see you. good bye Kiss the babies for me.

My Love to Ellen and respects to all Enquiring friends.

Your lovng husband

Thos W. Cahill

CHAPTER 5

"All is 'fair in Love war and Politics' "

September 1862–January 1863

Margaret to Thomas

New Haven Sept 23rd 1862

My Dear Husband

I recd a money package from you this afternoon containing 100 Dollars but I feel at a loss to know why you did not write me a few lines to "just say" you was well and as much more as you could find time to write. I saw Father Mullen yesterday. he seems very weak and quite lame. I also had a long chat with Father Smith. he wished to be kindly remembered to you and also sugested to me that it would be well on your part if you would have a subscription taken up in the Regt for him Father Mullen. that *he* thought it would appear well in the Eyes of our Revd Bishop and would give him F. Mullen confidence to go to his "Boys" again as he calls them. Now my Dear Husband for my view of the Mother. I had but a short interview with Father Mullen. I consider him an Exception of the Secular Clergy. I think he deserves it from the Regt and I know his constant wishes is with them or at Least with you. he attributes all they have done to you. all their *Victories* Every thing. in fact he says were it not for your perseverence the Regt would have gone to pieces Long ago and I know it well knew it Long ago but it is very gratifying to me to hear some one Else say. also He speaks of you as if you were Brothers. he tells me your wants. tells me what to send you and what is usless. he told me what he thought you stood in need of and I will send the first opportunity I have. I will second Father Smiths proposition and ask you to send him a nice Little Present.

Father Hart recd it from us when he went away for his health and Father Mullen deserves it from you all. he knows nothing of this. it is without his knowledge I write this and his words to me were "Oh what an unworthy Chaplain I have been but if I had been well I would have done much more goods." I like him very much. he and Father Smith Promised to take Dinner with me on Next Monday. I wish my Husband was home to help us eat it. I will ask Father Hart and Sheridan to come too. it is to be the Christening of your son Thomas Mathew.

your Last letter forbid to Look for you any longer so I will try and make myself contented but do not be afraid of the Cold. I have bought two New stoves. one for the kitchen and one for the sitting room and I have two ton of Coal. I did not have to get any more. they ask so high for it. I paid $7.25 but I believe it is $8 now but do not let that scare you. if you come home you will not freeze. Ill assure you I had to Pay $8.50 for one Barrell of flour to day. I wish you could send me home some Sugar. they ask 12/2 cets per lb for Conmon Brown Sugar 14 cts for white. I think that is horrid dont you? I have Paid your Insurance on the House and your Taxes. P. M. is having hard work to raise a Regt. he has his hands full and *never will* raise it. Thos McManus is in Hartford and him are having a great *clash.* Tom wants to be Colonel So does Pat. Pats Wife vows he must—good night God Bless you and bring you safe home.[1]

M. E. C

Margaret to Thomas
New Haven Oct 3rd 1862

My dear Husband

There is an other Steamer arrived since the one that brought F. Harts letter and no letter for me—but Patience is a virtue at any rate I must make a virtue of *it*.

I was going to call you my dear General but I am clear behind the *times.* I did not think of it while you was a Gen, and so Gen Sherman[2] has gone to take your Place, our people here feel terible about it declare it

1. Patrick Maher and Thomas McManus were in a dispute over leadership in the Twenty-Fourth Connecticut. Maher eventually became major of the regiment, while McManus became the adjutant of the Twenty-Fifth Connecticut Volunteers. *Catalogue of Connecticut Volunteer Regiments,* 808, 824.

2. Brig. Gen. Thomas West Sherman, a West Point graduate, was a career soldier before the war broke out and was appointed brigadier general on August 6, 1861 (backdated to date to May 17, 1861). He commanded federal troops at Port Royal, S.C., and led a division of the Army of the Ohio during the siege of Corinth. He was ordered to New Orleans in August 1862. Warner, *Generals in Blue,* 440–41; Tidball, *No Disgrace to My Country,* 53.

a great wrong to you. of course some are glad but very few, how do you feel about *it*, it may be the Means of bringing you home. Who knows: but I will not say any more about it. perhaps all we hear here may not be true. I trust that God will assist you in all your undertakings and that Mans plans against you m[a]y be frustrated as they have always been. My earnest Prayer is that God May help you and make your Labors light and bring you Safe home to us soon.

it is now dinner time and our dear little Eddy is standing at the front door watching for you to come. he came to me a few minutes since and said why don't my Papa come home. he made us all feel dreadful gloomy yesterday at noon. he seemed to positive you were coming home to din-ner. his affection for you goes beyond anything I ever saw an heard off. I cannot tell you half of his little sayings. Marry is more wise. She under-stands why you cannot Come. Father Mullen has a droll story to tell you about her. as soon as she saw him she says "I have a kiss for you Why didn't you bring My Father home." he was I think rather surprised but had to kiss her for she asked it the 2nd time.

he and Father Hart were taking dinner at our House. Father Smith was to have been here too but he had some company come from abroad just before the dinner hour. he sent his regrets. I will send them to you, so you can imagine how poor Father M felt when Mary asked him to kiss her before F. Hart—he told her that she could "Boast of that" for it was a long time since any person got "that." before she told him she had a kiss for Every one that came home and *Lots* of them for her Father. We had a pleasant little time. they seemed very well pleased with the dinner I prepared for them. I would tell you what it was only I do not want to make your teeth water—the only draw back to our having a jolly good time was your absence. your Chair was placed at the Table but vacant—I trust you will fill it over more.

Poor P. M. is having a sad time in getting up an Irish Regt. he com-menced as Capt raised a Company—Enlisted himself in order to get the Bounty. his wife says to help Equip the Staff Officers but it is the opinion of the people for his own Special benefit. they say too he had his life in-sured for 1,000/2,000. if it is true it tells the story of why he went in the Military at this Late date when Irish Cols are out of date. there is no Pros-pect now of raising an Irish Regt. they will either have to be consolidated with other Scattering Companies or form a Battalion. as the thing stands now there is two companies or part companies from N Haven. they were to go in Camp here on one Tuesday Morning but on the Sunday night previous there was a Dispatch Sent from Hartford to P. M to Report with all his men to *Major McManus* at Hartford to use his wifes words Pat was *sold* out. Tom McManus was superior Officer—P Made a fuss went to New York to See if Gen Corcoran[3] would accept them, he would but the men here would not go in his Legion. he would be sure to bring them into the fight—So you can understand how our 2nd Irish Regt is at Present.

I recd 100 Dollars from you, I wrote you Since.

 Your Loving wife
 M. E. Cahill

My respects to Dr and all friends.

Thomas to Margaret

Head Quarters 9th Regt Conn Vols
New Orleans Oct 7th 1862 Private

My Dear Wife

Your Welcome letters of the 22d and 23d of Sept Came to hand to day and what was more wonderfull so did Ms O Brien. well what a crazy mad Cap. good Lord I thought it was a ghost appeared before me when she walked into the office Early this Morning. what in the name of sense are the folks at home on what kind of a story must she have heard. I am sure I have written letters Enough since his accident to have satisfied annybody that Larry was doing well and will be on duty again in a few days. well I do not know what to make of it, it is a wild piece of business her Coming out. what good Could she do him. some one must have been verry discreet or somebody must have been more than usually Crazy: I can imagine poor Larry when she walked in to him. Even if I did not have a description from Capt Garvey who accompanied her to Carrallton to where he is in Hospital. well it is perfectly in Character for her.

so you are getting verry Economic with your Coal. I think I see you getting along with 2 ton of Coal with your two stoves. I tell you it would take more than 2 ton of Coal to keep me warm if I should Come home. I am afraid you were not wise in not getting more in before the winter sets

---

3. Gen. Michael Corcoran was an Irish nationalist who led the Sixty-Ninth New York. The Irishmen from New York stood strong as rearguard for the retreating federals at First Bull Run, where Corcoran was captured and sent to Richmond. He became one of the most recognizable figures of the Irish American experience in the Civil War, and after his release from prison, he was given authorization to raise an Irish legion. Ural, *Harp and the Eagle*, 66–80, 109–11.

in with the trouble in Pennsylvania.[1] I am afraid it will Cost more before spring. I do not know how I could get sugar home for you from here. if I should send it be Express it would cost as much as it does there. there will not be much sugar made in Louisiana this year and it will undoubtedly be high.

you speak of a subscription for Father Mullen. at present it is out of the question. the men or Officers have no money and to a certain extent I am glad of it. at present they are quiet. you know I am a mighty poor. hard to get money at anny time and it Certainly is out of my place to ask at the hands of our men. Father Mullen was but little known in the Regt and in Confidence was always a big load on the Dr and Myself, he never Could take care of himself he never scolded one of the men without repeating it all over to me and the Dr and manny a time I had a sore trial of Patience with him. you speak of his Coming back. the goodness gracious what for? now I have never seen but one priest I would put myself out of the way seriously for and that is not F. S. for Father Hart I would do a deal more than for anny other man living but I assure you that the men really have very little money Coming to them. the most of them have allotted their pay and they do not get it here not there and when we are paid it may not be for more than 2 months and between sutlers bills and Everything Else it goes mighty fast. it is Mighty Easy for Father Smith so disinterestedly to suggest but if he was in my place it might be different with him.

you speak of my not writing with the money. I had no time. a person was going to New Orleans Capt Curtiss to send home a draft and I got him to Check mine. I believe you aught to have some 8 or 10 sheets of letters from me by this time. you speak of Father Harts writing. I have not received annything from him by this mail. I have only recived one letter now. all this for your private Eyes and Ears. I am half inclined to think F Smith *Mischief* if his Craving for money was not unremarkable. Father Mullen has money at home. he was a verry Carefull and Prudent man and is not short so that it was necessary for him to speak of it. I do not think he asked him for anny yet. the fact of the matter is that I hold myself aloof from both Officers and men as much as it is right I should. I never am hail fellow with them consequently I am not one who is likely to get much from them. this is not saying I may not try but when I think of the source of the suggestion I do not like it. so keep shady for a while. may

---

4. This is likely a reference to the draft resistance and workers' strikes in the Pennsylvania anthracite region during 1862. See Palladino, *Another Civil War*, 102–3, 123–27.

be it is one word for Father Mullen and 2 for himself. I did not mean to
write so long a letter when I began but I have been scribbling for the last
½ hour without saying much. my respects to all *Friends*. my love to Ellen.
Kiss the babies for me. (Mrs OBrien *Kissed me* for them this morning)
God Bless you.

> your affatunate Husband
> T. W. Cahill

Margaret to Thomas

October 10th 1862

My dear Husband

Your letter sent by Mr Streits[5] has come to hand, I am glad you are
well but sorry you have so much hard labor to perform. Cant you *Play
Soldier* Sometimes? I think I would. Mr Streits said you were acting Brig
Gen when he left. he says if you go Back to the 9th as Col you must be
very *careful*. they do not like you because you will not allow them to drink
all the Rum they want and now that they have had such a Splendid time
under their other commanders. I would not be at all surprised if there
was some truth in what he sayd but you have such good judgement I
think you know about those things as much if not more than any Body
else. but for Gods sake my dear Husband do expose yourself in any of
their drunken brawls you are not obliged too.

I recd the Hundred Dollars you sent me. do not give yourself any
trouble about my wanting money the most thing troubles me is that I
have to lay out too much of it. every thing is so high that it would take
a little fortune to live at all. desert Flour is 8½ and 9 dollars per Barrell.
Coal 8 and over. I got two Tons at 7/25. I am afraid to get any more—
Common Brown sugar that we used to pay 9 and 10 cets for we now have
to give 12–13 for now—Cotton Cloth worth 10 is 25–30 Conton Flanell
37 cts per yard and all wool Flanell and yarn is out of the question entirly
and every thing. in fact 6 cts for a spool Cotton. I cannot see what the
poor people are going to do here—I wish you could send us home some
sugar but perhaps it is as high there as here—

I exchanged my cook stove for one that will burn less coal. I think I
am going to have Mr Countryman put up a high Board fence from the

---

5. Lt. Christian Streit, Company F and B as well as original band leader.

House to the Grape aslian. I cannot bear to have the place Look so for-
lorn. I have got rid of the most of those Brick if I ever get Paid for them.
Horrill has done nothing all summer but fuss about his two Houses Pav-
ing Painting Soding ornamenting and I don't what and indeed our Place
don't look any the better for it now. if I try to improve its Looks a little
you must not find fault with me. your being away and a General at that
makes it a very remarkable *shot.*

and what will I do with my little Pig? I cannot take care of him all
winter. I am afraid he will freeze to Death. I think I will have Mr Richards
kill him and have him salted and smoked and send it to you for your
Christmass Dinner. what do you think about it? I wish you would tell me
how to mix white wash the different kinds. if I knew how to prepare it I
could have cleaning done so much cheaper. I had Burns to do some for
me this spring and he charged me the nice little Bill of 24 Dollars. there
was some Painting done but I know he charged me too hig. I could say
nothing he said he charged the same as you used to—

Widmer[6] has gone as a private in the 20 Regt C.V. at last account from
him he was sick with Fever in Hospital at Washington. he never came to
see me about the rent although he got the hundred Dollars Bounty—his
wife went to parts unknown two nights ago with 20 Dollars of a Mill Bill
to be Paid. they are the *Genuine Yankee* don't you think so—our rooms
are empty yet no person has been to Look for them but Soldiers wives
and if I rent them at all I would like to rent them to a Man. I wish we had
some one in the House with us. it is so Lonesome nights. I don't know
what I shall do all winter unless something turns up to send you home—I
suppose you have seen Mrs Obrien before this. I wish I had her Courage
or some of it. I wont tell what I would do now. I hope she will have a
good time. Im sure she will. she found Larry well, there was a letter from
him yesterday. his poor father felt very anxious. he spends nearly every
Sunday Evening with us—

Father Hart and Mullen have written to you. you have their letters
before this. I could tell you a Bag full of nonsense about PM but I don't
know whether it would be interesting to you or not. he has not come near
us since he has been a soldier—you did not speak about your vest and
coat I sent you by Lieut Rolmen.

6. Their renter may have, in fact, been William Wightman, who served as a private in
Company E of the Twentieth Connecticut.

Write as often as you can I look for something Every Steamer—
Your loving wife
M. E. Cahill

Margaret to Thomas

New Haven Oct 12th [1862]

My Dear Husband

I wrote you so latly that I have very little to write about today. It is Cold blustering day here the leaves are beginning to fall and Every thing looks dreary however we Look very comfortable in doors and happy in a sense. I went to the Early Mass this morning. recived Holy Communion. Mary and Ellen has gone to Late Mass, Eddy is singing for his dolly and our dear little Thomas is sleeping yet.

Now I wonder what you are doing at Mass. perhaps you never told me how you get along since Fr Mullen left you. how are you off for a Priest? is there a Catholic Church near you so that the men can go to Mass on Sundays? but we know all the particulars particularly about yourself.

My dear Husband I commenced this letter last Sunday but delayed sending it because we were getting up a Box to send you. I thought I would wait and send all together but I am quite disheartened about sending it now at all, The one you sent home Came yesterday and although it was so strong and well secured every thing in it was Soaking wet and the Towls all Mildewed. the Guns are well Coated with rust. indeed they look hard at Present. the Pistol too is some Rusted but not so bad as the Guns.

Eddy and Mary are having a splendid time with the Paper Soldiers and Smoking cap. Mary says it was made for the Godess of Liberty. she is dressed in the White and Looks Beautiful with the Cap on. I will have your Guns put in order as soon as possible. I wish you could have seen Ellen and myself over the little Box. it was locked and no key to be found to open it. we imagined for a little while that there was something very nice for us in it. we hunted up a key and then you can imagine our disappointment when we saw the Pistol. we just then remembered you mentioned a Pistol in your letter.

but the best of all that has come yet is your picture. it gave me the greatest Satisfaction in the world to see it. it seemed that no persons that came home could tell me anything satisfactory about it. some say you are very *fat* and others that you are very *lean* and a thousand other things that I knew was doubtful but now I can judge for myself. Eddy knew it the

Moment he saw it and so did Mary. they were so pleased with the Horse. the Sorrell Horse they Call him. what do you call him? and tell us who is holding your horse in the Picture. his Cap shades the face so much we cannot tell who it is. I cannot call it a failure. and who is that other Photograph taken for? we did not remember Ever seeing him he is fine looking young man.

I hear the cart before the Horse this time. I began the last of my story first now I will begin again. I recd 3 letters by Mail from you last week. the one you sent by hand was mailed from New York on the 23rd it was written on the 10th. the other written on the 7th and mailed in New Orleans on the 9th Came next. there was but an hour or so between their coming. the scolding letter Last. I wished it had come first. I was all down in the dumps until Saturday Evening when Mr Terrell[7] Came with another letter and your picture. and then all was well with us again. now I had nothing to do with Mrs OBriens going out there. on the Contrary I tried my best to put all such ideas out of her head and so did Father Mullen and Father Hart. the only persons who encouraged her to go was Mayor Welch and Deacon Thompson and of course she Made everything appear very different to what it was to them or they would never have santioned her going. Mayor Welch told her to get some of her Friends to give her an letter of introduction to General Corcoran. She Came to me and tried to make me give it her. I to[ld] her to go to Pat Meagher. I then thought I had got rid of her but no. back she came and said I must do it. I told her I could not think of it. I thought he had enough to do and I did not know where to write too or how to adress him. I told her to go to Father Hart. she said she would not for he would tell her not to go and no Reason on Earth would keep her from going there.

I would not do it for her and off she went. you know how. well that was not the last of her. about 2 hours before she left New Haven she came after the few lines as She called them. asked if they were ready. I was in a fix then. I was on my way to the Post Office with your letter. I then told her I would see F. Hart myself about the matter. I met him on his way to the House. when I came back from the P Office I found her daughter here before me again and F Hart too. I told him what she wanted. he told her to tell her Mother from him to stay at home. I told him she was determined to go and her Dauter said she had spent a great deal of money getting ready and she would not stay for any body. so he told her that Gen

---

7. Pvt. Franklin Terrell, Company E.

Corcoran could do nothing for her. he was not in N York but down on Staten Island with his Brigade. he merly gave her Capt Baelins number and asked him to direct her to D. C. Tompkins office in New York. Now there was nothing about the accident in the letter F. Mullen brought to me but he heard of it in New Orleans before he left and told F. Smith and F. S. told Mrs OBrien and then go she would. I beged of her to wait for your next letter. I knew you would mention but if she done that she would be obligied to stay at home. her Husband told her the same but as Deacon Thompson told me and it is time for him She is the Man of the House. he gives her great praise. he said to me only think a mother of 10 Children going to N. Orleans to see her first Born—

Now I am now willing to shoulder any of the blame of her going there if there is any. you might know that when I would not allow her to be the bearer of a letter to you and no person here is to blame for it. she heard no awful stories at all only that Larry was wounded slightly and only one person told her that and it was F. Smith. I can see no harm in his telling her. you Could not Expect the Man to tell her an untruth. if he did not I would have to and then it would have been ten times worse. now the fact of the matter is this. if she did not have that for an Excuse to go down as soon as Larrys next pay came here she would go. she has tried time and again to urge me to say I would go and take the Babe and she would go with us as nurse servant or any thing for the sake of going. Manys the time Ive been told I have no right feeling in me and not by her alone and I hope you will pay very little attention to what she says about my wanting to go I have never Expressed any feeling in the matter to her or anybody Else. when I wish to Consult with any one about it it will be you.

you know I would Love dearly to see you and be near you always and you know it was always my Doctrine that you should never go anywhere without me and the Children. I wish we could be together but my true feelings about going down South is that I would only be only in your way and it would make you very unhappy to see me knocked about (as I should Expect to be) without the Comforts of a house. I have no curiosity to know what Every man in Regt is doing—saying—or things of you I scorn such measures—Now about the old women is bothering me so much to be candid with you. The one who troubled me most is in N Orleans and I wont cry for the time she may spened these but God bless us when she comes *back*. she will see what things that never happened and up at did take place wont be worthy of mention. I think you will wish I had written a short letter this time but I am not through yet More about the subscription for _____ _____. do as you see fit about it, it may be as you say Misschiefious and I do not mean to dictate to you what to do on an afair like that but I was given to understand that he had to Pay 3 Dollars per day while he was in Hospital (Sisters Hospital) in New Orleans. at that mater I Concluded he must be even poorer than when he went out with the Regt.

There has never been any allottment money recd here by me, Capt Garveys was the only Money Ever recd on the Allotment Books and that was the first Day recd on Ship Island.

Richard Connors was in to see us a few Minutes ago. he had his arm shattered a few weeks ago by a kick from one of his horses. it doing well he says now. his wife had a Tallon on her Thumb at the same time and will Lose a joint. he says so. you see there is trouble everywhere. did I tell you he enlisted, he bought a substitute and Revd O'Brien tells me his Business never was better and his own too. he had all the choice *jobs* this fall. Labouring men are out of the question. they are demanding enormous wages and so they are obliged to for they have to *Pay* for what they Eat these days.

Tell the Dr I had a letter from his wife a few days ago. she is going to have her Babys likeness taken and sent to him. I suppose I will have to follow suit will I send it. what become of the Mocking Birds Johnny was to send every time I get a letter? Eddy always asks where is my Mocking Bird Momma?

Now will you please tell me if there is a Wm Prior[8] in Co A? he enlisted with Duffy.[9] his little Girl comes here every week and sometimes twice in a week to hear if her Father is living. he has not written here in a Long time. his wife has Consumption is very ill and anxious to hear from him. his Dauter is a sweet Looking Child. I hope if he is living he will write soon and if he is dead have somebody write to his wife. I do not want to tell them bad news. they live in Lafatt Street I do not know the number. Poor O Laffin[10] and Michael Healy[11] was Prayed for in St. Patricks yesterday—Fr Sheridan is going to be rememberd and take Father Rileys Place in Hartford. F. Kelly is to go to some little place outside. do not call this a short letter. We are right. God Bless you.

your Loving wife
M. E. Cahill

---

8. There was no William Prior in the Ninth Connecticut.
9. Pvt. John A. Duffy, Company A.
10. Pvt. Richard Laffin, Company C, died of disease at Baton Rouge on August 9. 1862.
11. Pvt. Michael Healey, Company C, died on October 6, 1862.

Thomas to Margaret

Head Quarters 9th Regt Conn Vols
Lafayette Square New Orleans Oct 15th 1862

My Dear Wife

a man named Terrell who lived in Franklin Street is going home [illegible] I thought I would Send this by him. I will I think also send by him a box Containing some Odds and Ends I have picked up during the summer. there is a handsome Gun Box containing a verry handsome Double Barrell shut gun found in Col Allen of the 4th Louisiana's[12] plantation and another taken from a party trying to pass over lines. some towels and Pillow Cases a linin Coat One Pistol and etc. he knows to see it delivered to you. he goes with about 20 others discharged on the McClellan.

about your sugar. I saw Col Butler[13] a Brother of the Genls at his house last night where I went to see the Genl with reference to the allotment Rolls of our Regt as I wish to break up the allotment and let the men send home the money when they get it, the Col is speculating in Sugar. I happened to mention that I should like to invest in a couple of of Barrells at least for family use and he said if I would Come around to his place he would make me a present of a Barrell. you can see of course I will be like to Call on the Genl forthwith. I will try to send it by Addams Express if I can I will try to have it shipped. there [illegible] O'Brien is boarding in the City now. I have not seen her for a day or to it is verry Cool here for the Last 4 days almost as Cool as at home. we have had no pay as yet Expect it Evey day. I hardly know what to do about the Allotment Rolls. if I break it them up something will go wrong perhaps and if I can not I know it will. if the men see fit they can send it home. if they choose they can spend it here. I hardly know what to do.

Nothing remarkable has occurred since I wrote you. the Capt I spoke of Last time is not yet on trial. it is said that their Charges are lost [illegible] So I do not know whether I shall bother writing others or not.

---

12. Henry Watkins Allen, a Harvard-educated lawyer, was a lieutenant colonel of the Fourth Louisiana Regiment and military governor of Mississippi and Louisiana. For Watkins's recollections of the war see Dorsey, *Recollections of Henry Watkins Allen.*

13. Andrew Jackson Butler, Benjamin Butler's older brother, went to great lengths to establish himself as speculator in goods and trade in New Orleans during the Union occupation. Hearn, *When the Devil Came Down*, 183–96.

I send you the Photograph plate I got one taken here at a reasonable price whose Back I think I will: if you look verry sharp you can make it our recollect it is a Photograph Plate to print from and not a Photograph.

Well really i have nothing to fill up this letter with and as I have nothing to fill up with I wont start out to send out the sugar.

I have been down and got the sugar today. My Lord they are Charging 12½ cents a pound here by the Barrell and they say it will be worth 25 cts a pound soon at home. I have paid $11,00 freight out to New Haven. I will send the receipt to you. *did I Ever send you fifty dollars for a Boy named Warren of Co K?*[14] if not I have it myself, just at this moment in Comes your Letters of Oct 3 and 4th and Ellens letter of the 23d of July which has been all the way to Cairo and Back. O Lord what a blue letter but you feel better now thank God for it. well it did make my mouth water to think about your great dinner but never mind.

I had two good representations just at this moment. Father Harts letter of the 4th has arrived. a good long letter. it will take me some time to answer it but I will get about it at once. we have not been paid yet. I went to see Genl Butler about it but there no Government money here. if I can Break up the allotments I will send you a good deal but I understand our pay is Cut down Consdierably between forage reduction and per centages. you speak of my *generals* birth to ask how I feel. I feel well Enough. I have no desire whatever to be an acting Brigadier when I have all the work and none of the pay. the fact is that Genl Butler cant make Brigds and there is more here than he can take care of. he says he did not know they were coming but it is a little singular that none but Connecticut men Brigade of the 13th have been obliged to give way while Col Dudley is Mass Col is kept in Command. but it is rumoured that his Brigade is broke up. I scarsely know what to think of the prospect here; the secesh are Confidently Expecting intervention. I do not like that Emancipation Proclamation but think it must come to it Sooner or later.

I wish you would have the guns taken out and oiled and the Ranks kept together. the guns easily put together. give my love to Ellen my respects to the Reg Gents. Kiss the Babies for me.

Your Loving husband
Thos W Cahill Col
9th Regt Conn Vols

14. Drummer James K. Warren.

Thomas to Margaret

Head Quarters 9th Regt Conn Vols
New Orleans October 21st 1862

My Dear Wife

  your letter of the 10th of October Came to hand to day by the "Marion" but none from Father Hart or Mullen. I am surprised at this. it is the 2d or 3d time I have heard of letters coming but none here come from them. I have received one from Ellen and have an answer written and one to William Geary[15] although I have received none from him. why in the world do you listen to such nonsense from that old Dutch man Streit. as to anny danger from my men good Lord such an idea never Entered my head as fear of them. on the Contrary the men were Crazy to have me back. the Old dutch granny dont know what he is talking about. Our New Brigadier Genl Arnold lies verry low with an appopeptic fit has been unconscious since Saturday Evening: So that I have business Enough to attend to at present as I have to a certain Extent to take his place:

  You speak of the high price of sugar. it will be higher before it is lower. the Entire sugar crop of this Country is almost as good as last and the Cane will rot in the fields if the war last as it seems to me it will for a long time. Cotton will go up and whether or not it must go up it will never be as cheap as it wiss now within 25 per cent of it, I cannot understand why flour should be so high. it is verry cheap here 6½ and 7 dollars. I have sent you a Barrell of sugar But sugar is selling here by the barrell at 12cts so you see that it is as Cheap there as here. I could not buy here the freight is so high. it would not pay to send it home. all the trade is in the hands of Butler and his brother and they are making immense fortunes out of it. no one Else can get a steam Boat to go up the River after sugar, I am sorry you had not Cotton Cloth Enough to last you for 2 or 3 years but it cannot be helped now.

  I cannot advise you to lay out much on the house as I Consider property in New Haven very poor stock. it has Cost all it is worth for recipes for white wash for the bed Rooms and Basement and all but the hallway and front room and Keeping Room and front room and hall way up stairs. you can make a white wash of Lime in the usual way rather thin then take

---

15. William Geary was, along with Thomas Cahill, a member of the Emmet Guards, though he did not serve in the Ninth Connecticut. Murray, *History of the Ninth Connecticut*, 13.

some Paris white "which is a fine kind of whiting" and dry it in a bake pan on the stove. when thouroughly dried stir it in with the lime wash "which should be strained through a wine sieve before the whiting is put in." put in whiting say one third or Enough to thicken the Lime wash. put a ¼ pound of glue "white" into a little oven a quart of water in which it has soaked over night. bring it to a boil for a few minutes keeping it stirring put in the Glue sirpe at the rate of ¼ pd to about half a pail of wash. try the wash by putting a little on the wall in some Corner let it dry if it will not rub off it has glue Enough. if not add a little more glue untill it will not rub off. the great knack is it getting it to the right thickness. for work-ing the verry fine whiting for the front room we made by putting a large per cent of Dry Lime in with the whiting and which gives it that smooth hard appearance. but this costs a good deal. but I have of late used it more or less on all hard walls. it wants to be mixed with water before it is put in with the whiting. but you need not bother your head about it.

Well you have heard from your uncle at last and rather a singular letter it is too. what makes him speak of sending you money. I hope you have been writing to him for it. we certainly need not do that yet. it is a queer letter anny how. Mrs O Brien seems to Enjoy herself verry well. Larry seemed nearly as well as Ever.

as for your little pig why kill it and Eat it? what do suppose I can want of it out here.

I am sending home a good many discharged men. I cannot bear to see them lying about here looking like death although I know a great manny of them are playing on me and will be as well as Ever as soon as they get their discharges. but I do not Care. I would send the whole Regt home if I could and then go home myself. I wish I could do so with the whole Regt.

I will send this by Capt Liesegany of the Matanzas. Give my Respect to all Enquiring friends. Kiss the Babies for Me. God bless you all.

Your Loving husband
Thos W Cahill

Thomas to Margaret

Head Quarters 9th Regt Conn Vols
Odd Fellows Hall New Orleans Nov 5 1862

My Dear Wife

I received 2 papers from you a Times Con the Paragraph about the 9th in their War Paint and etc and the Herald but no letters. I received a

letter from Father Mullen. he speaks of Coming out again which I wonder at very much as he certainly suffered verry much while here and he
is verry weakly: he speaks of being at the house and of Marys kissing him
and saying she had a kiss for Every man on the Ninth Regt. well she is a
comical lassie.

I have not heard from Father Hart for some time. Mrs Obrien is talking
about going home soon. she may perhaps wait for the "Matanzas" Capt
Liesegang as I am in hopes if he is not crowded with passengers to get her
passage at a lower figure than one hundred dollars the price now asked
on Every boat for a Cabin passage. Larry is on duty and I have placed
him in Command of Co D old Coates Company and have written for his
commission as Capt.

I am well in health and spirits though kept verry busy as usual it seems
to be my luck to allways be working hard and at the same time always a
subject of Envy to some two and sixpenny Concern. but it is just as well
perhaps if I am not earning More Money I am always leaving more and
sure its all for Glory we are doing it:

So its all the same in the End untill this matter of Genl Arnolds is disposed of in some way. he lies in the same way as usual since he has been
taken down: all his work falls on my shoulders. he still continue in the
same condition and I suppose he will have to be sent home. he has never
spoken since he was taken to his house from the review. I see no chance
of relief unless another officer is sent by the Administration. they send
Everything that they cannot find use for at the North or that got shook
out of their places, owing other things that are said to be Coming down
are Major Fryes wife and Harrals Wife.

The fashion here is to take a confiscated house belonging to some
rebel or some one that has refused to take the Oath of Allegiance move
into it. they are some of them splendidly furnished with the House servants and Everything Ranos Library Pictures of the most magnificent
description. There will be some curious revelations made after this war's
over. how terrible will be the denunciations of these people of the de-
scrations of their Palatine Homes by the Vandal Yankees, such stories of
Robberies of household goods and wearing apparel as Every or nearly
every house is just as the owners left them. in fact some did not as I hear
leave them but were turned out of them by any one that took a fancy to
them leaving Everything as it stood no protection for them as they had
not taken the Oath and were therefore registered as Enemies, how would
you fancy that style of doing business if you were to come out here and
have me seize one of those Splendid mansions niggers wardrobes Bed

and Bedding Everything as the Luxurious owners left it. "whew" don't it make your mouth water;

I must confess for my part I have some old fashioned Compunctions of Conscience about it. me thinks we should see the "spooks" of the owners in our dreams. Verily the hand of the Lord is heavy on this Great City but I do not like this wholesale using of other peoples on what was their propertys: Major Frye has seized a splendid house. the Lieut Col has another and nearly every other of the same and even lower grades have seized houses and scandal is busy with the manner in which they are said to be used. this is especially the case with two splendid 5th Avenue Style of houses magnificently furnished. one of them the home of a very wealthy family. the daughters of the family are here and it is said that they declare they would never put their feet within it if it was given back to them. this house was taken by the Chief Commissary named Turner son of a wealthy man some where in Jersey. it is said that Genl Butler heard of the conduct of a *Lady* he had in with him. she used to come out on the Balconys and flaunt herself in the face of the neighbours and the daughters of the family. I prophesy that the fellow himself wont End well, the worst of this kind of work is in the provost department not among the Troops who are generally a hard working set of men but such of them as to get in too the Provost business and what great temptations.

you will probably want to know what the Dr and myself are about well. we Sleep in the Building known as Odd Fellows Hall[16] a very large fine looking Building the upper stories of which is devoted to the Old Fellows and other Secret Societies. the First Story to stores the Second Story has a Large and once was a very splendid Hall: the Great Ball Room of the City. one large Room which I use as an office another as an Hospital. 2 other Large Rooms with Brussells Carpets Stuffed Chains and Sofas a large mirror 4×8 feet on each side of the Rooms. these were used for Ladies Dressing Rooms and were very handsomely furnished and of a Cool Evening for we have had Cool Evenings. we have a nice Coal fire in the grates. we have our meals at the Ban House across the street at 3,00 per week. rather expensive but it is better than a Common Boarding house at 4,00. if we slept there it would cost 11,00 so we save something by having our own Rooms. Directly across the splendid paved Camp Street is Layfayette Square a nice little square just large enough for the mens

16. The Odd Fellows were founded in New Orleans in 1831 as a charitable fraternal organization. Odd Fellows Hall was located on the corner of Camp and Lafayette Streets in New Orleans and was completed in 1852. Rightor, *Standard History of New Orleans*, 320–21.

tents with a handsome high iron fence and just trees Enough to make it pleasant and room enough for a Dress parade. no one would dream that the Rough ninth were in it as it is as a grave yard and looks not unlike one with its tall white tents like tombstones in the moonlight and such lovely moonlight as we have here.

Mrs Obrien will have Enough to do to tell you all she has seen here for the Rest of the winter. you see we are very Comfortable. if they will only let us stop here—John Carroll has got a verry nice Locket and Chain he is going to send Mary. it has my likeness on one side and his on the other. but he has had a dorgh[17] taken of himself but he cannot get his Eyes taken. mine is said to be a good one. I have about 800 hundred dollar being 4 months here and 120 dollars in gold. I hardly know how much to send you as my Expenses are of Course much more than when living on Salt Junk in the field and I do not know when we may get another pay but think I will send 600 home and perhaps 700. I do not like to spend the gold so will have to keep more on that account. the health of the men is very good now. Remember me to Father Hart and ask him to write me as often as possible. I am desposed to be down on you but Expect something by Roanoke which left the 29th.

your loving husband
Tho W Cahill

Kiss the Babies for me as usual. the Dr gets no letters from home. he wishes to be remembered to all at home—

Thomas to Margaret

Head Quarters 9th Regt Conn Vol
Odd Fellows Fall New Orleans Nov 11th [1862]

My Dear Wife

your letter dated Oct 12 but mailed on the 20th came to hand by the "Parkersburgh" this verry so I commenced my letter at once so that nothing may happen to hinder my writing. I am obliged to seize every spare moment and it is only at this late hour when every body is asleep that I am like to be free from interpution; well now what have I been saying to you that you speak of a scolding letter? I had no intention of any such thing; I was annoyed at the Idea of folks at home kicking such a row about

---

17. Daguerreotype photograph.

Everything that occurs here; and to think of the Risk. Mrs O'Brien ran to say nothing of the Expence and trouble without waiting for something definite. of Course it only shows the state of morbid Excitement which much Exist; and which is of Course nature but verry unpleasant,

but Enough of this or you will Call this a *Scolding letter* and it is not after receiving such a good long letter that I wish the reputation of scolding, now which part of your letter will I answer first, well about the Photograph. I do not recollect sending a picture of any one but my own. it may have been my Adjutant Kattensworth[18] as he gave me one in full uniform and I dont recollect what became of it and I suppose I sent it home. he is a verry fine young man.

so you fancy you can decypher the Plate? well I think your imagination must assist you unless it attend on the Passage but I did not Expect much from it; It so happened that on the morning we marched from Camp Parapet that in Riding by a little shed used as a Photograph Saloon I observed Major Frye trying very hard to have himself and horse "took." The little Sorel as the Children rightly named him would not keep his head still so when I told the man to aim at me one of the 9th who was having his Picture "took" took him by the bridle and think Rascal shut his Eyes and held his head down he being with his rider troubled with modesty. he is a bright red sorrel Pony of the Country. of no particular value but an easy rider.

The Picture was taken without any preparation in the Bright sunlight and I do not suppose it can be printed from but it is verry correct. it is almost impossible to get a good picture of a horse as they will not stand still in "fly time." but it might perhaps be framed as it (could some body who knows about it) it was taken as the "Times Correspondent" said of us as we marched in our "war paint" just as we started for New Orleans. I do not know the boys name. *Johnny* says it ought to be him. I wish it was it looks like him had I intended to have it taken in that way I would have had him.

I intend to send you my "head" taken by Jacobs of this City but I dislike to send word before hand and did not mean to thus; as something might disapoint me,

so Eddy Keeps fretting about the Birds. but we could not raise them: I do not know what to send the little dears. John Carroll is going to send

---

18. Henry Kattensworth enlisted as a private in Company I and was promoted quickly through the ranks.

Mary a Gold Chain and Locket with his and my likeness, then I am again telling what I am going to send (well it slips on me). I want to send you and Ellen and Eddie something but really can find nothing that strikes my Eye that is at all peculiar, I am sorry for your disapointment about the Pistol Case. well did you not allways say you wanted to learn to shoot a pistol and cant you learn and keep it for yourself (but dont let Capt G's folks see it as I took it from him bye the bye he has resigned again)? I wish he would go home).[19]

I had a long letter written to send you by Lieut McCusker but failed to get it to him in time, how happened it that Terrell did bring the Box with him I am always sorry for trusting it to him, In one of the letters you will receive I have given a history of the house seizing business here but do not make it public as it was written for the family and Father Hart. I do not care what he sees as he knows what to say though I am provoked at not having a letter from him; in the Old trunk of Ellens which I propose to send home by Ellen's a large spy glass taken at Pass Christian; also a Rebel Flag. I wish I could get some memento approate for Father Hart and Mayor Welch and Deacon Thompson but really Every thing is snatched up here by Curiosity and Trophy Hunters and I am fairly tourmented in my Capacity as Commandant by the Navy Officers hunting after Every thing. I cant have an old gun in my Quarters without them asking me for it. and the men are getting so cunning that they hoard up Everything they can their hands upon and sell it for a Trophy of some field. But what I have are Come by honestly for war times I am going to send Ned O'Brien a gun.

Johnny Riley is going to send home a splendid violin which you must take care of for him also a Claranet. I am also sending home a thrice cocked hat which you can make a splendid trophy of. I also send you 4 or 5 bunches of some kind of gimp or lace for Childrens dresses which is used here a good deal and which I think a *peculiar.* in fact I send you Everything I pick up around Loose more for the sake of saying they came from here then for any value which they are not. The Fancy Mosquito Bar however is a nice article. they are used universaly here over Every Bed and would not be bad at home in summer over the Bed.

In case any Auctions by the government of Confiscated property of which they are seizing such immense quantities here Comes off any one that had money might bye a great deal for little or nothing. I cannot

---

19. Capt. Patrick Garvey, Company B.

imagine what the government mean to do with all this property now how it Can be got away certain we poor soldiers will not get it. I might write for a month and I could not give you my ideas of things here. I cannot find Language to Express myself and perhaps I had better not try as the least said is the soonest mended. if possible I will give to Father H my Ideas at length some time as it is I think I wrote too much. I wish you would let me know if you suspect any of my letters miscarry as they might get into bad hands. I intend to send you all my old letters which if you had nothing else to do you might arrange acording to subjects and dates. at any Rate send them carefully. but you dont get one think of them as I am continually writing. but dont scribble as bad as this. I must scribble or I never would get through. this makes 4 pages since ½ part two now it is 12/ past 12 o clock. now good night.

You ask how we get along without a priest since Father Mullen left; There is no trouble about that in New Orleans as there is plenty of Clergymen here and I believe that there are no other than Catholic Churches open. at least the main Churches of Every other denomination are Closed: by order of General Butler. St. Patricks Church is across the Street a block above the Camp. The pastor of the Church is a bitter secesh. he refused to speak to Father Mullen who made up to him as a namesake in a Catholic Bookstore a few days before he left but his Curate Father Riordan is a verry fine man and is verry kind to the men;

So you had a nice time of it with Mrs O'B and her letter to Genl Corcoran. well to be sure she must think that officer had verry little to do to be able if he was inclined to look after passengers to New Orleans; I tell you she has flew around some here and it will last her the rest of her life. the wonders she has seen, although she declares she will Come out again before spring and bring you with her;

now about your coming out. there is nothing this world would give me more pleasure but the Lord only knows where we might be Ordered to any day and then what would you do to be left here alone among strangers and such a wicked set; and what I really almost dread as much I should be obliged to do as all the rest of the officers do seize a house and furniture, and I honestly look upon it as a hard piece of business in more ways than one, true it is war at war time and the old adage all is "fair in Love war and Politics" may help to Cover the matter.

There is not a man living detests the Course pursued by these people more than I do and I do not begrudge to see others do what I might hesitate to do myself out of a fight in Cold blood; in fact I would rather shoot them in a fight than live in their houses unless it should be in that of some well known and leading traitor though I suppose I might Easily find such a house; now I do not say this to discourage you from coming out but simply to show up the main features of the Case. God knows nothing would do me as much good as to see you here Except to see you all at home as when I left; but hence are a large number of other Officers wives coming out, among others Mrs Major Frye is here to day by the Cambria with her Bloomen and Curls, and Mrs Major Whittlemore of the 30th Mass and the wives of the Major and Lieut Col of the 72 New York, the sister of Dr Brandt 1st Surgeon and the wife of the Quart Master of the 26th Mass, and some few others whose names I do not recollect. the 75th New York is now absent in the advance with Genl Weitzel and they are here alone. none of them have any Children with them and I believe with the Exception of Mrs Frye have none; so that I cannot consider any of them Cases a parallel with yours.

So that with all the facts and circumstances before you I am satisfied to leave the matter entirely to your usual sound discretion.

Nov 13th 10 O Clock PM

Nothing hs occurred as yet to Change the usual state of affairs. I am verry busy to a late hour every night Comparing and Collecting the Muster Rolls for October 31st. Major Frye made the last muster and the Paymaster Came near refusing to pay on them and has not ceased swearing about them. Yet Some of the Officers of the 26th Mass who Eat at the Hotel with us are under the impression that they are going to Galveston Texas and that we are going with them. I do not believe it s the Programme a few days ago was to send the 6th N York (Billy Wilsons) there. My own impression is we will remain here some time. the men are behaving verry well indeed. there are no men absent from Camp Except those who are in the Parish Prison. there is about thirty of them and how they do beg to get out. they Embrace the hard Cases of the Regt and you may believe they will stay there as the Regt is all right when they are out of the way.

The Prisoners taken from the 8th Vermont Regt about 100 of them arrived and reported to me to night they are "Paroled" and will have to be sent home. the 17th Vemt left to day to relieve the 6th New York this is the Regt that had their Colours taken from them for their Conduct at Baton Rouge.

Speaking of Baton Rouge Jacobs the Photographer has a government Plate of the Plan of Battle which I will ask Genl Butler to allow me an impression of and if successfull will try to send it to you. speaking of photographs you like the Plate I send you be Carefull of it. I think it a good one and so secured it. I have only 3 or 4 of those Pictures as I only got a Dozen printed and some of my men want me to Exchange for theirs and as I would like to make an army album so that I may want some of them sent out to me. I send you Drs and Dr Bradt of the 26th promises you his if I get it will send it. Lt O'Brien has his taken. do not think it a good one.

Lt Carroll has heard his wife is dead and has applied to day for a furlough for thirty. dont know where he Expects to get his money from as he has none now. wants to be gone 30 days.

Thomas to Margaret

Headquarters U.S. Forces in New Orleans
Nov 27 1862

My Dear Wife

your letter of nov 9th and 11th Came to hand on the 24th. Every thing remain as usual here no new excitement unless it be the now being kicked by a *Regular Battallion of Artillery* which has received an Order from the War Dept. to recruit from among the volunteers to fill its empty Ranks. Every Drunken Rascal that gets on a spree goes off and joins the *Regulars.* it is making a good deal of Excitement among the volunteer officers of Every grade:

nothing has occurred during this war as yet which has raised such an opinion of Contempt in my mind for the Administration as this little affair which looks small Enough in itself, but which is utterly at war with Every thing like Military discipline. it makes me feel that the men that Could issue such an order were not fit to manage anything. Just think of it. a fellow goes off from the Camp or quarters of his Corps. he gets drunk over stays his pass and for fear of punishment he goes off and Joins the *regulars.* he comes back and sauces his officers demands his papers and away he goes, he comes back a dozen times perhaps with some pretense or another bothering Every body. I have shut some of the gentlemen up to cool their bones in the Parish Prison for a while, but the principle of the thing is abominable and the Officers who have ordered it have shown that they do not know their business. if there be anything on the face of this Earth that I will confess to hate and despise it is a *regular,* those that I have chanced to see are the most contemptible puppies it has ever been my fortune to have observed.

This matter must affect the state verry sensibly as Every man that goes out of her Regiments decreases her quarters on the field and it makes me laugh sometimes to think how the game works. as Every man the Regulars steal leaves one more man to be raised by the state and there they are paying some 2 or three hundred dollars per man to make up the number Called for and here they are stealing them from the state without saying by your leave. The thing really looks ridiculous and Enough on the face of it but as the little girll said they did it themselves. it is a small thing but nothing has occurred yet which has made me feel as much like throwing up my commission as it has it is so *foolish* there is *nothing to redeem* it for the sake of a few thousand puppies. this tremendous Volunteer Army is to be insultted. I am not sure I wont do it yet between the deaths and discharges and enlistments into the Battery. our regiment it get pretty well down in numbers. some thirty have been discharged to day. I am not sorry. let the poor devils go home, sometimes I wish I was one myself, I think I made a mistake on the heading of this letter. it ought to be addressed to the governor instead of to you but I must let of to somebody, so never mind;

I have signed James McCarthy[20] papers to day and Tom Colwells[21] and Mrs Sharly sows and Tom Starkey[22] and a host of others will try to get McCarthy off on saturday,

the Coat and Cap and sigars come to hand all right, I like the shirts very much and the Cap fits; the Coat is rather small but will do for all I shall want. you dont say anything about receiving the Brl of sugar I sent you. I paid 11 dollars freight on it; you did not send me the Boots Mrs O'Brien said you were going to send. I send you Johnny Reillys Picture for him; I did not send you any money for the Boy waverd. I have paid him here; you need not send McDermotts Bank Book yet as I have sent you some more money for him. you must do what you think right about the subscription for Father Hart. I wish it was for himself and I would not be grudge the amount. let it be what it might, I have received another long letter for him. will try to answer it to morrow if I can make time. if I can get McCarthy off will send this by him. it is mighty hard to get a man off from here. what do you think of my Picture? I suppose Mrs OB has got home before this so you have been hurting the dignity of Wm P. M. Major what made you do it? *too bad who cares.* never got an answer from Geary to my letter. got none from P Merring and but one from Father Mullen to but I answered. am afraid I dont get those. they say they write. am afraid they dont write. get all yours. curious I get yours and not theirs.

20. Pvt. James McCarthy, Company E.
21. Pvt. Thomas Colwell, Company B.
22. Sgt. Thomas Starkey, Company A.

give my love to Ellen. my Respect to Father M and Father Hart. Kiss the babies for me as usual and I am your Loving husband.

Thos W. Cahill

Margaret to Thomas

Nov 28th [1862]

My Dear Husband

I commenced my letter with a blunder as you will perceive by the heading. well its no wonder. I am a soldiers wife you know and had to go on a *bit* of a Spree when I got my money but F. H.—will tell you all about it and what is the use of me telling on myself when you write him. ask him what he is teaching me.

I recd no letters by the two last arrivals. I hope the Malanzes will arrive soon. I am sure to get news by her. We expect Mrs OBrien too. we recd our allottment money last week for two months. theres $240 for me and 200 for Mrs Gallagher. Mr Scharnley sent to me for Mrs Galghers order and sent me 50 and the rest to her. I wrote her telling her about it. it is strange the Dr does not get her letters. the last one was mailed from her be F. hart.

I would like to have you tell me what to do with this money I have. F. Hart tells me I had better deposit it by the 1st Jan. I have Richard Connors fifty Dollars today on that old account of Cook sand. Paid all my other Bills. there is about nine hundred left including what I had in the House before this money came and one in the bank that I never took out. I have nearly all we will want for the winter in the grub line in the house. but what will I do for Coal? it is still on the. I recd 42 Dollars by Express for John McDermott. I will deposit it. is Johnny or Carroll going to abld any to their Rile—

they are watching daily for poor Claffe[23] and McKennas body. the Emmetts had a meeting Tuesday night to make arrangements for McKennas funeral. Michael Fahy was here last night. he wished to be remembered to you—this is Ellection day here. there is Terible hard work and hard feelings to. I have just got a Register so you will be able to judge how Politics are here. We are all well. our little Babe grows splendidly. oh dear when will you see him—he spent Last Evening at mrs Gearys she had one of her grads Suppers—

---

23. Lt. Patrick Claffee, Company C.

Willie Geary is going to have a Party tonight. he sent a written invitation to Mary and Eddy but I think the best place for them is in their beds. they are now eating their Bread and Milk and will soon offer up their little Prayers for you. do send us home a good likness. I will try to Tommys taken and send it to you but he has a blue eye and perhaps it will be like Carrols no eyes at all. has Johnny Eddys Mocking Bird yet? he makes a great fuss when we get letters from you. he thinks the Bird ought be in some of them. I almost forgot to tell you a Box Came to me by Express from Philadelphia full of Horse Trappings. what on Earth are they for?

Father Hart has just been in to see if I would him have some money for John Carrolls Wife. he says they are in a starving condition. she is a perfect maniac and cannot live long. I hope if he will send money to her it will get in F Harts hands. he will see that it is used properly used. Hamills Mother is taking care of her. I gave him fifteen Dollars for her. he said if Carroll was not pleased he would make him pleased for she had neither fire nor food in the House and owes 4 months rent. I hope he will not forget his two poor children. what misery the cursed grog has done among our people. what a happy family that might have been but for it. F. Hart says you have his letter before this so him and I are looking for good long letters.

from your Loving Wife
M. E. Cahill

Margaret to Thomas

New Haven Nov 29th 1862

My dear Husband

I intend sending this by Mr Hale. he called last evening to tell me he was going out by the next Steamer and would like to carry letters or Papers or any Small Parcel I would like to send you. he lived in Trumble St you know him I suppose.

And So Mrs Obrien has arrived in New York. well done for her. She telegraphed from New York last Evening. Mr OBrien went down. she will go to Philadelphia before she comes to New Haven. I hope she is pleased with her visit. I long to see her. Father Obrien has another niece dead at his House. the wife of Tom McManus of Hartford it is said she was dying when he went away and joined the Irish Batallion. he was shifted from his Majorship in that and was then appointed Adjutant of the 25th Regt C.V. I think I will go to her funeral tomorrow morning from St Marys Church.

did I tell you that Mrs McCarter lost another of her children? Bernard the finest of them all. a splendid large Boy. he was sick but a very short time. his disease was croup. she is a most heart Broken woman. Joseph Kennedy's[24] wife came here to ask me if I would ask you to find out from Cogan[25] what has become of her husbands watch. She says She recd none of his things that she wrote to Cogan twice but recd no answer. the poor creature has gone to work in the Shirt Factory.

Write as often as you can to us. good night my dear Husban. God Bless you and bring you home soon to us.

yours

M. E. Cahill

Thomas to Margaret

Headquarters U.S. Forces in New Orleans
New Orleans, LA, Dec 14, 1862

My Dear Wife

Yours of Nov 28th came to hand on the 11th instant. you do not tell me how you got along on that spree you speak of but that Father Hart will: I am afraid of I want for him to tell I will never get the acount as I get no letters from him or in fact from any one else but yourself. The Dr has reced but one letter mailed from New Haven and that was 5 weeks ago. he has Rcd one from home since but not by the last mail.

do not know what to advise you to do with the money sent you unless to deposit it. what you do not what to use that is if the Bank pays any interest and is not a going to break, what have you done with those Coupon Bonds I sent you from Ship Island: they bear interest themselves and I do not know whether the savings Bank pays interest on their deposit. I should suppose not; I have I think sent you some "one Demand" notes. I perceive that kind of note is worth a premium of there 5 per cent. I believe there was none in the last I sent you as were not paid in that kind of money. if the Government gives them to the paymasters they do not give them to us. the difference in the notes consists in the words "on demand" being printed on the face of the Bill. on the 5s it is on the figure if you have any of that kind do not part with them.

24. Corp. Joseph Kennedy, Company A.
25. Lt. John Cogan of Company A.

I still have the $120,00 in gold with me. I keep it for an Emergency though the high Rate for Gold tempts me some times to part with it; I do not understand what you mean by paying Connors 50 dollars on Cooks act you did not tell me that Cook had paid you anything on that bill of his, you need not be afraid to draw on Carrols Money if the Bank will let you have it. he sent an order home by Wm O'Brien. he is an infernal Old Rascal and is kiting around here with some young woman making his braggs that put $50 in his fist the other Evening. he was Officer of the Guard the night he says she gave it to him at last was the night he told of it and he got drunk of Course and my Field Officer of the Day reported him as being absent from his post. it will be impossible for me to save him much longer:

There is a rumour that there are six of Banks Transports in the River and one has come up as far as Algiers. Larry O'Brien boarded her this Evening and they told him on board that the 24th was in the River so I expect to see Pat tomorrow. O'Brien will board her as soon as she arrives, this is Sunday Evening and I am writing in my shirt sleeves with the windows open and a Bunch of Roses plucked in the open air on the table. there fragrance is delightfull. you did not speak of Mrs O'Briens having arrived in your letter but John Healy got one of Dec 1st which did. so I suppose you are all right now about the picture I guess. you had better get the mocking bird from Tom Starkey for Eddie. I did not know in time that he was going to take any home or I would secure one for him;

Saturday Dec 15

Major Maher arrived on the "New Brunswick" Yesterday and called on me in the afternoon and slept with me last night and left to day with five or six other regiments for Baton Rouge. his presence brought back old times to mind. I feel verry Lonesome since seeing him; at 12 pm to day the *Thunderbolt* fell and General Butler is supersed [superseded] and retired. what revolutions this war brings about. nothing stands still Long and verily we know not what a day may bring fourth. Every thing is in suspense and the Excitement runs high:

at 12 pm. today Commanders of Divisions Brigades and Posts and Regiments about the city in the Army of the Gulf were presented to Genl Banks[26] the New Commander in Chief. it was a verry cold formal affair.

---

26. Gen. Nathaniel P. Banks, born in Massachusetts, was a lawyer before the war and was elected governor of Massachusetts in 1858. Appointed major general of volunteers, Banks commanded Union forces in the Shenandoah Valley and was defeated by Thomas

The Staff of both Commanders were present in addition to the officers indicated above. after the Presentation Gen Banks and Staff (after a verry short speech turning over the Command by the Old Genl and one Equally brief in reply by the new) withdrew and officers of the Old Army of the Gulf were alone with Genl Butler. it was an affecting scene he proceeded to read his fare well address. a brief but Eloquent recapitulation of work done and sufferings Endured, it will probably be published.

Saturday Dec 15 9 O'Clock P.M.

Mrs O'Brien has made up her mind to go on Tuesday next by the "Parkersburg" and Herrity is going too, I am not sorry. he has been drinking a good deal this summer and has given me a deal of annoyances and I am not sorry to get rid of him: I am of the opinion you will have an Easy time of it when Mrs OB gets home as she can talk to all the old women and men for you; as she seems to be in the confidence of a big crowd: nothing new has occured here:

I expect Billy Wilson[27] here in a day or two when I shall be releived from my Extra duties in Command and shant not be sorry for it. there is a large amount of small work to do and it has kept me verry busy and I get no benefit or Credit for it; I do not know how it may be taken at Hd Qrs nor do I care. Billy must take hold. in my next I may tell you how it works. there are 2 or 3 more lady arrivals here to day by a sailing ship from Boston. one is the wife of the Qm Master of the 26th Mass, they are stopping at the Park House. have not heard of them taking any houses. dont know whether that game has played out or not. it might do it verry suddenly, as the major genl might at any moment order them all out if he saw fit: and he sees fit to do anything he has a mind to. he is the most singular compound I Ever saw, I intend to send you Copies of some of his late orders particularly the one about the officers being found drinking in Bar Rooms. of course this will not have any serious Effect but it makes some of my lads growl because he wants them to take their Liqour like men; or what they are supposed to be gentleman. what a terrible hardship it is for them.

"Stonewall" Jackson during the 1862 Valley Campaign. After that, he was transferred to New Orleans. Warner, *Generals in Blue*, 17–18; Hollandsworth, *Pretense of Glory*; Cozzens, *Shenandoah 1862*.

27. Col. William "Billy" Wilson, commander of the Sixth New York Infantry. New York State Military Museum and Veterans Research Center, New York Civil War Units.

I keep on writing not that I have any thing to say but rather because I have nothing so I keep open untill Mrs OB gets ready to start when I will seal up, Capt Wright and Wiliams are not on duty yet tho Genl promised me to send William back to duty last week but has not done so yet; I have not Called on Mrs Frye yet although invited, the fact is I have no time and not much inclination as you will probably saw. I never had for visiting good night.

Sunday night [December 16] 10 PM

have been at Genl Butlers house all evening. wanted to see him on business. he was down the River at a Plantation with the French and English Admiral spent a pleasan Evening with a few of the staff. The Genl did get home till late; he is a singular man to see him here Chumming with these French and Englishmen and the way he handles the consuls, when he sent those Episcapal Ministers north the other day he told Laycock the Englishman that he did not propose to *die* until he had a chance to *publish General Order no 28* in the streets of *Liverpool.* I suppose that will be published in the Lines and will make "John Bull" howl:[28]

I understand he intends to buy a house at auction in a few days so as to live in a house of his own. this looks as though his ideas run somewhat according to mine about the houses and he may order these officers all out of them, This is a mighty dull City here. we get no news. I suppose there is none Except to the Elections north which it is rumoured here are going Democratic, The Matanzas has not arrived and it is said she has been taken off the Line. the Creole is Expected; about all the Excitement is waiting for the mails and I am Expecting a good long letter from Father Hart. I dont write to him this time because I dispair of getting this one finished. you must turn this over and try and make it answer both and each send me one just as long. mind that John Carroll has heard of his wife death and [illegible] to send you an order for the money he sent home so as to have the Children taken care of. I dont think you will have much cause to Com[plain] of not having a letter this time.

Monday [December 17] 2 Oclock PM

nothing new. no mail as yet and I close my letters to Nate Wilson[29] has not arrived yet. I have not given Mrs O Brien any money here. I wish you

---

28. John Bull was a common reference to England, much as Uncle Sam often refers to the United States.

29. No Nate Wilson served in the Ninth Connecticut.

to give what you think right from what you have at home: as I have only a little over a hundred dollars in treasury notes with me. I sent home you by the Potomac and I did not get it insured. I shall not send so much by one ship again as I am afraid it is too many Eggs in one Basket if anything should happen.

I am too busy to write more so I must stop give me regards to all enquiring friends, my Love to Ellen Kiss the Babies all round—for me. tell New O'Brien I have sent him a gun. dont let Father Hart of[f] from writing.

Your Loving Husband
Thos W. Cahill

No one knows but the New Commander what will be the next distribution of the troops. hence all is doubt and uncertainty and conseqeuntly unpleasant; there are many more Regiments to arrive one steamer is reported as lost but the Crew and troops saved; I had no opportunity to go on board Major Mahers vessel and Conseqeuntly saw no one but himself, John Murphy[30] and John Shaw.[31] the latter is left behind and may be Cashiered for being absent without leave probably what he desires:

The "Columbia" Mail steamer arrived last night from new York Dec 6th but brought me nothing. I really expected a letter from home as we knew here she would leave on that date. I suppose the Public at the north will be surprised at Butlers removal as we can find no indications of a knowledge of it in the paper of Dec 6th. for myself I must own I was surprised at the Radical nature of the change although if you see mayor Welch after McCarthy gets home he *may hint* to you privately that I thought some Change in Certain matters might be advisable;

and a few Paragraphs in a Leading Editorial in the last Times you sent me on the sugar taken in the La Tourche Country gave me an idea that some of the work going on here must be known at home. of Course not being in the way of handling any of these Pickings myself I can afford to Laugh at those who by this Range see their anticipated "Piles" snatched out of their hands. Even if what they have already grabled be not Carefully looked after: as it may possibly;

I must say that I have often been more than vexed to see the spoils won by the blood and sufferings of those of us who have been in the field going into the hands of vagabond confers who have hung around

30. Three John Murphys served in the Ninth Connecticut, in Companies B, D, and I. It is unclear which Cahill is referring to.

31. Lt. John C. Shaw, Company C.

Head Quarters living on and Enriching themselves at our Expense and through dangers in which they never participated. it Could not last for Ever and it ought not; Even since this Sugar Crop has Ripened speculators in the Army and out it who were in the *Ring*.[32] that is with the sequestration Committee have been grabbing sugar plantations wherever they could find a fit one with the machinery and wood all ready and seizing all the runaway negroes they could get and taking off the Crop only to think of it with sugar worth 10ct by the 1,000 lbs; I hardly think the Ring have succeeded in so arranging things as to Cover up Every thing; the blow has been too secret and sudden, although it is said that they got a hint of it some 4 weeks ago but that they supposed it had blown over. many of these men hold no Commissions in the U States service although noted as Col this and Lt Col that and Major some thing and any quantity of Capts to Lieuts *Shaw*. they were as plenty as young *toads* after a Shower in summer and Equally as *toaddy*. O dear it does me good to see them get a kicking though it will indeed be strange if some who gave in no cent do not suffer.

A short time ago I was placed on a Committee as Chairman to settle the Liability of the united States because the genl let all the negroes out of the Parish Prison without paying the Jail Fees amounting to some 3,000 dollars. now some of these negroes went into the negro regiments but the greatest portion went I think into the hands of the fellows who go the privilege of taking off the sugar crop and I suspect into the hands of those who paid for the getting of them. If I am let alone i may find out who got them and I may help to make them pay instead of the tax payers.

Dec 17

no news as yet of the 16th Conn Came in to day. they are going into camp at the Parapet. we have not yet received any orders for Changes. Nims Battery has gone to Baton Rouge. some of the old Regiments must undoubtely go into the field with the green horns: all the staff of Genl Butlers are upset. If we are ordered off I will try to let you know—will leave a letter in the officer here the Regt are so much scattered that it will be some little trouble for them to relieve them to send them off particu-

---

32. Benjamin Butler granted permits to clear cargo from the port of New Orleans to a number of speculators who flooded into the city after its fall. Col. Andrew J. Butler (the general's brother) made nearly $1 million from sugar speculation during this period. Winters, *Civil War in Louisiana*, 138–40; Hearn, *When the Devil Came Down*.

larly with green troops and officers. I had an Eye to this when I made the distributions. I do not think we will be sent away but nothing is certain.

Good Bye and God Bless You all

Thos W. Cahill

Margaret to Thomas

New Haven Dec 15th 1862

My dear Husband

I sent you a few lines on Friday evening and your Weekly Papers. perhaps this will be in time for the Same Steamer. While I write there is a Terrible Battle being Fought. Oh dear it fairly makes me Tremble and how will it End. God alone knows but this much we do know—that there has been a great *slaughter* already on both Sides. I have cut out all the latest news to send you but will keep this open for the next issue.[33]

We had the Right Rev bishop at vespers yesterday. he Preached a good long Sermon and recommended to us a Prayer for Peace in our Beloved Country. it is *high time I think* for something of the kind to take place. I firmly believe that nothing else will bring Peace to us but the Prayers and fastings of good sane Minded Servants of God.

Mr Res of the Conn Savings Bank is dead and I am sorry to hear of it. he has been very kind to me since you went away, he has often asked me if he could be of any service to me. he was always willing for your sake to assist me in all Business transactions and always so agreable whenever I had occasion to meet him and so feeling in all his remarks about your absence. Many will have cause to regret him. Ellen went to Beg for The Fair last week. she called upon Mayor Welch. he complained of having a great many calls for money and among others P. M. he gave him One Hundred Dollars to help equip him but he was very much disappointed

---

33. This is a reference to the Battle of Fredericksburg, which was fought December 11–15, 1862. Union forces under Gen. Ambrose Burnside attempted to cross the Rappahannock River and dislodge Lee's Army of Northern Virginia from its positions around the town of Fredericksburg. A major Union defeat, in which the Army of the Potomac sustained 12,653 causalities to the Army of Northern Virginia's 5,377, this even had serious repercussions on the Irish American population, who saw the losses of the Irish Brigade there as evidence of the misuse of ethnic soldiers. At Fredericksburg, noted one observer, the Irish were "slaughtered like sheep, and no result but defeat." Another noted that the Irish brigade was "the most dejected set of Irishmen you ever saw or heard of." Ural, *Harp and the Eagle* 134; Rable, *Fredericksburg! Fredericksburg!*

in him regarding his influence among the Irish. good for him wasnt it! He had no business to risk so much. He wished to be remembered to you. Said he would write to you soon.

Mr Herity came to see me twice. he is well and Hard Herity still. And our brave Mrs Obrien is not alone traveling yet. she is now in Bridgeport and going to New York to Buy the Capt some Clothes. by the by what shall I do about your Pants? you told me to send you one Pair—I sent you the ones you Send Home. will they answer or will I have another Pair Made; I ordered you a dark blue Vest and a Pair of Boots. they will be done the later part of this week. I must go and see Capt Ward and find out if he will take them to you. I hope he will for I do not like those Express Agents here. they are a most contempable sort. Capt Ward will tell you you what I mean—

Terrill called here today. he looks miserable has the chills quite often yet he is going to write and send you papers this week. he wished he had not come north this winter—you are a great favorite of his. Wm Geary answered your letter two weeks ago and they are all well. Mrs G is going to give you a great dressing down, you say so little about our dear little Thomas. you know she is his Godmother. She thinks Mary must be your favorite because all the little Presents was for her—*but Mother says* Mary is deserving all the love you can bestow upon her and out darling Boys too. I know they are as dear to you as her.

Oh when will we all be together again? only think of our second lonely Christmass. but my dear Husband I do not mean to complain. God has been good and merciful to us in sparing your life but perhaps it would be well to attribute some of it to the Prayers of our little children. their constant Petition is to spare you and bring you home safe to us and I hope you will let no opportunity go by to do so, as [f]or my going to New Orleans I hardly know what to say. if you wish me to go I will do so by all means. whatever you say I will do but I cannot go without *all* the babies and Ellen too. I would only make you miserable if I went without them and would it be Prudent to expose them when it is not known how long you will be in the same Place. Please answer this and I will be guided by it.

Now I will tell you of an incident which occured on the day of Mrs Ferys departure from her home as told me by Mrs Palmer. She left her two girls at a Boarding School in Bridgeport. her little Boy 7 years old she took to Brooklin with her and left him with a relative of hers to take care of him until she came Back from the South. in her hurry getting ready to go on Board of the Steamer the poor little fellow was forgotten—at night he was missing and could not be found. they had him advertised but to no purpose and where do you think he was found in his own home or where his home ought to be in Bridgeport. he had 2 shillings—made his way to the New Haven depo in New York and paid his fair to his home. I think he has more common sense about him that Either Father or Mother don't you—I have just recd a note from Mrs Palmer saying her Husband has sent for him to come out by the next steamer. she is in New York engaging her Pasage. she wants me to spend a day with her before she leaves and send you a Something by her. That old *Jew* sent your Vest home this morning but it is made of such poor light cloth I do not like to send it. he shall make a better one or I will take none from him. I am afraid you will get out of patience waiting for it.

I rented our rooms yesterday to an other half Dutch and half Yankee the woman. says she had Irish Blood in her not spunk. I hope they lived in John McGuires house in this street. the woman could not agree. I hope we will not have the same story to tell. they have no small family only two douthers the youngest 13. they wanted only 3 rooms this winter thinks they will be able to Pay more rent in the spring and take the whole floor. I keep the front room and they are satisfied to use the Back stairs until they will be able to furnish the Front ones. they can only pay 4½ dollars a month but I think that itself better than to have it empty all winter. it is so lonely nights. he looks like a steady man. works in WhitneyVill.[34] they get Paid off on the 15th of every month so I think I will be sure of the rent—

I would like to send our Babies likness to you but you said the others made you homesick and I do not like to make you feel bad. I have one of the Drs Baby you can tell him if I *should* send one of my Baby it would put his little Girl clean in the shade and I do not like to do that. I wrote to his wife last. She has not answered my letter what is the matter? Drs fret you never told me he had any disease but it is a current report here that he has they Pronounce it *Gout*. perhaps you are troubled in the same way. but if you are you are only getting Paid off for the way you used to laugh at it me.

I am sure if you could only see our little Tommys legs you could not say anything else but that he was gouty too. sulch stumps you never seen on a Chap 5 months old. yesterday F. Hart knocks great fun out of him. he says he is going to give you a scolding for Bad writing. every letter you send is worse than the last. he says the more you write the worse you write.

---

34. Whitneyville is a part of the town of Hamden, Conn., and home to the Whitneyville Armory, one of the largest armories in the United States in 1861. Rockey, *History of New Haven County*, 1:304.

I don't know what he would say if he seen mine but it is a consolation to know that there was no little Fortune paid by to _____. He wrote to Mr James E. English[35] on your merits and let me read the answer—it was very complimentary to you very much so indeed. I suppose he will tell you all about it and in better shape than I can. hoping this will find you enjoying the best of health and will bring you a happy Christmass and the only and best way to do that it so secure the Blessed Sacrament. we will join with you in doing the Same at home. God Bless you and bring you home soon to us.

from you Loving wife
Margaret E. Cahill

Thomas to Margaret

New Orleans Dec 20th 1862

My Dear Wife

Nothing new has occurred since the mailing of my letter to you on Tuesday Last. The new administration are verry secret in their movements and they being strangers to all the officers there is not much gossipping going on between them, we have had rumours of Genl Corcorans being on Ship Island a few days ago but have head no confirmation of it since, have not heard anything from Major Maher since he Left for Baton Rouge. One of the steamers that took up troops returned from there just at dark this Evening but have learnt nothing of any news she brought if any.

The Secesh here are quite jubilant over Butlers removal.[36] whether they will have any ocasion remains to be seen, you will see Genl Order No 110[37] that it looks as if Genl Banks intends to look after the houses

---

35. James E. English was a contractor in New Haven who was engaged in a number of enterprises, including clock making, the lumber business, and shipbuilding. English served as a member of Congress, the governor of Connecticut, and a U.S. senator. Hill, *Modern History of New Haven*, 2:22.

36. Butler was removed from command in December 1862. Warner, *Generals in Blue*, 61.

37. When Nathaniel Banks took over command of the Department of the Gulf from Benjamin Butler, he undertook a series of policies designed to reconcile with the Southern population, which had been alienated by Butler's leadership style. Banks "ordered the release of political prisoners; he forbade further auctions of property; he continued to feed the destitute; those who wanted work were found a job; he ordered elections for two congressmen to be held; he restored many private homes and other private property; and he reopened the Episcopal churches of New Orleans." Cahill misspoke above when he wrote

occupied by the officers and that they are to be restricted to the Regulation allowance. the new Quarter Master seems also to be advertising for a house for himself instead of *taking* on. all this indicates a change of Policy taken in Connection with the stoppage of sales on behalf of the Govt so called. it may mean nothing more than to gain time to examine matters. but I think it means none but Mr Jonas H French the Provost Marshall Genl has not been removed. I cannot understand that. however so far as I am Concerned they may overhaul or underhaull old affairs here as much as they are a mind to. it can make no difference with me, I have had no finger in any "Rich Pies" that may have been pushed around among the "sellect" nor have I occupied any big house so let them work at it "how cares."

I have been Expecting marching orders but have not received them. the 30th Mass did but begged off on account of the Reduced Condition of their Regiment although they report more men for duty than we do. but we have not begged off yet nor do I think we will let things Come as they May.

I have not had a letter from home since the 28th of Nov and am afraid I will get none this side of Christmass. O dear this is the second Christmass away from home. sometimes I feel the blues thinking of it. it is a long time to look ahead yet what can I do? I turn the matter over in my mind Every way I can but can see no ready means of escape. if I was home what could I do? I could not remain there idle more particularly as all Eyes would be on me; and all avenues of industry must be stopped and I might be glad to take some inferior position and when I think how much reason I have to be thankfull and how well Everything has gone with us notwithstanding the thoughts of as Resignation Comes up verry frequently before me and there is a possibillity I may have recourses [illegible] it though I am almost ashamed to allow myself to think of it:

Dec 22d
No Change yet will keep this open so long as I can.

Dec 23
it is said a mail leaves today. nothing has changed with me as yet. have not heard that Corcoran is at Ship Island yet but learn on good authority

---

"General Order No. 110" because these issues were addressed in General Order No. 113. Winters, *Civil War in Louisiana*, 147–48.

that he is Coming out here. it is said that there will be 12 Brigades made in this Command and 4 Divisions. one old Regiment to each Brigade and senior Col to Command.

Genl Banks I think will try Concilation as far as it will do. it is singular what a difference there is in the air of the people. Every one of the secesh is gay. Father Chalon Called on me yesterday. he is in Extacies. says Banks and staff were at Cathedral on sunday he expects great Changes in the Policy I can write no man no news from home yet it seems so strange [illegible] the immense number of vessells. but of course did not know where they were going.

Kiss the Babies for me. God Bless you all at home and a Merry Christmass to you.

Thos W. Cahill

Margaret to Thomas

New Haven Dec 25th 1862

My Dear Husband

I wish you a very Merry Christmass. We are all well and are happy if not verry. the Children hung their stockings up last night for the first time. it is quite a task to make them believe anything about Santa C. I took them both up Town yesterday. they were delighted to see so many Toys. I feared we would have a fuss in Chappel Street with Eddy. he wanted me to Buy Every thing he took a fancy to and when he found I would not he was determined to stay looking at them as long as he choose but poor Mary consoled herself with mama. will Buy them when Papa comes home.

O dear have you any idea of how much we miss you? I cannot find courage enough to cook our cook Dinner. I think we will save Labor and have Dinner and supper together. perhaps someone will come along and help us eat it. I fear it will be hard work to keep our little ones up to eat it with us. they are up since 5 Oclock this morning and well pleased with their stockings full—we met Mrs and Miss Mary Hillhouse yesterday. they were peased to see the children. gave them some little Presents and enquird particularly after you.

My dear Husband we spent the evening very pleasantly. Mr Sheridan called to see us. Mr Flood and two of his Daughters Larry and Jim Cooney and Father hart left company at home and came to spend an hour with us. he knocked great fun out of Tommy teaching him to smoke if you please. I am anxious for McCarthy to come with my letters. there is not news of any importance. I will send your Papers with this today. hoping you have spent a very happy Christmass and that this may find you in the best of healthy. I will finish with remaining your Loving wife.

M. E. Cahill

Thomas to Margaret

New Orleans Dec 28 1862

My Dear Wife

Your letter dated the 15th Came to hand by the "Marion" to day: so far things remain as of my Last dates in this place. I have not ascertained anything as to the proceedings in Contemplations. I hardly dare to hope to be left here. it is too nice a place for one who has the name of an Irishman. one satisfaction I have that I have Embraced the opurtunity to scatter my Companies all over the place and it will bother them to relieve them.

So you think the more I write the worse I work? well I cant spare more than ten or fifteen minutes to a sheet and then I steal the time for sleep. I have a Confounded sight more writing than I want to do for it is work I never liked. Ellen is at work at me about answering Morrisseys letter. I never received any letter from him Except one Enquiring about a soldier which I turned over to the Captain of his Company. if he took the trouble to write me a personal letter he would have some Cain, I have received none from Wm Gearvy but one, none from M Fahey none from the mayor. I think these folks are only Codding you. I get your letters why not theirs if they write them?

so you are getting Jealous of me about Mary and the other dear ones? well I dont deserve it. Carroll sent the Locket. I wish I was there with you all, I do not need the vest nor the pants verry much nor the boots the last as much as any; though I have not mended those I have yet; If I am to go into the field a gain the less I have the better I cannot carry them. if I remain here I may want them in a month or two.

you do not say a word about the Barrell of Sugar I sent you by Express on the 11th of October. I have the receiprt but why dont you answer about it? I have written several times about it and I dont like to be repeating. besides I told Mrs O'Brien about it. it went on the "Ronaoke." I paid $11 freight on it. it was to have been delivered to you in New Haven by Addams Express. what is the matter with you and the Express? why dont you tell me? I may never see Capt Ward again. you cant tell when these

Navy men go to when they leave port. Addams Express has always done my business as well unless the sugar is wrong.

I may take it in my head to Clean out from here in some way. nothing but the dislike to leaving the men keeps me here. I do not think there is a shadow of a chance for a furlough and they need not accept a resignation. if I write it I wish I was sure they would, they would think it was in consequence of Butlers going and would be glad of a chance to snub me.

Father Hart has not given me the particulars of the letters between himself and Mr English. I am under many verry many obligations to the former and also to the latter. in one sense though I sometimes wish he had not helped me into this affair yet what is the use of weping? I only make these observations that you may readily understand I have no particular pleasure in the life. I am leading against my will; I never expect to be happy in it and wish to God I was at home. though better off than 2 thirds that are in it, the officers here are awfully down on the new men. I will try to send you the orders so you may understand some of the reasons. not many Resigning though. in fact there is no use of talking about resigning unless a man has strong cause though. I believe the people are getting tired of the war verry fast but it Cannot stop yet. I suppose if the democrats carry the states as they are like to do in the spring the absent ones will be apt to catch the raps.

I do not think the soldiers aught to vote. if they vote against the governor they will catch the Rap. if they dont they will from the Demos. I should not want my men to vote. dont want the bother of it. the soldier has no interest different from any other citizen. if they are tired of the war we have a deal more reason to be thorough many will be worse off after it.[38]

I do not know as I would be able to get a living at home if I went there. I have tried to look around here to see if there would be any chance here for making a living, what do you think of it? they will need a new population down here after the war. it was a mighty bad one they had before you see.

I looking ahed—just ½ hour at this letter

---

38. As Warshauer in *Connecticut in the American Civil War* notes, the constitution of Connecticut mandated that "electors had to meet in their respective towns, and when Governor Buckingham asked the state's Supreme Court justices to consider the constitutionality of a law allowing soldiers to vote in the field, he was told without qualification that it would be unconstitutional." This was changed in an 1864 amendment to the state's constitution (107).

Thomas to Margaret

New Orleans January 8th 1863

My Dear Wife,

I am here yet not having been releived. The two Cols next me in Rank had a dispute as to seniority. in the mean time the unfortunate affair of Galveston occurred.[39] This with the horrible Gloomy accounts received from Tennessee may have changed the Programme. I have taken advantage of this lull to present an application today for a Leave of Absence for 60 days to run home. on my being releived at this Post, I saw Genl Banks personally he was verry Civil and gave me hopes of granting it. But his Adgt Genl is an ugly curse apparently, so dare not hope too much. the Secesh is in estacies over the horrible news from the north. Banks suppressed the report of Rosencrans[10] surrender which makes it look more gloomy. it is horrible and I verry much fear the *union* has *gone in*.[11]

Major Maher is well. I hardly think they will attempt much by way of Baton Rouge, do not think it can be done. he has lost his horse. it died on the passage, as also the Lt Col of his Regt. he desired me to remember him as he has not written. he has had no pay yet, I have all my things packed for a move. hope it may be home. no Mails from home since 20th Dec 2 Steamers over due May be the Alabama gotthem.

you need not believe any stories about my health. have to do something to get an excuse. keep it up though so I shant have to play it too strong when I get there if I do. you need say nothing about my application, but I am verry sick, which is true Enough of something. The Dr. is well as is every body else. Garvey has not been paid this time dont know the cause. The weather is delightfull here. hate to leave it but think this my best Chance. am afraid I'll freeze to death if I get home but am willing

---

39. Union efforts in the Gulf extended to Texas, where federal forces had secured a foothold in the state in October when the navy captured Galveston. On January 1, 1863, Confederates defeated and captured the small Union garrison and wrecked ships in the harbor. Winters, *Civil War in Louisiana*, 212.

40. Gen. William S. Rosecrans, who was born in Ohio, graduated fifth in his class from West Point and was "praised for his ability as a strategist and tactician" in the years before the war. Jones, *Generals in Blue and Gray*, 101–16. See Moore, *William S. Rosecrans*; Lamers, *Edge of Glory*.

41. The Battle of Stones River, fought from December 31, 1862 to January 2, 1863, between Braxton Bragg's Army of Tennessee and Rosecrans's Army of the Cumberland, was a Union victory. Reid, *America's Civil War*, 250–55; Daniel, *Battle of Stones River*.

to try; it will cost a pile of money though. hope to get a letter in a day or two. I would Rather stay here untill April if I could but am afraid if I got hitched on to another Brigade it would be hard to get away from it when I wanted to Could hardly do it.

The men were paid off and went on a bus as usual but there were not many of them in the City so did not show so much; I sent you 2 hundred dollars and 46 for scully. John McDermott Co K sent you some for himself to. he put with the others. Old Carroll had 50 cts left of his pay they tell me the old scoundral, but the most of them are near as bad.

We are looking with anxiety for news from the north though these steamers will not bring dates as Late as we have them to 2nd Jan and it is said the suppressed news to 4th. Oh it is terrible bad news from Vicksburg and all around.[12] am afraid the north is Done up. The loss of those vessels at Galveston was a Miserable affair. I am afraid there will be something of the kind at Mobile where one of those great Iron Clads that were to do so much not built yet I suppose now wont be untill the war is over or we are all well whipped. it is rumoured here that the "winona" gun boat was sunk by the Batteries at Port Hudson[13] and 1. 3. and 7 disabled. no news of Corcoran yet. wonder if he is coming here. hope not Enough I here I think unless a tremendous force is sent. there is not more than 12000 men in the New arrival. all small regts. my own men as large as any. give my respects to all friends. Kiss the Babies for me. Love to Ellen and yourself.

Thos W Cahill

Thomas to Margaret

New Orleans Jan 14th 1863

My Dear Wife

Your letters of the 19th and 25th of Dec. came to hand on the 12th as likewise the papers. I remain here as yet *I am on the sick list as you will understand by my last letter.* I applied for a leave of absence on the 6th after a personal interview with General Banks who gave me to understand I

42. Cahill is referring to William T. Sherman's failed attacks at Chickasaw Bayou as Union troops moved on Vicksburg in the winter of 1862–63. Stoker, *Grand Design*, 224; Dougherty, *Vicksburg Campaign*, 63–66.

43. Port Hudson was a fortified city on the Mississippi River. See Hewitt, *Port Hudson*.

would get it. on the Contrary I received an insulting refusal from his Adgt Genl who directed me to report to my Brigade at Baton Rouge. I did not go yet. the idea of Ordering a sick man on duty and that to organise a new Brigade of Raw troops. I have had all the organizing I wanted for the last year Especially for a Colonel pay. So I just sent in my resignation to the Mr Adgt Genl on Monday the 12th and have not heard from him since. I do not Expect it will be received but I think my letter will give him to understand that I do not intend to be trifled with.

I do not like to leave the Regt but they have ordered me away from it so I had that point in my favor and I intend to make the most of it. the Dr gave me a rousing Certificate of Disability and he drives Every body away from the Room. he is what you may Call a bully man and is bound to Carry this thing through but I have not much hope of succeeding. however you can see that there is no foundation for your assertion or hints that I am not as anxious to get home as you can be to have me.

I had worked verry hard to keep the Regiment in good Quarters this winter using every particle of power while in Command here to Effect it But they are bound to keep us in the front if they Can. I have baffled them a little but of Course they have the power; to day an order came assigning the 9th temporary to the Brigade for the City. it is called the 2d Brigade of T. W. Shermans division which I am senior Col so that I am in Command yet *only I am sick.*

I had a letter from Major Maher a few days ago. he is well and all is quiet up there. he is trouble about the loss of his horse and they are somewhat scarce here as there is so many to mount and but few horses. I think I will lend him one of mine. he wished me to see the Quarter Master for him about the loss of his horse but I have not been able to leave My room since he sent me word but I do not think there is any Chance for him to review anything for him.

Why does not Father Hart write to me? I hear our troops are fighting at Berricks Bay or Brushean City. that is down near where Matt Young[44] said he was going to be Married at Breax Bridge. *Every body is in good health here not except myself.* I expect to be bye and bye, a Mr Thomson who used to drive a milk wagon in our neighborhood Called to see me several times this week. I have been of some assistance to him. he said he would call and see you when he went home which he expected to do in a few days.

---

44. No one named Matt Young served in the Ninth Connecticut.

you need not be *frightened at what he says* as I had to pull the wool over him. he went to see Genl Banks with a letter from me. my love to Ellen and Kiss the Babies as Usual.

Your Loving husband

Thos W Cahill

Thomas to Margaret

New Orleans Jan 19th 1863

10–30 PM

My Dear Wife,

The transport St. Marys Sails to morrow. Dr. Lines our 2nd Asst Surgeon has been ordered home by the state authorities. I do not know for what reason he has not been mustered into the United States service so is under their control: I have not received an answer to request for a furlough on sunday. the Adgt Gen sent over note wishing to see me about my resignation. *I was not able to go* so I sent the Dr. he was told my resignation could not be accepted but was given to understand, I might renew my application for a furlough. I have done so but no answer yet. The Medical Examiner to whom was referred my Case has *Endorsed the application so it is all right so far:* I am not fit for *active service.*

I am afraid some of those mail steamers will be caught by the *Oneto.*[15] rumour reaches us of another disaster at Galveston in the loss of the Brooklyn Sloop of War. it is said she has grounded and thumped to pieces on the Bar. the navy is going to the old boy.

I am disapointed in not receiving my Leave to day. it was sent in this morning. true it is almost to soon to Expect it. all is quiet at Baton Rouge. these 9 month fellows[16] are crying about going home already.

I had not letters by the Last mail of sunday by the Columbia. there is three steamers now due here if the Alabama or Oneto has not caught them. they will Catch some of them soon. I see it is states on the authority of the naval officer before Mobile that the Oneto is in that Harbour. I

---

45. It is unclear which Confederate ship this refers to.

46. As part of Lincoln's call for troops in August 1862, he requested three hundred thousand nine-month volunteers. Failure to furnish these men would result in the implementation of a draft. Nearly half of the federal force in New Orleans in 1862 were composed of nine-month men. With their terms up in the spring of 1863, Nathaniel Banks faced the possibility of losing approximately twenty thousand men from his command. Winters, *Civil War in Louisiana*, 212; Warshauer, *Connecticut in the American Civil War*, 90–91.

know there has not been an ocean steamer within the last six weeks. she is in the Gulf and they will find it out pretty soon it must have been her that sank the Hatteras at Galveston. The Dr. is well and sends his regards. all are well here but disapointed in the last mail. Give my regards to all Enquiring friends. why does not Father Hart write me? Kiss the Babies for me. Love to Ellen. I hope to be with you for a while soon.

your loving husband

Thos W Cahill

CHAPTER 6

"All my command are on detached 'provost Duty' "

April–October 1863

Thomas to Margaret

On Board Steamer George Peobody
Off Coast of Florida Saturday April 25/62[3]

My Dear Wife,

Expecting to arrive at Key West to morrow. I commence this with intent to mail at that place though it may reach you sooner than if mailed at New Orleans. Still there is a chance for it. So far we have had a splendid Passage we left the Dock at 9.30 AM on Sunday last.

The Commencement of our voyage seemed Ominous of ill luck and ere we reached "Sandy Hook" I had serious misgivings (so far hapily dispelled) On going down the Bay we picked up the schooner "Mary Steadman" Which we were to "Tow" to N. Oreleans Often getting a "Hawser" to her and getting under full head way we were ordered to "Come to" by a gun from the Revenue Cutter: this brought us up all "Standing" and before the schooners headway could be stopped she ran into us fortunately without causing much damage. She drifted against us two or three times: in addition to this we were among a fleet of Sailing vessels among whom we butted about and fortunately for them and us save the smashing of a small boat on a schooners stern without much damage to them or ourselves.

Our boat having returned from the Cutter We commenced our voyage. I came on deck on Monday Morning to find the sky overcast and symptoms of a heavy storm during that day and untill Thursday we had clouds and a heavy wind to sea without Rain, On Thursday it cleared and since have had lovely weather. The Steamer has proved herself an excellent Sea Boat verry steady: I have not been at all seasick. at noon on Thursday the first "Observation" was taken since leaving Port We were then about off Hilton Head.

Since yesterday noon we have been steaming down within a mile of the Coast of Florida. How singular it seems in this apparantly over crowded world to see this Coast for hundreds of miles apparently without a human inhabitant or a habitation. A Country in all its primeval Solitude as "Ponce De Leon" found it in its Virgin Verdun and so practically named it the "Land of Flowers." we are running sufficiently near the shore to be able by the aid of a good glass to see the trees well defined though not always able to say what kind they are unless the well marked species as the Palmetto or Cabbage tree and the Pine; but it is one Endless Primeval forest; neither can we see the Flowers;

So much had I written when the cry of "Sail Ho" brought all hands on deck; after a while the Glasses pronounced her Ensign "Winson down" a Signal of distress, What could be the matter was she on a Reef of which these treacherous seas are so full. The Captain thought not: On Coming up with her she proved to be the U.S. Transport Ship "De Witt Clinton" with 2 Companies of the 48th Mass Regt and the 13th Mass Battery in all 240 men and officers and 120 horses on board; they were 27 days from "Fortress Monroe" and had been twelve days in sight of Cape Florida without being able to gain a mile on her Course to New Orleans:

they were on Short allowance of Water; and had but two days supply on board when at that we Came in sight. So that it must have seemed like a direct interposition of Divine Providence to them our happening along as we did. had we been a few miles outside of them we could not have seen their signal of distress or had we passed in the night it would have been the same. What a cheer went up from her decks when in answer to her Captains Statement of her Condition Capt Atwill of the "Peabody" said he would take her in Tow to "Key West." after a good deal of hard labor her Hawsen was taken on board and we started on our Course:

with a big Ship and a schooner hitched on behind we cut quite a swell on Old Oceans bosom. after being a few hours under way our Cabin Passengers amused themselves by Rigging up what they designated a submarine Telegraph in this wise. A large bottle Containing the latest Papers and a written Communication was attached to a line and allowed to float towards them. when they Picked it up and when they placed their Communications in the bottle and by means of our End of the line we pulled it on board, in this way correspondence has been going on all this Saturday Evening and Sunday morning as I am now writing. In addition to the Bottle Containing dispatches or an intimation from Our side to which they answered that they were as dry as their horses. a Demi John with a supply of the "Mile of human kindness" was sent to them: The return dispatch was profuse in their expression of thanks; should the morning land breeze die out as usual they are to send some of their Officers on board to dine with us this Sunday noon; our Captain is a jovial fellow and a thorough Sailor and Enters into the sport of thing with a hearty good will. he had had thirty years experience in the Seas, I will reserve the other sheet for what may happen between here and Key West about 80 miles off.

325 PM Sunday

have just made Key West Light distant 10 miles, our friends from the De Witt did not seceed in getting on Board as we could not stop for them without taking in sail. it has been a verry warm day thermometer over 80 degrees although a good deal of air stirring in the shade. The Captain has treated me with a deal of Kindness giving me a large bed and Room to myself in what he Calls his Bridal Chamber. the Board has been verry fair and Every thing verry pleasant. so far as Soon as we reach Key West I will ascertain how long I can keep this open and will write more if I have time.

10 O Clock P.M.

in Key West. news of Great success near New Orleans some 2,700 Prisoners taken and the Queen of the West retaken but you will have all the details before receiving this.[1] the 9th remains as I left them. Billy Wilsons Regt said to be in serious disgrace; its said that 15 of his officers are in prison and a large number of his men: and himself under arrest. these items I have from an "aid de Camp" of General Banks who came on here with dispatches and orders at Key West and the Tortugas have been added to General Banks Command.

he says that a large number of Troops are to be sent out here this summer which will be needed if they are to hold all the new territory recently taken in with its Head Quarters at "Opalousas" the new Rebel Capital of Louisiana. this would imply that we have taken up an immense Extent of Country. The aid tells me that we have lost but few men in this movement which is wonderfull if true cannot learn anything about the 24th Conn Major Maher as he knows nothing of that Regt the small loss

---

1. Cahill's reference is to Nathaniel Banks's Bayou Teche Campaign against Confederate forces in Louisiana under Gen. Richard Taylor in March and April 1863. This was part of Taylor's attempt to cut off Banks from New Orleans. During this campaign Banks moved on Thibodaux and attempted to push Confederate forces out of the Teche Bayou. Winters, *Civil War in Louisiana*, 221–35.

in the agregate would indicate that Even if Engaged they could not have lost much: My Respects to Father Hart and all friends my love to Ellen Kiss the Babies for me good night and God Bless you

Your Loving Husband

Thos W Cahill

Thomas to Margaret
New Orleans May 6th 1863

My Dear Wife

We arrived here safely on sunday morning after a slow but pleasant passage: the Dr and all our friends and acquaintances were well. Capt O'Brien is down for a few days from his Parish. Everything is going on well with him and the people are extremely pleased with him. he anticipates a very pleasant time. The men and officers of the Regiment are all well and doing nicely being all on the same kind of duty as when I left although some changes have taken place in their location. Capt Healy Co C. and F are at Pass Manchac[2] and Company B Capts Sheridan and Wright at the US Barracks and at Proctorville and H along the River below New Orleans D at Algiers K and I at Lafayette Square. Major Frye is at Pass Manchac he has been under arrest once since he was stationed at Hickons Station and he was relieved and sent to Pass Manchac. he is about half crazy as it is not a verry desirable place:[3] his wife has left and he was not allowed to come in to see her off and he naturally feels sore over it.

---

2. Pass Manchac is a waterway that connects Lake Maurepas to Lake Pontchartrain. During the war there was a railway embankment that served as the only way to move troops through the swampy areas north of New Orleans. Confederate forces operated in and around that area during 1863 from their base in Ponchatoula. Winters, *Civil War in Louisiana*, 166.

3. No mention of Major Frye's arrest remains, but it is clear that duty at Pass Manchac was difficult. Frye wrote of his time on station: "The moccasins and rattlesnakes are quite abundant, and apparently old settlers, as we killed one with nine rattles. They are quite a protection against a flank movement of the enemy through the swamp; the alligators actually stick their noses into the tents, in hopes of stealing a biscuit or a piece of pork. And then, all night long, the soldier is lulled to sleep by the most infernal croaking of tree toads, and kept asleep by the buzzing and biting of myriads of mosquitoes and yellow flies. One knows not how it is; but though every soldier has a mosquito-bar; still, daylight will find as many inside as out; and then innumerable green lizards about four inches long, harmless but spotive, gambol and catch flies and mosquitoes freely upon your face and body." Murray, *History of the Ninth Regiment*, 140.

Father Larnaudis Called to see me to day. he is stopping in town for a few days. Father Chalon Called when I was out. left his Card, he left word with Johnny that he wished me to Call to see the Arch Bishop which I propose to do tomorrow. Johnny is well except a slight touch of the shakes. The Dr has been fitting up his Regimental Hospital in great shape. he had all his mattresses Emptied and refilled with new moss. he has a fine set of new Iron Bedsteads clean new sheets and Blankets and fine white Mosquito Bans and his Hospital Cooks Elegant. A Medical Inspector General from Washington visited it a few days ago and complimented him highly on its appearance and condition.

There is great Excitement here over a general order ordering all Regimental enemies to leave the department by the 15th.[1] This has been qualified since by allowing such as choose to take a verry stringent oath on Condition of them remaining. Of course the secesh are Cranky over this as they must leave all their property behind them as they have never been allowed to sell or dispose of it, they will go forth beggars. What a terrible infatuation has seized these people So proud and haughty once; in their wealth and extravagance. The veriest beggers are happy in Comparison with them, since they have never known wealth of luxury. What a fate has befallen them and yet they are as insolent as ever.

By all accounts they have grossly imposed on General Banks kindness and leniency and seemed to have construed it as so much cowardice. now they feel the consequence of their insolence as they have succeeded in stirring up the sleeping Lion. and he will let them know who they have over them; General Banks is pushing on through the Country at a terrible Rate towards Alexandria with every prospect of tremendous success. he has already seized a verry great quantity of Cotton and sugar it is said more than three hundred thousand bails of Cotton and sugar without limit and he has only commensed his opperations. this is through the celebrated Tuckipaw Country said to be the Richest in all the south; and it is said with immense quantities of Cotton all of which will be sent in for the government and I think General Banks will see that it does not go as last years work did;

I believe he is honest so that the Government must be immensely benefitted if he is lucky, and it is a terrible blow to the Rebels by far the worst blow they have received during the war; and worse for them than Capturing Richmond. take in connection with this the desperate and

---

4. General Order No. 35 stated that "registered enemies of the United States are hereby ordered to leave this Department on or before the 15th day of May." "Later from New Orleans," *New York Times*, May 8, 1863.

successful Raid of the gallant Colonel Grierson through the whole length and breadth of the state of Mississippi cutting Every Rail Road in the state and burning all the Bridges.[5] this Raid beats anything in Military History ancient or modern as an offensive movement by such a handfull of men: the damage it has done cannot be measured as it will prove the vulnerability of Rebeldome and this can be done again and again and it should be. what if these men had been captured in comparison with the amount of damage they have done; they have done more than twenty thousand men could do anywhere Else. Banks and Faragut will now operate against the Rebels on the Red River and the chances are verry good that the Rebels will not have so much Cotton to give Johnny Bull for his money: Cotton taken from the Enemy now is better than lives or dearly bought victories in the field;

the prospect is glorious after all the gloom. if we have troops to stand by what we have on if we only strip the Country completely of every vestige of wealth if they will not submit; this is the method to subdue them and take Vicksburg and Port Hudson not by rushing men on Fortifications prepared for their slaughter. they cannot live on the air; and they must be starved if they will not submit. we continue to hear the most terrible accounts of their suffering in some places from hunger, flour is worth two hundred dollars per barrell on the Coast of the Gulf. it cannot be bought at any price. it is said that absolute starvation exists in Mobile and the cutting of the Bridges on the Rail Roads will not help them. in addition to the immense amount of Cotton and sugar Banks has seized all the horses and mules said to ammount to thousands upon thousands so he will not be behind hard for transportation or Cavalry or Artillery horses and if he drives all the non producers out of the Country into the Rebel Lines he must add immensely to the number of mouths they must feed or let them starve and let them Eat ever so little. it will take a great deal from them and no one pretends to say they have anything to spare in the states East of the Mississippi River: so that as a war measure every person sent to them hurts them and the brave men of secesh will show their bravery by calling yankees names can have a chance of something Else to try their teeth on as well as the insolent hussies of women. let them go and then conscript the men who are left behind on their oaths

5. Grierson's Raid, which took place in Alabama and Mississippi under Col. Benjamin H. Grierson's Union cavalry in the spring and summer of 1863, diverted Confederate attention away from Grant's movements outside of Vicksburg. For a full account of the raid see Brown, *Grierson's Raid*, and Lardas, *Roughshod through Dixie*.

this will fetch them to their senses to a certain Extent. you will think this a crazy letter and these are crazy times;

well good by give my respects to all Enquiring friends to Father Hart and say to him I intend to write him a good long letter soon, my love to Ellen and Kiss the Babies as usual for me,

Your loving husband

Thos W. Cahill

Thomas to Margaret

New Orleans May 9th 1863

My Dear Wife

I wrote you from Key West and again on Wednesday last from this place but it is said that the Boat of Wednesdays wont get there in three weeks so I drop you this that I may say I am well. I wrote Father Hart to day. Dr Bradts sister is going home next week. she promises to stop and see you. she is a verry good hearted lively girl and you will like her. she has consumption and has spent the winter here for her health, Dr Galagher is a little under the weather with the chills but is doing well. I mentioned all particulars about friends and acquaintances in my last. have not heard from Carney. yes O'Brien has gone back to his place I have not been paid as yet but Expect it next week:

I have resumed my old place in Command of the 2d Brigade Shermans Division that is in Command of the Troops in the city. it is not much more than a nominal command as I merely transmit orders from General Sherman. I would not have assumed command but Col Farn who took my place began putting on airs sending me back my morning reports because I did not sign them. which I could not do as a Junior Officer:

So I just notified Shermans Adjutant General that I should take command of the 2d Brigade as senior Colonel of the 9th if I received no Orders to the Contrary. this on the 8th so to day I received a formal order to do so. In addition to the scattered states of the Regt this will probably assist in keeping me in the city. Every thing is going on Gloriously in this Dept. Banks is sweeping Every thing before him and Porter[6] having passed Vicksburg. we hear to night that he is at Alexandria

---

6. Adm. David Dixon Porter commanded the Mississippi squadron that operated in conjunction with Grant's in taking Vicksburg. Tucker, *The Civil War Naval Encyclopedia*, 1:767–69.

on the Red River helping Banks who is probably at that place, perhaps they will Catch Theabald. it was there he wrote me from and Grant[7] has Crossed the Mississippi[8] to the East side and taken into the Country after Capturing Grand Gulf to cut off the Rebel Rail Roads and destroy their connections. everything is looking splendidly. I do not see what can save Vicksburg now or Port Hudson. both I think must fall without fighting for them:

Major McManus Called to see me. he says Major Maher is well, the 24th has had no fighting yet. McCarten's well doing finely. Admiral Faragut is said to be in the City to night having come down the "Actafolaya", not with his ship though. she is to big for that water: Logan is going home. Every body in the Regt is well. Capt Healy is in an unhealthy spot Jones Island at Pass Manchae. I am striving to get him away from there but Sherman has not trust any 9 months men there he is down on them:

I have this minute from forwarded a letter for Mary Huss Healy from John. it has just come in with one for myself. John Rielly is all Right and generally Every thing is well. The men and Officers were verry glad to see me and are denouncing Col Dick. he tried his hand on the Dr but got beat as in fact he did in almost Every thing else he tried. it is getting verry late and I must close. I believe I left a list or Roster of the officers of the Regt sent me from the Adjutant Generals Office Hartford. if so send it to me or any letters or copies of letters I may have left on the subject. I have not received the Commissions I asked for when at home and suspect the Adjutant is playing me false in the matter.

give me Respects to all enquiring friends to the revd clergy. I have written Father Hart. give my Love to Ellen and Kiss the Babies.

    Thos W. Cahill

---

7. Gen. Ulysses S. Grant, Ohio native and West Point graduate, distinguished himself in the Mexican-American War and spent some time with the army in California before resigning his commission in 1854. When the Civil War broke out he was given command of the Twenty-First Illinois before being appointed to brigadier general of volunteers. His victories in the winter of 1862 at Forts Henry and Donelson and in April 1862 at Shiloh propelled him into the national limelight. In the wake of the capture of Vicksburg in July 1863, Lincoln brought Grant east where he took command of the Union war effort. Warner, *Generals in Blue*, 183–86. For further reading see Grant, *Personal Memoirs*; Waugh, *U. S. Grant*; Longacre, *General Ulysses S. Grant*.

8. On April 30, Grant's army crossed the Mississippi River at Bruinsburg, south of the Confederate position at Grant Gulf. This marked the beginning of the campaign that would ultimately capture Vicksburg. Stoker, *Grand Design*, 263–65.

Thomas to Margaret

New Orleans May 12th 1863

My Dear Wife

I have to day left in the Express Office a package containing one thousand dollars in 20$ Green Backs and [illegible] three dollars in New Haven money: I took a receipt for one thousand dollars on which you will pay freight and insurance amounting to $15. I hated to risk so large an amount "for us" without insuring: nothing new has occurred since my last. I have taken my old place in command of the City but have not much to do as nearly all my command are on detached "provost Duty." so I Expect Easy times, Col Farr of the 26th Mass who took my place did not like to give it up but I thought I would take it:

The Dr has recovered and is about. he is writing to his wife. he has not had any letters from home lately. I tell him he does not deserve any; as he seldom writes himself. he excuses himself for not writing to me by saying he did not wish to lead me astray by any remarks of his: My Six months pay to 30th April 1863 amounted to $1144,30 so I have 144 with me, and as while I am detached from my Regiment I command my pay every two months. I think I have enough to spare;

the men and officers of the Regt are all well. Terence Logan[9] goes home tomorrow in the Matanzas as also a man named Dennis Brennan[10] of Capt J. G. Healys Co. I will probably send this by Logan,

The Arch Bishop Called on me to day and as I was out left his Card: I have called upon him once and this I suppose was in return. I have written to Father Hart describing Church affairs. please say to him that the French Priest who preaches such strong abbolition sermons is named "Lemaitre" not Maest as I wrote him.

I have nothing new to write about. we are receiving verry contradictory stories from Hookers army in Virginia; yesterday the secesh Papers had Hooker badly defeated and half his army prisoners to day.[11] our paper has it just Exactly the Other way and all Jacksons Rebels killed and pris-

---

9. Pvt. Terrance Logan, Company F.

10. Pvt. Dennis Brennan, Company C.

11. The Battle of Chancellorsville took place from April 30 to May 6, 1863. In the battle Robert E. Lee's Army of Northern Virginia defeated Joseph Hooker's Army of the Potomac at Chancellorsville, Va. Union forces sustained 17,197 casualties to the Confederate's 13,303. In the wake of this victory Lee turned his attention north, invading Pennsylvania, where he was ultimately defeated at Gettysburg by George Meade. See Gallagher, *Chancellorsville*.

oners. so we do not know what to believe though we hardly dare hope for much good from Virginia: We hear good news so far from who has got in behind our old spot at Grand Gulf and so far seems to harass the rebels. sadly some of our boats have been amusing themselves bombarding Port Hudson without Ellicciting a reply:

it is possible they may be concentrating against Grant to overwhelm him. he is in some what a precarious position in the heart of the Enemies Country. unless he can live by foraging on them. Banks seems to be having things his own way in Louisiana so far he had gone over an immense amount of Country with verry little fighting. I do not see what is going to feed Port Hudson and Vicksburg and it seems to me they must fall unless we have serious reverses to our armies in the front. I have not heard from Major Maher yet and have not written him as I really do not know precisely where to direct to him only that he is some where about the La Tourche. Capt Kelly[12] is sick in the St James Hospital but I believe is getting along well. the Weather is delightful here so verry much cooler than it was last year at this time.

The Regiment are Jealous of me as I am not at their head: but I think it just as well for me where I am as long as I can stick to it as I am not likely to be sent off on the confounded little scouting expeditions here and there although there is some fun in them after all. Capt Sawyer[13] has managed to furnish me a splendid bay horse since I have been gone. he would be worth a good three hundred if I had him. he is a splendid saddle horse. I am in some hopes the Dr will get a chance to run home although it is doubtfull as good physicians are scarce here.

give my Respects to all Enquiring friends. no news from Johnny Carney yet.[14] Give my Love to Ellen and Kiss the Babies as usual for me.

Your Loving Husband
Thos W. Cahill

Thomas to Margaret

New Orleans June 13th 1863

My Dear Wife
Your Letter of May 17th Came to hand on the 7th. you complain that you have received no letters from me since the one written at Key West.

---

12. No one named Kelly served as a captain in the Ninth Connecticut.
13. Capt. Silas W. Sawyer, Company H.
14. Corp. John Carney, Company B.

yet as you will see by the number at the head of this I have written seven to you, neither do you say anything about receiving the thousand dollars I sent you, however there is no fear of that, It is true I have been verry full of business as I have been obliged to work hard to make up for lost time. I wish it distinctly understood however between our selves that I am tolerably well satisfied on (*your account of course*) to be where I am.

The siege of Port Hudson drags it slow length along. the Rebels are making a terrible defence. I am in hopes of hearing something before I close this letter, as we have been Expecting another assault for several days. Banks must Either take it or leave it before this reaches you I think. Your letter took a great weight off my mind about poor little Tommy as from what I had heard from others I had serious misgivings for him, but am more hopefull now. do not give yourself too much anxiety as it cannot do any good to worry too much. God is good and his will must be done, and those that die innocent die happy, and Escape many sore trials.

I notice what you say about the Consolidation. General Banks is too busy just now to give the matter much attention but he may soon. A great many of the most influential Planters in the adjoining Parishes are Endeavoring to have me appointed Provost Marshal instead of General Bowen[15] whom no one likes it seems though I do not know why, as I do not know of his doing anything, perhaps that is the reason. The Planters say they have an agent a verry influential man whose name I have forgotten a heavy land owner and Planter here and who also owns a vast amount of Property in President Lincolns Neighborhood and with whom he is said to be verry intimate. There is another influential man who who owns a verry large Plantation down the Coast and who resides in New York who it is said is working for the same End, but it is to be kept verry secret. This mans name is Bradish Johnson,[16] for myself I have but verry little hopes of their succeeding but it is pleasant to have the good will of the People, the position is a verry responsible one and I suppose makes too much money to be given to me.

---

15. Gen. James Bowen of New York was appointed provost marshal—general of the Department of the Gulf in 1862. Bowen's command was marked by harsh treatment of African Americans, whom he often detained and "marched off to forced labor" if they had "no regular habitation of Employment." Williams, *I Freed Myself*, 185–88.

16. Bradish Johnson was born in New Orleans in 1811 but relocated with his family to New York City. During the Civil War he "played a significant role in Louisiana's reentry into the Union. . . . He was a member of a group of conservative Unionist slaveholders who were ready to repudiate Louisiana's secession but 'earnestly hoped' to preserve slavery." Young, *Emma Lazarus and Her World*, 49.

I wrote you that I have a new Commander here since Genl Sherman went to Port Hudson and has come back badly wounded for which I am verry sorry for although a sharp severe Officer I believe him to be an honest man. The new commander is General Emory.[17] he has kept me humming Ever since he has been here. it seems to me he never stops fretting and expects the Enemy are going to attack us Every night. I have no time I can call my own Except when I am asleep. but I stand it bravely. I have been in this Command so long that I have the advantage in some respects over the new General who is not so well posted.

the Arch Bishop and Father Chalon have left their Cards but I have not been able to return their Call as yet. I have had me a dress Coat made of light Flannel Cloth verry nicely got up which has cost me 20,00 my other coat being too heavy. Dr Bradt made me a present of 4 pair of white linen Pants, and John Carroll bought me a Dress hat with Gilt Cord and one Feather which cost him 9,00 but as it required 3 feathers and a bugle I had to put them on which cost me 5,00. but then he made me a present of a white vest so I am square with him. I [am] pretty well provided now. O'Brien made a present of 4 linen Handkerchiefs, He is up at his Parish and is growing like a young Elephant. I am glad to hear that Carney is all right, Capt Healy and Sheridan are all right as are all the officers and men. we have had no deaths in the Hospital in over two months which is remarkable. you ask what you are to do with Dillons.[18] perhaps give them to Old Wm Moloney, I am glad you have got James Cooney in the house, I have not received the letter you speak of from Father Hart. I wrote you three letters before his.

I promised to write a letter for Johnny Reilly to night but it is near twelve oclock and I have to take a bath. tell her that Johnny often speaks about her and when he gets some money he will send her his picture.

John Carroll tells me that he has seen a letter from Carney saying he was at Annapolis waiting his Exchange. I have not heard anything from the Dr. since he went up to Port Husdon. I think he is in a General Hospital but he never thinks of writing a letter. I heard nothing from Major Maher since I came. Expect that he is well. no wounded men have been sent here from the 24th and I cannot learn that there are any.

---

17. Gen. William H. Emory served with distinction during the Peninsula Campaign and at the Seven Days Battle before being transferred to the Department of the Gulf. Norris, Mulligan, and Faulk, *William H. Emory.*

18. Pvt. John Dillon, Company A, died of disease on December 1, 1862.

I cannot write any longer. good night God bless you all. Kiss the babies as usual and keep up your Courage. Give my respects to all Enquiring friends. tell Father I am waiting for his letter. I am waiting for a chance to send you and Ellen some queer little Trinkets.

Your Loving husband

Thos W. Cahill

Thomas to Margaret

Head Quarters 2d Brigade
Defenses of New Orleans
June 28 1863

My Dear Wife

Your welcome letter of June 9th Came to hand last Sunday Just as we were marching off against the Rebels on the Lafourche district so I did not feel it safe about it after reading I destroyed it, I recollect however that you spoke of the safe arrival of the Birds, and of your anxiety about the $1,000 I sent you home. of course I wish you to invest it with Father Heart. I will send you all I can spare if I can get my pay to 20th of June promptly but wish you could manage Even by borrowing temporarily untill I can send it to you. you must use your own judgement about these things as I am too far away to direct all operations, I am Glad the Birds got home safe as they are verry fine birds. I will try to get a pair for Father Hart. The[y] are difficult to find however of the right age to send. Wm Slakney got them for me.

We came verry near getting nabbed on the La fourche country. The history of the affair is this. during the week before last Genl Emory got some what alarmed about our communications by Rail with Brashear City[19] as he well might, but he had no troops to send out there save the garrison of the city, so he ordered us out along the line of the Road from the Mississipi River to Lafourche. well the Enemy came down upon 800 of our troops who were in Camp at La fourche Crossing under Command of Lt Col Stickney[20] of the 47st Mass though there was not a man of his Regt with him he had a few of the 176 NY 250 of the 3d Conn 1 Co of

19. Now Morgan City, this town controlled the pass over the Atchafalaya River and the road to New Orleans.

20. Lt. Col. Albert Stickney of the Forty-Seventh Massachusetts was placed in command of Lafourche Parish in June 1862. Pena, *Scarred by War*, 234.

the 42 Mass 2 guns of the 25 NY Battery and about 400 men of the 26 MA all men of my Brigade Except the first 2 named. on the night of the 21st of June the enemy attacked them with a terrible uproar but they were repulsed with great loss leaving 53 killed on the ground. I arrived on the ground the next morning with part of the 9th Conn 26th Mass and 2 more guns of the 25th N York Battery. to their relief the Enemy did not renew attack on the second day and on the night following they fired 2 shots about 10 pm. suspecting that it might be a signal for attacking I pushed a reconaisance forward to a place called Thibodeaux which they Entered and found the Enemy had Evacuated leaving their sick and wounded and same time I sent the 9th Conn up the Rail Road in another direction and the[n] came a few of the Rebs and took four prisoners, I did not pursue but made preperations to return to the where I now am. the 9th lost one man wounded severely I think he will die and four slightly none of our acquaintance.[21]

The Dr Returned from Port Hudson in time to go up with me. he is well. he had a great deal of Professional duty up there and gained great Laurels. all the officers are well 2. Expect O'Brien in tomorrow. remember me to Father Hart. I will answer of June 11 as soon as possible. I received it while on the march. Kiss the babies as usual for me. My love to Ellen.

Your Loving husband

Thos W. Cahill

---

21. This was part of Gen. Richard Taylor's attempt to cut off Gen. Nathaniel Banks from New Orleans. With three thousand men, the Confederates were successful in their advances in mid-June, occupying Thibodaux before stiff resistance by Stickney's men at the Lafourche levee stalled their progress. Cahill arrived from New Orleans and took command from Stickney on June 22. The Confederates moved down Bayou Teche by boat, around Cahill's men, and landed at Brashear on the morning of June 22, surprising the federal garrison of some seven hundred men (only four hundred effective) and causing considerable anxiety among the Union high command. Winters, *Civil War in Louisiana,* 285–92. Correspondence from this period illustrates the confusion regarding Confederate feints on Thibodaux, southwest of New Orleans. Reports reached Gen. William Emory that rebel forces numbered some seven thousand men in the region and had captured the town of Brashear on June 24, 1864. That same day, Cahill was ordered to spike his artillery pieces and retreat by rail back toward New Orleans, destroying bridges along the way. Emory seemed confused as to Cahill's delay in retiring from the area, ordering him at ten o'clock at night: "If you cannot bring your horses, kill every one on the spot. Kill them with a knife, so the enemy will not hear your guns. Don't let anything fall into their hands. Destroy all the bridges, including the one at La Fourche, after your rear has passed. . . . Destroy the telegraph office and all its records. Blow up your caissons, but make no fires until your main body is at least 10 miles off." Gen. William Emory to Thomas Cahill, June 24, 1863. *Official Records,* series 1, vol. 26, 594.

Margaret to Thomas

New Haven June 1863

My dear Husband

I recd yours of June 4th yesterday morning. you Say you have recd Father Hearts, well that is Strange. you ought to have one from me by the same Steamer. I think they went in the Same mail from here. at least I intended they Should but you surly have it by this time and another one too. I am very much troubled about you. I fear they will drive you up the Missisippy again. We have very discouraging accounts from Port Hudson and Vicksburg. if you are ordered up I hope you will form some excuse or other and not go.

There is a perfect Panic here among the Men liable to the first Call[22] namly unmarried men. Some are being married and consider themselves Save but the majority are running away from it is a great pity for Times were never before so good here. Father Hart is down on their runing away so soon at least he advised them to form into Associations and have a fund and if necessary buy each other off but you know how excitable our people are.

I was very glad you mentioned Major Maher in your letter. it was reported here that he was killed. send him word if you can that he has a fine little Daughter. all his family are well. I recd a Package of Money from you and one from Johnny Rielly. I deposited Johnnys. Barney Lynchs wife recd some from him. She is very gratful to you for it. Mrs Galaghers sisters wedding is to take Place today. I had an invitation but could not do.

dear little Thomas had another Hard day yesterday. poor little dear had seven more teeth cut 4 double teeth. The Dr says it is unusual for one so young to cut so many at once. he is as bright as ever. today you would think there never was anything the matter with him. I have every hopes of his being sparred to us but he will require the closest watching. he grows more Lovely every day and is Large enough to [be] 2 years old. he would have been walking now were it not for his teeth. I will try to send you his picture. I must not put of[f] having it taken any Longer. Eddy and Mary is well and strong. they always Pray for your Safe and Speedy return.

---

22. This refers to the first call of the draft, which took place in Connecticut in the summer of 1863. Of the 11,530 Connecticut residents called in the draft that July, only 248 actually served. Warshauer, *Connecticut in the American Civil War*, 131.

Sincerely wishing that may soon take place. I will close for the present—Ellen sends her Love. we are very anxious to see that nice present from you.

Your Loving Wife

M. E. Cahill

My dear Husband I feel very grateful to you for writing to us so often. it is such a Comfort to me. now please continue to do so write every day where you can.

Yours M. E. Cahill

Thomas to Margaret

Head Qs 2d Brigade
Defences of New Orleans
June 29th 1863

My Dear Wife

Yours of June 16th Came to hand to day. I have already one in the mail for you in answer to one of about June 1st which I received while on my way to the La Fourche County. in that I answered what I could recollect of your letter for as I was then in the Enemys Country I destroyed it. I will try to get my two months pay tomorrow in time to send it home by the 15th July. I would advise you if you have not Enough on hand to make a thousand dollars to try and borrow some temporarily as I shall certainly get it home for you within a few days of the 15th. I am sorry to hear of Tommys Continued troubles but continue to hope for the best.

I had a narrow escape from the Enemy at the La fourche Crossing but succeeded in getting Every man away Except those in Hospital. Seargt Peter Donnelly Co C[23] and Hospital Attendant Porter Corcoran[24] and a man named Robinson[25] who Enlisted in New Orleans were left in the Hospital. have since come in all right having been paroled. I was fearful for Robinson as they have Every man who Enlisted with us down here. Corcoran brought off the Dr Clothes swearing they were his own. he also took apart the Drs Pistol and Concealed it in his stockings and brought it away. I was obliged to leave poor Francis Judge[26] who had been badly

---

23. Sgt. Peter Donnelly, Company C.
24. Pvt. Peter Corcoran, Company A.
25. Pvt. George Robinson, Company C.
26. Pvt. Francis Judge, Company C.

wounded that morning behind as he could not be moved; also a number of the 23rd Conn in the same Condition and their surgeon remained with them to take care of them. Dr Gallagher wished to remain but I could not spare him and brought him much against his will.

The Enemy were in overwhelming force over seven thousand and 13 pieces of Artillery but I just saved my "bacon." I had about 1,500 men and I made good my retreat to this City without loss of men but Banks has lost Brashear with an immense supply of stores. "O such Generalship." the first Order I gave when I was ordered to the front was for the stores to be brought in but it was too late the Rebels had cut the track. In one hour more I would have saved two heavy trains, Brashear City was 28 miles beyond where I was.

so Capt G did not call to see you? so much the better. The seargent that went home with was a decent fellow and I am so glad he got the birds home safe. look out for them or someone will steal them from you. you must thank Bill Starkey for them. I have received a letter from Michael Fahey and a paper from Mrs Morrissey. poor Michael also sent me two Heralds. the poor fellow is in great trouble about the draft and I do not see how they are going to get out of it.

Capt O'Brien is in town and will probably remain while the Enemy are about. The Dr is well and busy. Capt Sheridan has a touch of Chills. all others are well. we have but one man by sickness since I came out. The Box number is changed it is now 500 not "2558." Tell Father Hart I am setting myself to write a good long letter. give my love to Ellen. I will try to home the letter present by Express this week. Kiss the babies as usual for me. God Bless you all at home.

Your Loving Husband
Thos W. Cahill

Thomas to Margaret

HdQrs 2d Brigade Defenses of New Orleans
July 10th 1863

My Dear Wife
Glorious news has reached us yesterday. a dispatch from General Grant to General Banks announced the capture of Vicksburgh to day.[27] General

27. Confederate forces under John C. Pemberton surrendered to Ulysses S. Grant on July 4, 1863. The fall of Vicksburg gave the Union control of the Mississippi River and was

Banks announced the Capture of Port Hudson.[28] all is joy. the revullsion of feeling here is tremendous, within two day and for three weeks past the Rebels have been threatening New Orleans and that too with some prospects of success as we had Comparatively few men to go around and our immense lines Calculated for twenty thousand men and we had about three. really it looked hard for us.

I have not had much sound sleep in four weeks but now all is Joy and the prospects are that the Rebels will "skedaddle" in a lively manner. the Rascals had nearly cut off all Communication with Port Hudson with their Batteries on the River and things began to look bad true they had got into the City the Navy might shell them but it would not be an agreeable alternative. We are all well and in the best of spirits. the men and officers in good health. we have not heard from poor Judge whom we had to leave at La Fourche Crossing but was along at the last account.

I write this at my Official desk with any quantity of Officers all around me all wanting something attended to but hearing a rumor that a steamer leaves to morrow I scratched this off in haste. the seargant that brought you the birds came in last night Expect a letter by same boat. it is not yet distributed.

I sent you a Copy of Oder 22 so you may imagine that I have occasionally something to attend to but I have no idea of Complaining. far from it I am well satisfied. The City is full of struggling Officers and soldiers. I will bring some to their business.

Good bye God bless you all. will write to night if I have time. Kiss the babies as usual for me.

Your Loving husband
Thos W Cahill

---

a serious blow to the Confederate war effort. For a full account of the Vicksburg Campaign see Ballard, *Vicksburg*.

28. Confederates surrendered their last fortified position on the Mississippi River, Port Hudson, on July 9. Ibid., 401.

Thomas to Margaret

Head Quarters 2d Brigade
Defences of New Orleans
9–30 PM July 14th 1863

My Dear Wife

All is well and Glorious with us and it is to be suspected it is so with you. we had dates to the 4th of July and if the Gettysburg Affairs turn out all right things will begin to look better,[29]

we had 92 Officers sent down prisoners from Port Hudson to day and more are coming. I believe we have about as many more Coming, The Enemy have not yet left the La Fourche and I believe Genl Banks has sent a force down there to look after them. The Hartford and the Gunboats are all down here and things begin to look as they used to do.

I have not had a letter from home in three mails. what is the matter, OBrien had a letter by the Creole to the 28th of June and nothing being said. I suppose all is right, I have not heard a word from Major Maher in a long time, but as there has been no fighting since the 14th of June. I know Every thing is Right, I am plugging along here as usual, I have but a small force and a large amount of Guard duty to perform as well as stragglers to look after,

I sent you a copy of the Order appointing me Military Commandant of New Orleans. this was done to give me Control of all straggling officers and men and I have a Commissioned Officer and twelve men on patrol duty looking after Officers and men. I have some fun having officers Explain how they happen to be in the City and without side arms and such a buying of swords as there has been, These sneaks have had a warm time of it, It serves them Right, and they are beginning to make tracks out of the City,

I carried of a bill of fare from the dinner table to day and enclosed it to you to give you an Idea of our living at 1–25 per day, I intend to get this in the mail in the morning. the boat leaves at 9 A.M. Tell Father Hart I intend to send him a Role of Louisiana Tobacco called "Perique" from a

---

29. Robert E. Lee's Army of Northern Virginia battled George Meade and the Army of the Potomac for three bloody days, July 1–3, 1863, on the fields of Gettysburg, Pa. The Union victory, which came at the cost of more than forty-six thousand men killed and wounded, has traditionally been seen as the high-water mark of Confederate military efforts. See Guelzo, *Gettysburg.*

little spot in the Parish of St James the only place in the state where they raise it, it is said to be good.

Give him my Respects. I am looking for a good long letter from him. Give my love to Ellen. Kiss the Babies as usual for me.

Your loving husband

Thos W Cahill

P.S. A story is around to night that the drunken imbucile Col Farn of the 26th Mass who is home on leave is coming out a Brigadier. if so I must leave my place but I do not believe it though those are the kind they make them of.

Margaret to Thomas

New Haven August 2nd 1863

My dear Husband

I recd yours of the 22nd. two days ago I mailed one for you on last Wednesday. Now don't you attemp to threaten me with not writing to me so often, how can you do so, when you know your letters is such a comfort to me. You say you write your letters to me when all others are asleep. now I know that right well if you did not do so we would have the same pitiful faces that we see so many off and we would be very apt to believe every absurd Story that people may see fit to invent. The Sheridans are in a great fret about Terry. they do not hear from him regular at all and Some one wrote home that he is married to a rich Lady of course.

I told you in my last that Peter was Drafted.[30] well he is Exempt on account of one of his great Tow nails it grows down in the flesh I believe. *rich isn't it.* M Fahy is all right too. he has Disease of the Heart and Tom Cunningham[31] the Same. There was but one Man Drafted from the 5th Ward. his name is Murphy a shoe Maker. he must be of Some importance to the Ward they are going about begging money to buy him off.

They came here last night nothing less than five or Ten Dollars would do. I told them I would give them one. the were indignant. I gave them three very reluctantly indeed, and I hope they will not come on such an erand again. Your Tax Bill came in this week. 21.71. I have not Paid it yet think I will do so tomorrow.

---

30. It is unclear who this is.

31. There was no soldier named Thomas Cunningham in the Ninth Connecticut.

Gen Corcorans wife is dead. he sent a Dispatch to F. Hart to attend her funeral but He was not able to go down. he has had a very hard turn of Cholera Morbus. he is better. The Weather is extremely hot. we are fairly worn out with heat and want of Sleep. Thomas is doing fairly. Eddy and Marry is well. they continually prattle about you and are always making calcula for your return. I wish it might be soon. I get all your letters and do not Stop writing as often as possible. I will put the Latest news in this for you. don't you need Some fine shirts. let me know in your next.

From your Loving Wife

M. Cahill

Margaret to Thomas

New Haven August 8th 1863

My dear Husband

I recd yours of the 29th of July this Morning. now you may believe it or not but this will be my third letter to you since August came in and Sur[e]ly Father Harts long letter must have reached you before this. What makes you suspect that I will say Some person picks my letters out of your Box? Surly they can be of no Earthly use to any person. Father Brady is staying at Harts and he [illegible] hear from the Dr. he offered up a Mass for you the Dr and his brother who is a soldier on the Potomac a few days ago. it was very kind of her to remember you. Mention him in your next to Father Hart. He too offered a Mass for you a week ago and would not allow us to even Thank him for it. Father Brady is very uneasy about Mrs Galagher. her health She has failed very much and the Baby is some what troublsome. now to things I suppose I did not ask permission to tell you this. it is their own affair but I do think if she recd more letters from her Husband she sould be more cheerful and stand little trials.

Mr Clarks son called here. he said he had a letter from his Brother and that he mentioned you said you were very well. the old people are very kind to me. they send me a great many little luxuries from the garden and better than all they furnish me good milk for our dear little Thomas. he is weaning it out well and the heat here so extremly hot too. I keep the little ones almost naked to keep them indoors during the heat of the day. I wish you could see me. I am nearly melted away I never so suffered so much with heat. I often think of you. how do you stand it in that hot climate and you are so confined to indoors? but perhaps it is better than to be exposed to outdoor heat.

there was three persons died here from Sunstroke yesterday. one of them was Michael Smith who was Leaving in in Tom Healys place. I have not heard who the others were yet. it is said here that Capt Healy is coming home on leave of absence. his people will be delighted. I wish you could get away again. it is untrue about M. Fahy runing away from the Draft. he went to New York on Business. was gone two days was here when the Draft took place and was among the Drafted but is exempted on account of some disease. heard nothing about McGowen but indeed I do know very maney who did run away and are starting back now begging for work and fortune seems to favor them to for there is plenty of work to be had. there seems to be more men passing our House to and from work than I ever saw before.

one of my Birds died. it never was well since I had it. the other one is very healthy but does not make any remarkable noise. it may be to young. the noise it makes is exactly like any young bird. perhaps the old man played me a trick in sending me two Female Birds. they tell me they never sing at all.

Mr Herity called here today. he said he had written to you to ask you to get your Adjutant to send him the Dates of the Soldiers Deaths who were in debt to him. if not he cannot get his money from he sent you coppy of the Document he recd from Washington and he requested me to mention this in my letter to you—he has a Livery stable and is doing a small Business in that way. his Daughter Kate has graduated. We are all well. I wish it was cool weather.

your Loving Wife
M. Cahill

Thomas to Margaret

Head Quarters 2d Brigade
New Orleans August 8th 1863
8–PM

My Dear Wife
I take advantage of Capt Healys going home to drop you a few lines just to say that we are well and in good spirits. I received nothing from you since the 3d of July but received one from Father Hart on the 25th in which he says you are all well but that Tommy had a slight attack from which he had recovered. nothing new has occurred since my last. Every thing is quiet in this Department since the fall of Port Hudson. the 24th

has gone to ship Portland but has left a lot of stragglers around the city which I am picking up and sending off as fast as I can. 2 or three of our officers are going home for the conscripts. We want 400 to fill up with. we send home 6 men for same purpose among who are old Mll Slankey and Ned OBriens son in law Jim English.[32] I dont suppose we will get a great many of the Conscripts but here now do I suppose a great many many will be got by it only way now. in short do I Care whether or not if they dont come. I may be mustered out for which I suppose you will pray, but I dont find much fault as yet, as I am honestly getting on Easier living than Ever before and more money for it.

They have not got me out of here yet and do not know as they will. though I do not know what they find for so manny Brigadiers to do down here without Commands. I see by the papers that Brigadier Genl Strong Butlers old adjutant General has died of the wound received at Fort Wagner and that Chatfield[33] was wounded there again. well so far I am as lucky as any of them. Thank God Major Maher went off unexpectedly. he was down the day before. he makes great Braggs of all the money he sent home within 50 cents of $1,000 he says doesnt know what Mary Ann did with it but he sent him home, I can not learn that McCarten has been brought down from Baton Rouge yet he is sick in Hospital. I tried to get him brought down and Capt Keely[34] promised to send for him but they went off in such a hurry I suppose they could not. I will take Care of him if he comes down here.

I see that Garvey and Eagan escaped as well as more of the Copperheads.[35] so much the more pity the fellows that the lieut Col appointed Quarter Master while I was at home has just been dismissed the service dishonorable, the fellow it is said had been in the Louisiana penitentiary for theft before he was Enlisted, The Lieut Col feels awfull sore over it and says he will not make anny more appointments without my consent. he wants to make his Brother Q Ma but I refused my consent on the grounds that he was not a proper Character which he admitted but [il-

32. Thirty-year-old private James English was a native of Tipperary. English left his wife, Mary, home when he enlisted in September 1861.

33. Col. John Lyman Chatfield of the Sixth Connecticut Volunteers died during the assault on Fort Wagner. Wise, *Gate of Hell*, 106.

34. It is unclear whom Cahill is referring to here. There were no soldiers in the Ninth Connecticut by the name of Keely.

35. "Copperhead" was the name given to the antiwar movement during the Civil War. See Weber, *Copperheads*.

legible] for him. I told him if he placed him in charge of anny property he must hold himself responsible for it.

I wrote Father Hart that I found that a lot of my officers had signed a petition for a Brigadier Generalship for Col Farn the fellow who took my place when I went home. they Explain by saying they thought it a good joke and thought it well to humour it and get the drinks but I consider it a contemptible piece of business of all concerned. so far as I am concerned I care but little about it. The health of the men Continues good remarkably so. several of our officers are trying to get home. Capt Sheridan is rather unwell at present but not serious.

give my respects to all enquiring friends. give my love to Ellen, Kiss the Babies as usual for me.

Your Loving husband

Thos W Cahill

Why dont you write I stop after this?

Thomas to Margaret

New Orleans Augst 12/63 11-PM

My Dear

It never rains but it pours. to morrow morning Lieut. Garrey T Scott leaves on a furlough. The Dr is writing home and I think is Encouraging Mrs G to come out here. he says he had advised her to call on you and to have you come out too. I tell him it is altogether a different question to move a wife and one baby and moving a wife a sister and three babies but if we can find a furnished house of the Right kind and location.

I am verry much tempted to say come anny how always supposing we are to stay here as I think at present we will we are to have another "Army Corps" down here. the 13th under Major Genl Ord[36] of Grants Army. Genl Franklin[37] will have Command of the Army or what is left of it after the 9 months men go and Genl Banks will Command the Whole Defenses of New Orleans to be a seperate Command and to report

---

36. Maj. Gen. Edward O. C. Ord, a West Point graduate and Pennsylvania native, commanded forces at Vicksburg before being put in charge of the Thirteenth Corps in the Department of the Gulf until his transfer east in 1864. *Civil War Trust*.

37. Gen. William B. Franklin, who was blamed for the defeat at Fredericksburg, was ordered to Louisiana on June 25, 1863, where he was given the opportunity to "redeem his reputation." Snell, *From First to Last*, 265–94.

direct to Genl Banks. I rather like this arrangement as it looks like our remaining here and if Genl Emory remains as it now looks shall like it all the better.

I think a trip south would help Ellen as I think it would all of you. the question of Expense is of course a heavy one. I do not know what they would charge for the Children nor what they Charge for Adults from New York but it is not less than sixty dollars. Scott will Enquire as he goes home and let you know what he learns. he used to be our Hospital Steward and is a fine young man. you can trust to what he tells you.

If I can learn anything by the next mail from the Quarter Master here as to whether I can get any favours from them I will also let you know. I have no Expectation of our getting board and rooms here less than $5 Each for adults. I think I can have a splendid furnished house here from the Quarter Master for thirty dollars a month. that would be for me $10 a month and 12 for the Dr. I allow $3 each week for us three (36 per month 18 and 36 is $54 for month say sixty). it costs me now forty so that I think that with hiring a house together we can live cheaper than now and better than now if I can get the house which I will commence Enquiring about at once. I think we can do it particularly while I have the Brigade which brings me about fifty dollars for Commutation and things promise to be Cheaper if the river keeps open, so that if you have Courage to try it I think we may say come as soon as I can fix it here, and our winter cant Kill us any how. it will not be such a terrible job for you as you can not be on the water more than 8 days any how.

I suppose you will be troubled about the house but I do not think it will hurt it to stand Idle one winter. I suppose it would be necessary for you to bring the bedding and some table furnature as I do not Expect you would find them here Even if we got a furnished house. still we might do so. I will set two or three wives a feeling soon. we might make a better arrangement with some family here than that I have spoken of and we have two months yet to work in. I think the Dr will bring Mrs G out any how. I do not see why he should hesitate. I would not in his circumstances. whether we move or not. I think you had better get the Mortgusan [it is unclear what this refers to] record and look about you to be ready to move at short notice if we can get things to suit here.

it is getting late and I must quit grieving. love to Ellen and Kiss the babies as usual. I wish you could have one winter out here. I do not think you would ever want to leave it.

Your loving husband
Thos W. Cahill

Thomas to Margaret

Head Qrs 2nd Brigade 4th Division
19th Army Corps
New Orleans Aug 18/63

My Dear Wife

You will see by the Change of heading that a change has taken place in the organization of the troops here the 4th Division however are all in or about New Orleans. My brigade being in the City and Consists of the 9th Conn 12th 13th 15th Maine and 1st Louisiana, The batteries are not yet designated but at present are the 25th and 26th New York 12th 13th and 15th Mass so you will see it is a verry handsome Brigade in fact is an object of Envy to the others. but I fancy the greatest source of trouble to them is that it is pretty well understood that we are to retain our present position in the City of New Orleans. Of this I have no doubt whatever and the next campaign will be over before there is any probability of a another reorganisation so that our Chances are good for a long stay here.

Well now are we not the luckiest of the lucky, it is astonishing The 26th Mass are ordered up the River to Port Hudson and their Col will have to quit manouvering for the Brigadeership and turn his attention to the begging off his Regt so much for manouvering.

I intend to send this letter by the River for a chance though as we have Officers going home I may send it by them if they have a fast boat, I have been to anxious in view of the Changes taking place up to this A.M. to give my attention to the subject of a house as I wrote to you about. but as I feel quite secure now for some months or more I shall begin to day, on the quartermasters as well as if I can get track of them from Private persons. I think I can make the thirty dollar a month arrangement that I spoke of for a furnished house; it is on Carrondlet St in the Center of the City has two Parlours and 5 or 6 Bed Rooms with beds but not linen or quilts or table furniture. I may do better. the Dr is moving quitely in the same Enquiries.

I Commence another Court Martial to morrow with a higher Rank of members than the other which has just adjourned after sending in 17 Cases hard ones too. I have business Enough to keep my mine active. give my love to Ellen and Kiss the Babies as usual for me.

Give my full respects to Father Hart

Your Loving Husband

Thos W Cahill

PS The Conscripts had better volunteer for the 9th as it has the best Chance for a quiet time of anny Regt in the service. plenty to eat good quarters and nothing to do.

PS I have got Killoy Pardoned.[38]

Thomas to Margaret

Head Qrs 2nd Brigade 4th Division
19th Army Corps
New Orleans Aug 26/63

My Dear Wife

I wrote you last night and forgot to say that I have received the Papers sent on by Mr Herritty and that it will be Extremely difficult for me to do as he desires. I am not Connected with the Regiment in a Regimental sense and have not been since last October, Consequently have no Control over the Books or the Officers Except in the line of their duties. The acting Adjutant is a young man who knows but little about his business and would hardly be competent to do the work he desires even if willing, however if we seem likely to remain here I will try to get it finished up for him Even if I am obliged to pay the Adjutant for it.

nothing new has occurred since last night. I have had not Explanation as yet for the marching Orders Received last sunday but do not anticipate that they can be carried into Effect. some body must be left here and my Command is so scattered as not to be available for a move and I think is intended for the defense of New Orleans and surrounding Country.

there is quite a Quarrell going on in the 1st Brigade of this Division between Col Birge of the 13th Conn[39] who is now in Command and Col Morgan of the 90th New York[40] this one is at present under arrest and

---

38. Pvt. Michael Killoy, Company E, was charged with violating the Ninth Article of War. On September 26, 1862, he was ordered to dress for company drill. He "did say to 2d Lieut Thomas McKeon commanding by Jesus Christ I will drive my bayonet through you." He was confined to hard labor at Fort Jefferson on Tortuga. Court martial of Michael Killoy, RG-153, KK-629, National Archives and Records Administration, Washington, D.C.

39. Col. Henry W. Birge of Hartford was first appointed major of the Fourth Connecticut before resigning to recruit for the Thirteenth Connecticut. Warner, *Generals in Blue*, 33.

40. According to historian John David Winters, the war career of Col. Joseph S. Morgan of the Ninetieth New York was, perhaps, most notable for drunkenness, which led Morgan to misdirect an attack against Port Hudson on June 14, 1863, and severely impacted his leadership skills a month later during a skirmish near Fort Butler. Winters, *Civil War in Louisiana*, 292.

being tried by Court Martial but he vows as soon as he gets through he must have the Command, It is fun for me as this Birge is working like a beaver for a Brigdrship. he is a nephew of Buckinghams so I suppose will get it. at present I am all Right as in the Command I have. I get what none of the other Cols Comdg Brigades got. that is my commutation for Fuel and Quarters. so let them work at it. I say nothing about it as I do not want to call their attention to it, This is owing to my serving in the City, I do not think it is fair but it is the Law, and as they are all so confounded anxious to Command Brigades why let them do it for nothing if they like, the money suits me better but Lord how they would flare if they knew it, but I am Cock of the Walk as far as the Cols are Concerned as I am senior to them.

Major Maher wants me to let him know what he can do to urge my claims as Brigadier when he gets home, but I dare not say much to him or in fact to anyone about it, although I feel myself Entitled to it. all I can say is that if a Connecticut man Junior to me in this department gets it before I do I shall verry probably resign and come home. but I do think I am Earning my pay verry Easy at present particularly with the Commutation.

All that I have written to you about Coming out is of course left to your own discretion. I should be glad to have you do so if you think you can arrange affairs and make the children come right I feel quite positive that we are to remain her some time,

I must close this to get it on the mail.

Your Loving husband
Thos W. Cahill

Margaret to Thomas

New Haven Sept 2nd 1863

My dear Husband

I recd both of yours of the 18 yesterday one by mail and the other by John Welch.[41] he called the morning after he arrived. he told me you looked so very well. he says they may not go back sooner than six weeks or two months. I was not at home when Kenedy Called. Lieut Scott[42] has been to see us three times he came to see us from the Cars and before

41. Pvt. John Welch, Company A.
42. Lt. Gary T. Scott, Company A.

he went to see any of his own people. I think a great deal of him I think he is very faithful. he is anxious to get back. he is fearful something may go wrong in his company while he is away. he has had the chills two or three times. the weather is too cold for the season and consequently very unhealthy nearly every one is complaining.

I have had more trouble with Rheumatism for the last week than I have had for the last three years. the children are well Baby gets on fairly has a mouth full of teeth.

are you realy in earnest about our going South? if you are you know there is nothing that could hold me here. I would be delighted to go if everything would be agreable to you. I can be ready by the 1st of the next month and will go if you say come.

I expect Mrs Galagher here tomorrow and then I will write again and tell you what her arrangements are: now if you want clothes made here you ought to send me your measure and I can have them made now. and you will please name the articles I ought to take with me. I mean outside our clothing and will the children require any heavy clothing.

will I order you a cap or boots. light or heavy. I can bring you Cloth if you would prefer having your clothes made there. how much Table furniture would we require. there is one thing. I will here suggest that we live by ourselves as much as possible. you know it would not be pleasant for any person to live with us. our children are so young and you are very likely to have a nice Christmas present of another. it seems to me to be a splendid idea of the Drs to have us come he fears his ___. I will say no more on this subject until I get you both together but indeed I have many a good laugh or rather a Grin at whats coming. write often. F. Hart has written to you again.

    from your Loving Wife
    M. E. Cahill

Margaret to Thomas

New Haven Sept 4th 1863

My dear Husband

I recd 3 letters from you this morning. the Dates are 23rd 25th and 26th. I see you still encourage us to come and I can see nothing to hinder us unless the expence alone. and if God Spares your life to us we will never want friends. I think I would be willing to suffer a great many privations to be near you. and then I sometimes think you might choose to remain in the South after your time of service will have expired and it will be a good chance for us to live there and make up our minds within the next year what is best for us.

James Cooney is taking his family to Brooklin today to live. he is going in *Business* there. he will never be worth a Dollar. he is too unsettled. Joseph Millers Brother is going to move in his place the 1st of October. he is a good steady man. the family consists of himself wife and two children. he has lived in one place 5 years and I consider that a good recommendation. I have agreed to let him have the apartments for one years and the use of the Garden next Summer in case I would not be here for 6 Dollars a month. I thought it better than have it entirely idle and a very good mark for a Bonfire. I hope you will approve of my plans. what do you say about my renting the Basement in Case I went away or let Miller rent it to some of his acquainces.

I am anxiously waiting for Mrs Galaghers arrival. I recd a letter from her but there was nothing definite about her going South. she seems to think it will not be safe to go before November but I consider that nonsense. if I go I will certainly leave here by the first week in October on the Second at furthest. F. Brady has wrote for her to come on and I will write as soon as I can learn what she intends to do.

poor Scott is tired going to the P. Office looking for a line from somebody. he is very anxious to get back. he wished me to ask you if the Dr is Dead. he is very anxious to help us go out but I doubt if he can wait for us. he is uneasy about his company papers. I saw Kenedy last night. he reports to Gen Hunt[13] in Chapple St this morning. he told me he saw the Gen and he told him that they were going to fill up the Regts in Virginia first and that he and his men would have to go in camp and do Duty while waiting for Men. he says he can get a great many to Volunteer but he has no authority to enlist men.

you do not say anything about getting F. Harts second letter. he is very anxious for the answer to it. he says he asked you some questions in it and he is almost impatient to hear from you. he said if we go he will clear out too. he says you never intended to come back to live here. we are all well. poor Starkey is very sick. The Creole sails tomorrow. you ought to

---

13. This is possibly Gen. Henry Jackson Hunt, commander of artillery for the Army of the Potomac. See Longacre, *Man behind the Guns.*

have two letters by her from me. good bye and may god grant we may be
to gether soon is the wish of your Loving Wife.

   M. E. Cahill

John McAlan is Drafted[44]

Thomas to Margaret

New Orleans Sept 16 1863
9-15 PM

My Dear Wife

   I take up my pen to say that Every thing remains as when I last wrote.
our search for a house so far has not been successfull although the Dr has
succeeded in getting a promise from the agent of Flanders as soon as he
gets his business arranged,

   I went to see the Chief Quarter Master to day but he is Sick. Col Chandler[45] who was attending to his business temporaly assured me I should
have one. that he thought Col Holabird[46] the Chief Quarter Master could
get me one. I forgot to say any thing about Lt Scott. I think his Co affairs
are all Right. Lt Mullen[47] has charge of his remains. it is necessary for him
to report to Dr Jewett and get a Certificate of disability to travel in Trip-
licate. send me one Copy, send one Copy to Adjutant Generals Office,
and retain one himself.

   I see Healy has put in for an Extension. in that way I have received his
first certificate. tell him so, so there is not much Chance of the Officers
and men sent home for Conscripts getting back, not I suppose is there
any great chance for the Conscripts. you say Kenedy says he could get
volunteers. why can he not take them on? is recruiting forbidden there?
I could get recruits here if the State of Conn would pay the men the same
bounties when raised here as she paid when they came from Conn.

   as it is a United States recruiting agent sent out here is getting quite
a number of men. refugees Coming in from Texas and down the River;

---

   44. It is unclear who this is, though he was likely a family friend.
   45. Lt. Col. J. G. Chandler was the chief quartermaster of the Nineteenth Army Corps.
Official Records, series 1, vol. 53 , 608.
   46. Col. S. B. Holabird was an assistant quartermaster of the U.S. Army and in charge of
the supply depots in New Orleans. Ibid., 609.
   47. No man named Mullen served as a lieutenant in the regiment.

he has some 400 on hand now and says he is going to raise a brigade of them.

The Expedition sent from here under Major Genl Franklin to Sabine Pass[48] were repulsed with the loss of two gunboats the Clifton and Sachone. this has not got into the papers yet the Expedition has returned and is now going to Brasher City over the same ground General Banks went on his Teche Campaign.

the 24th finally got off yesterday so I suppose all will be happy. they have a better reputation than the most of the nine months men and have behaved verry well indeed, Their Col appears like a gentleman. The major has Carried himself through the Campaign verry creditably indeed as I always said he would whenever he felt the call of duty. and when I have said that it is all that he said for the Irish officers the reputation of the rest is verry bad indeed. particularly the Major of the 25th and the Irish officers of the 24th will probably be pretty well ventilated when they get home.

the "Chawaba" sails to morrow morning and in it goes a good for nothing ingoramus sent out here to us as 2d assistant surgeon from Conn. his name is Winser and he is the most good for little Curse I Ever saw, and the Dr is mighty glad to get rid of him, now the medical director wants to send Avery back but the Dr does not seem to care for him. I do not think he will ask for him to Come back.

did you ever receive a mocking bird from Norwich Express? a member of Sawyers Co H named Irwin[49] has been home and says he sent you a mocking bird and Cage by Express from Norwich about a month or six weeks ago.

has Mrs Lynch told you how much money Barney has sent home this summer. he tell me he has sent home $580. if so that ought to satisfy her for a while. speak to Father Hart about Larry McCarthys moneys. he is after me all the while about it. I sent you $300,00 a week ago. how much

---

48. Sabine Pass links the Gulf of Mexico to Sabine Lake, bordering Texas and Louisiana. It was a vital avenue of trade before and during the war, and as the Union blockade grew stronger, it became an important passage for blockade-runners. In early September 1863, Maj. Gen. William B. Franklin, a native of York, Pennsylvania, graduate of West Point, and veteran of the Army of the Potomac, embarked with the Nineteenth Corps to capture Confederate fortifications at Sabine Pass. "The entire operation," concludes historian Mark Snell, "was a complete fiasco," as Confederate batteries decimated federal infantry and naval forces. Snell, *From First to Last*, 281–83. Cotham, *Sabine Pass*, provides an excellent overview of the Sabine Pass Campaign.

49. No soldier named Irwin served in the Ninth Connecticut.

have you on hand now or how much altogether, Give my respects to all Enquiring friends. My love to Ellen and Kiss the Babies as usual for me.

    Your Loving husband

    Thos W. Cahill

Thomas to Margaret

New Orleans Oct 14th 1863

My Dear Wife

I succeeded in getting a splendid house to day after a long search, it is in the center of the City on the Corner of Dauphine and Custom House Street. The house belonged to an old Cotton Broker and Planter J D Hill, who is out in Rebledom; the house is splendidly furnished with statues and Paintings and the furniture is magnificent in its way: there are 4 or 5 grand large beds, but no sheets or coverlids or pillow cases, but we shall not want many of these as the Dr has plenty of New Blankets and I have my own.

I do not think you need bring anything but 3 or 4 sheets and pllow cases; there is an Excellent Range and Water and gas all over the house. We have not had time to Examine verry closely but I am afraid there is not much table crockery. there is plenty of Chamber Crockery and plenty of glasses of all kinds. I do not think you had better bring out any Crockery as think they can be purchased at the auctions here verry Cheap. knives and forks and spoons and small articles not requiring much room you might bring. do not load yourself down with baggage. there are fine quarters. all the Rooms and the house is beautifully completed all through. The house has 5 handsome furnished Chambers with best and splendid bedsteads. a verry large parlor. well furnished a dining room and library and Billiard saloon; and good kitchen.

I sent Lieut Goodman[50] to Copy the Inventory to day. he filled 4 pages of foolscap and says it will take 3 more to complete it. as soon as he finished it tomorrow we will take possession and make a closer examination and let you know the rest of things if any that we shall need besides the bed clothes and Crockery. but I do not care about anything but the bed linen and knives forks and spoons. there were a good many Closets and some rooms we could not get into to day and we can tell better what there

---

50. Lt. Louis H. Goodman, Company F.

is when the inventory is finished; I receipt for all there is in the house and have a guard there,

I send you this by the Parkersburgh a slow boat. the "Morning Star" leaves here on Saturday morning. I will write you again by her. Capt Healy says you intend to come out by her. she is a good boat as are all the Regular boats running here and some of the Quarter Masters boats are verry good. Mrs Frye has arrived. the weather is verry cool here. now below 6o degrees.

I have not seen Capt J G H[51] but once since he came out. I am sorry you did not write as I can place but reliance on what little I am told, Everybody is well here as I am told you are at home. I hear that Col Binge of the 13th Conn had been made a Brigadier genl, he is a nephew of Gov B so I suppose it is all right. If I am to *remain* in the City all *Right if now well* then something Else *"This is private."*

it is getting late and I must finish by what I hear. you may be on the way before you get this. if so you are right now as I have the house. it has given me a deal of bother from my anxiety about my communication and houses are getting scarce. that is furnished ones. I got this outside the military from the US Marshall. have made no bargain about the Rent and do not mean to pay any if I can help it. do not think I shall be asked. o hurry up your cakes and get out as soon as possible. the suspense and anxiety of the last month has been terrible. have you seen Old Carroll yet? he went home on the "Evening Star." I am in hopes you might have started in her. make arrangements with Father Hart to send out all letters that Come to the house while you are gone;

you will get one more letter on next saturday and not another untill I get one from you. give my kindest regards to Father Hart. my love to Ellen. kiss the babies as usual for me untill I see them.

    Your Loving husband
    Thos W. Cahill

---

51. John Healy.

CHAPTER 7

"My plan is to get home and there if I have a *choice express* it"

July–October 1864

Thomas to Margaret

New York July 18 64
On board Steam Ship
Empire City
11-PM

My Dear Wife

We are on board this Craft, and Old Aspinwall or California Liner, with mighty poor accomadations for Officers. the Cabin completely stripped of furniture, no sheets or Blankets on beds as yet, the niggers say there is none, have not seen Either Captain or Steward though we have been on board all the morning, hardly think we shall leave to day, I suppose somebody made something by sending us off on the saturday night boat because they may have less passengers on that night. nothing worthy of note occurrd save the usual scenes of Drunkeness and disorder and straggling. Except just as we left the boat this morning Mrs O B appeared in a terrible state looking for *Fahy*[1] who was running away. she said do not know whether she found him or not.

The *Quarter Mast* says he ordered a barrell of Rice sent up to the house, so look at if comes. let me know I have all my baggage on board. Every body is looking for their baggage and can not find it. we have a good many stragglers who comes. some come down this morning by cars. we are undoubtly for New Orleans as there are quite a number of recruits for New Orleans from here and officers. no more at present from

Your Loving Husband

Thos. W. Cahill

---

1 Pvt. John Fahy. Company H.

3-PM

I open this letter to say that at this moment our destination has been changed to *Fortress Monroe.* so it seems the 19th Army Corps are at Washington. if we had been three hours sooner we would have gone on to New Orleans. well it may be all for the best.

Your loving husband

Thos W Cahill

I suppose I will send home the Money I have with me as I can not use it here.

I would sent it from here but it is sunday and Cannot Express it from here to day.

Thomas to Margaret

Somewhere on the James River
On Board "Gen Woll" July 20th 1864 9–AM

My Dear Wife,

We have been navigating the James River since 4-P.M. of Yesterday. this much more of a stream than I had supposed having I should judge an average width of two miles and in many places wide Bays on the "Right Bank." Coming down the land is high perhaps twenty feet above the River and showing cultivated farms in many places on the left bank is flat. it seems strange to see any signs of cultivating in a country overrun as this has been by large armies for so long a time. not that there are not Evidences Enough of this dreadfull war as we can see stacks of Chimneys standing here and there along the Banks. mournfull Evidence of the devastating presence of hostile armies. a few moments since we passed a Rebel fortification abandoned, close to what appeared to me to be the remains of an ancient church. all along on Each side are the remains of wharves destroyed.

Transports are constantly passing us coming down from the front. some of them large Ocean ships. the ship we Came on could not come up as she was very heavy laden drawing 16 feet so we were transfered to this miserable old thing. A north River propellor Barge which shakes so I can hardly write.

we found the 26th Mass at Fort Monroe. they preceded us up the River Dr G going up with them. It seems Barge has command of Our Brigade. it is said to be Composed of the 26th Mass 9th Conn 12th Maine 14th

Maine 14th New Hampshire. we have only 294 Enlisted men present with us counting Band and Drum Corps and all not a very heavy force to commence a campaign with, but of course we have nothing to say only that the Regiment will the sooner get through unless the state sends on more men which I hardly think she can. with a severe draft is enforced a not very likely prospect.

the 26th Mass takes in 600 men. Dr Brandt is with them again after burying his only sister and brother the first the day he left home. I cannot tell what has become of Liet Kenedy Connors and McKeon. they all left the ship without asking my leave or saying anything to me about it. I suppose they will come and join us, it will depend on superior officers as to how it may go with them. if they report as soon as possible they may escape with a reprimand. quite a larger number 117 are either deserters or absent without leave since we came from New Orleans. of the 40 new recruits 11 have left, of course there was a great feeling of disappointment when we learned of the change in our destination. but it seems to Entirely worn away both among officers and men all.

the 19th Corps are it is said to be brought here it is said for Butler. I am not certain of the latter part but presume they are coming here. I have pretty much made up my mind to send home the most of my money from city point but may if not pressed forward at once. take a few days to see whether I can use it any way with profit.

It is said that Adams Express are in daily Communication with the front from City Point. for the present I think our address will be 9th Conn Vols City Point Via Fortress Monroe. Give my Respects to Father Hart my Love to Ellen and Kiss the little ones as usual for me.

I remain your Loving husband
Thos W Cahill

Thomas to Margaret

Head Quarters 9th Conn Vols in the Field near
Bermuda Hundreds July 25th 1864

My Dear Wife
We still remain here in a state of perfect quiet, doing nothing but Endeavoring to make ourselves as Comfortable as we can which is nothing to boast of as we are verry much straitened for Canvas both for Officers and men. The Line Officers being allowed only what is called a shelter tent this is simply two pieces of a very thin canvass Each piece about 5 feet

square. these Button together in the center and are when put up slightly Elevated in the Center by being thrown across a small stick. two men then crawl under it. the only difference between Officers and men is that they allow two pieces to an officer and one to a man. for the Field and Staff we are allowed 3 small wall tents the same size as were formerly allowed to Line Officers. This for seven of us. is rather short allowance and what is worse is that we have but two of them myself.

the Dr Adjt and Dr MacNeil are all in the same tent as also the Adjt Disk so that we are considerably crowded for Room, this is because we arrived here without our own Camp Equipage and only succeeded in getting three miserable old things, only two of which we can put up, if we knew we were to remain here any length of time we might manage to make ourselves a little more comfortable by Errecting bowers but the Extreme uncertainty of our stay and the Extra labour it imposes on the men disinclines us from laying out much labour for the present, as the woods are some half or three quarters of a mile from us and it is heavy work to lug the timber so far,

I am afraid Father Leo will find it rather rough quarters and poor living. we depend alltogether on the Commissary and find it pretty costly at that. meat fresh being 17 cts per pound ham 19 sugar the same coffee 47 cts, however if we are let one we may worry out three months more without much trouble unless they get up some crook upon us to hold on to us which I do not think they will.

I find the Officers here very much opposed to Butler and many are strong McClellanites. I hope you have received my Trunk before this as I forgot about the 400 belonging to the men which was in it or I would have sent it on by Express. though I believe it would have made but little difference as to its safety either way. let me know just as soon as you receive it. Our address is still the same. 9th Conn Vols 1st Birgade Div 19th A.C. near Bermuda Hundred via Fortress Monroe,

your Loving husband
Thos W Cahill

Thomas to Margaret

Deep Bottom on James River Va July 29th 1864

My Dear Wife
as you will see by the heading we have changed our "Base" since the date of my last letter. we left Butlers front yesterday morning at 3–O clock

arriving at 6–30 and immediately going into Line behind a breastwork from which "Hancocks" the 2d Corps had driven Longstreets corps the day before.[2] to whom we report for the present but there is talk of our going to Washington where the rest of the 19th are Certain it is that 4 Cos belonging to the 14th Maine of this Brigade which were on the way here have been sent to Washington, which is said to be threatened again, I forgot to say that the identical Regt which the 9th Relieved was the Old 69th New York or what there is of them. that look hardy and well. I did not see any I knew save John Bull a boy that used to keep Bar for Corcoran.

Matters change here so Rapidly that it almost impossible to guarantee anything to remain one way. five minutes since commencing to write news comes that we are going away probably to Washington so that our own and the other Regt labourin on the Earth works are thrown away. though they may help to cover some other poor fellows.

I never saw such workers as these glorious fellows of the 2d Corps. they are the greatest workers I ever saw. of course I need say nothing about their fighting but they will work all night and fight all day. I do not know what are the particular stragetic Reasons for retaining this place but presume it makes the Enemy Extend his line and consequently takes more troops.

The Dr came up from Butlers to day. he is well as are all others. The Mail carrier has just come round and I must close.I have writen you that I send you $600 by Adams from Bermuda Hundred and then was the Soldiers money in the Trunk also which I did not think to take out. My love to all.

      your Loving husband
      Thos W Cahill

---

2. The First Battle of Deep Bottom was part of Grant's offensive outside of the Richmond-Petersburg front during late July 1864. Hoping to compel Lee to withdraw forces from around Petersburg, Grant attacked north of the James River with the Second Corps under Winfield Scott Hancock and cavalry under Philip Sheridan. The threat on the Confederate capital worked, and as Lee withdrew his forces to meet the Second Corps, Grant attacked around Petersburg in an offensive that began with the explosion of a mine underneath rebel lines. Both attacks were, ultimately, unsuccessful. Bearss, *Petersburg Campaign*, 2:xiv–xv.

Margaret to Thomas

New Haven July 30th 1864

My dear Husband

I recd your welcom letter of the 23 yesterday Morning. I need not tell you that we are very much encouraged by your Cheerful letters. I have written to you two letters. the directions was symply Bermuda Hundreds VA. in your last you tell me to Send by way of Fortress Monroe and that I have not done so you may not get them.

Father Leo left or was to leave to join you Last evening. he called on me and very kindly offered to take anything I wished to send you but poor man I cannot conceive how he is going to carry all the stuff he has with him. he is not well pleased with somebody in Church St. they did not treat him the best. he had to Borrow 200 Dollars to fit himself out. I think from what he said that the Sisters of Mercy must have been very kind to him.

I told him to send you home very soon to look after your little Children. he answered by saying he would keep you with himself and at the same time saying he was ready to meet his Maker at any time. well that is all very well for him to tell about but you must remember you have a great responsibility here below to look after. but I know you will try to come home as soon as you can get away and Father H—often tells me so so I feel quite encouraged at that part of it.

but you must be very uncomfortable being out under the Burning Sun and in such weather as we have now. only about Two hours rain has fallen since you left home and (private) F H tells u that he thinks the real Asiatic Cholera has visited us he had several bad cases in the last week.

your Friends here cannot understand what it means about your Skedadling (have I spelled that word wright?) from the Regt. Some one credulous enough to believe all that is told them but I do firmly believe that that young gentle man from the *Front* is at the bottom of all the Slanders you have suffered from since the Regt left here. I told you who *he* was in the letter preceding this and also sent the article cut from the Paladium.

I have a whole News Bag full of stuff to tell you. but is it worth while? but I will forget it all when you come home. It seems to me *Somebody* is very much afraid you will come home at all. *that* I think is the great Trouble. well that is in the hands of a greater Power than they can control or *wire-pulling* for (as they call it). our Earnest Prayer *night and day* is that you will come home safe to us.

now please dont say from the tone off my letter than I am a very silly woman to pay attention to anything that is said but we feel so lonly without you and every word not true fairly stings us.

F H is becoming tired waiting for a line from some of you he says. I think he depends on you most for he knows you are a punctual writer; drop him a line soon.

Monday 31st

I just recd your letter dated July 25th. I have answered the Receipt of your Trunk and Package—all—wright—The Trunk stands in the Hall yet I did not think it contained money beloning to Soldiers. I will have it opened tonight. I wish you sent all the money you sent home to us in it. it would have Saved the neighbors from *Gregson Alley*.[3] Congratulating me on the Exact amount—recd a nephew of theirs is in the office in this city.

Baby is not well. her teeth is going to trouble her as Tommys did I fear—I hope you will be home soon.

from your Loving wife
M. E. Cahill

Miss Dawson Sends her Love

Thomas to Margaret

Head Qrs 9th Conn Vols
On Board Steamer "Prometheus" Potomac
River Monday August 1st 1864

My Dear Wife,

I dropped a Short note for you last night at Fortress Monroe but you will probably receive this as soon from Washington.

We have been kept pretty busy Since we landed at Bermuda Hundreds. Either under arms or in the March all the time. on the night of the 27th at an hours notice we broke Camp at 1–O'Clock AM and Marched to the Extreme right at Deep Bottom or rather Strawberry Plains. at this place the 2d Corps Hancocks had the day before attacked and routed

---

3. Margaret's suggestion, here, is that the families will be left on the street, and it is clear here that Gregson Alley would have been a place Thomas would have recognized.

Longstreets Corps in an Entrenched position taking 4, 20 pdr Parrotts in Battery Longstreet was re Enforced and we the 1st Brigade 2d Div 19th AC were sent to Hancock, who sent us to relieve his left Div.

the 9th Came in in front of and relieved the 69th New York, we went to work at once strengthening the Old Rebel Works. the Enemy having a very long and heavy line of works in our front and both having a heavy picket line with constant firing. on the night of the 29th at 10 PM I received an Order to Picket and Occupy the Line of Works held by the 2d Corps preparatory to their withdrawl.

I at once deployed my little Regt and Covered at least a Mile of already abandoned works. so silently had these indomitable veterans withdrawn that although their left lay within 20 feet of my Right not a man in our Regt knew they had left. They still had a Picket line about 20 rods in advance of the Earthworks close to the Enemy and we must Cover and Conceal their withdrawl. no easy task in the face of a vigilant Enemy. as soon as I reached the Regt this work commenced and just Ended at Day break and we commen[ced] to withdraw in a single thin line of skirmishers Extending diagonaly across the Strawberry Plains.

we got off apparently undiscovered to the works covering the Pontoon Bridge which was held by the 12th Maine who followed us across the Bridge. it was a delicate and dangerous movement but we were lucky as usual. we then marched to our Old position in Butlers front and at 1-AM again broke camp and Marched to Bermuda Hundreds and at 10 A M was on board this boat bound for Washington or Elsewhere. the men havent took the work surprisingly, notwithstanding the Enormous loads they carried in their knapsacks for which they were laughed at by the 2nd Corps men who literally carry nothing. Myself and Officers stand it well although a little foot weary for want of horses.

There is no truth I am sorry to say in the report of my appointment in the Veteran Reserve Cops. I presume it grew out of a similarity of names with the man in New Orleans. General Brige had the same impression and so left my name out in the Orders for the first March from Bermuda Hundred.

as the matter of the remuster of Officers is understood here ours does not amount to anything and it is said it is discretionary whether we go out or not with ourselves. the Lieut Col and Major say they will go out, as also some of the others, but we can perhaps tell better about this when we get near Washington and the opinions there,

I have had no opportunity of getting my Clothes washed but I still have one change of flannels and several pairs of stockings not used. I have nothing with me but the valise and what I carry in the Bag and I think that too much. it is so much trouble to look after them. I think I will send home another hundred dollars as I am obliged to carry it in my packet day and night. Give my respects to Father Hart. My Love to Ellen and the Children.

> Your Loving Husband
> Thos W Cahill

The Man Williams[4] is a deserter. tell his wife that he must apply to me in person for any money he may have in my hands.

The Man Condon[5] can have his check sent him and he can Endorse it over to you and you can get it cashed and Express it on to him and charge him five dollars for your troubles if you wish to do so.

Margaret to Thomas

New Haven August 3rd 64

My dear Husband

I recd yours of the 1st this morning. I am very glad you have heard from us. I sent my last day before yesterday. the *Old Boy* is a witch if you dont get it with some exageration. there must have been a whole mile of Directions on it.

You must have had a constant worry of mind ever Since you left us. you must be nearly worn out with Fatigue. I do hope you can have some washing done very soon. I feel uneasy about your runing short of flannells but if possible Buy some at Washington when you get there.

Mrs Williams has not been after any Money latly. was I not luckey for once not to give it her. I hardly like to hear anything to do with that Condon Mans Check. if you can conveniently drop him a line do so but if you wish me to send it I will.

Mr OBrien has been here two or three times. he has not heard from the Capt since the 4th of July. he was there in New Orleans and was to go up to St James on the 5th. We had a letter from Johannah this week there was no news in it.

---

4. Likely John Williams, Company H, though no records indicate that he deserted from the regiment.

5. Pvt. Maurice Condon, Company H.

Mary and Eddy was delighted with their letter from you. poor Eddie carried it about with him the most of the morning and has put it away so careful in his Aunties room.

Marnie had a severe attack of Cholera Morbus last night and to day she is a little better now and I hope will be quite well tomorrow. there has a very cold Rain set in and I am sure will cause a great deal of sickness after so much hot weather. the rest of the little ones are very well. Nellie had her turn of it night before last but she is nicly over it now. Eliza went away sick Sunday morning. I expect her back in a day or two.

Mrs Cooney is back and her two little neices and two Babies and young McCugh and says her sister and Larry is Coming soon so he wont be very lonly. over *heard* anyway. our Tax Bill is Presented 22 Dollars and 88 cts. our Anual subscription for the Church debt took place on last Sunday. our not been Called upon for the Last two or three made me feel a little in debt so I offered 10 Dollars but Father Hart alow us to give but 5 Dollars. he says he will try to make all bear the Burthen alike if he can.

he is complaining at your not writing to him before this. he goes in a Retreat next Monday evening and will be gone a week. he goes to Western Mass. he will be very lonly while he is gone. he comes often to see us. I will send this to Washington for you may not get it.

good Bye from your Loving wife
M. E. Cahill

Thomas to Margaret

Head Qrs 9th Conn Vols
Tennallytown D.C. August 5th 1864

My Dear Wife

As you will see by the heading we are still here. nothing has occurred to break the quiet monotony of our lives since we arrived. we are just sitting on the top of the hills and looking around us, nobody seems to know where the Rebels are at present, and the weather is too insufferably hot for us to desire a foot march for any distance to look for them. we are well satisfied to lay as quiet as we can,

This whole country is terribly parched up. not a green blade of grass to be seen. nearly Everything in the shape of vegitation is dying from the long continued and severe drouth, I should Judge this could be a fine looking country in an ordinary season. it has a beautifull rolling surface is verry Elevated, but at present Every thing is so burned up that it looks very miserable, this makes Every thing in the way of living very high. we are paying 50cts and 75cts Each for inferior meals in private houses. rather Expensive living, We have Excellent water here from natural springs, of course we do not know the moment we may be ordered off and yet I should not be surprised if we remained in this vicinity for some time.

They must it would seem to me desire to have some troops called veterans here to mix up with the new men. though for my part I should not be surprised to find the new troops behaving just as well as those we have here.

As to my personal affairs, I am getting along very well but find it rather Expensive as in addition to price of food Even Every Rag we get washed costs us ten cents a piece and I am trembling for fear I may be compelled to buy a horse, which I do not desire to do, but I do not see how I can get rid of it but will stave it off as long as I can.

I am Examining Enquiring into the subject of the officers remuster. I have just succeeded (this day) in getting a sight of the instruction to mustering Officers on the subject I have not yet had time to study up the subject, but believe it depends on the Division and Corps Commanders. as to the Officers who may be retained in service after the Expiration of the original term of the Regt this is rather indefinite as it also speaks of the Reduction of the Field and staff without saying how the reduction is made or in what is consists. I will let you know as soon as I can what information I may obtain on the subject. Give my Respects to Father Hart. my love to Ellen and the Children,

> from your Loving husband
> Thos W. Cahill

P.S. This is the 3d letter from this place and Washington. the Dr and all others are well Except Lieut Kennedy who is in Hospital in Washington but it is nothing serious.

Thomas to Margaret

Head Qrs 9th Conn Vols
Tennallytown D.C. August 7
3-P.M.

My Dear Wife

So far we have remained quiet and Sheridans Cavalry[6] are coming up or at least part of them, and are going somewhat in our front. Father Leo arrived last night and we had Mass in Camp this morning. he is staying at the College house for which I am thankfull as there is positively no accomodations for him in Camp in the way of tent or cooking,

He tells me he has brought a trunk and valise besides other bundles. for that I am very sorry as it is very doubtfull if we can carry them, and he cannot afford to lose them, I have some hopes of being able to get pay for the horses I lost on ship Island and I wish to look up a report and findings of a Board Survey appointed by Genl Phelps on Ship Island with reference to the loss of the horses of which Captain Wright was president. My reason is that I sent it home in one of the Boxes from Ship Island.

I am making a copy from one in the possession of Dr Brandt 26th Mass and it may be sufficient without the original Copy to which I refer as being at home but I wish you to ascertain if the Original is in my possession as I suppose it to be; in case I need it, It will be a *God Send* if I can collect it now as it will not cost me anything to do so if it can be done while I am here, and will assist me in getting another horse, which I feel that I must do if as only to carry some of my luggage on. I do not want to by one if I should help it in hopes that I may get out in November. but if we have to move around much the horse would almost pay for himself before that,

The question of going out in November is a delicate one. So far as I can trace it now, it rests with the department, Division and Corps Command-

---

6. Gen. Philip H. Sheridan graduated from West Point in 1853. When war broke out, he was appointed chief quartermaster of the Army of Southwest Missouri until May 1862, when he was appointed colonel of the Second Michigan Cavalry. He was promoted to brigadier general in September 1862 and then to major general on March 16, 1863, after the Battle of Murfreesboro. His victory over Confederate cavalry general J. E. B. Stuart at Yellow Tavern in May 1864 propelled him into the national spotlight and compelled Grant to give him command in the Shenandoah Valley. Warner, *Generals in Blue*, 437–39. For extended reading see Hutton, *Phil Sheridan and His Army*; Coffey, *Sheridan's Lieutenants*.

ers, who (whether all or any one of them I do not know) are to say who shall be re Mustered at the Expiration of their Original term. at least that is said to be the way the matter is understood at the war dept. now then apprehend that if *Every Officer* who has not been promoted during the last three years, should, at the Expiration of his first term say he would go out, then they might be short of Officers and they would then begin to contrive some way to hold onto them, But if my next two Officers should desire to remain then they might be ready to let me off. But again the fact of their admitting that an officer must serve his first term before he can be re mustered implies that it discretionary with himself to whether he will or not be remustered at that time,

Still I think it will be as well to keep close as possible about the subject to avoid all Excitement so that I may take advantage of circumstances as they arise, before of course there will be the same amount of talk no matter how I get out, but I desire to place the *order* of my leaving on the *Govmt* if I can rather than to take it myself, I think I may be mustered out because the Regiment is so low in numbers a result of course for which I shall be very sorry. *that* is *between ourselves* but of course I cannot leave against their will,

I recd a letter yesterday from O'Brien. he is out of the Provost Marshall ship and was on temporary duty in New Orleans. I expect he will be ordered back to his Company. I understand such orders have been issued to all the Officers of the Corps in New Orleans so he may arrive any moment though he says nothing about it in his letter. I will keep you informed as closely as I can about Every thing that transpires.

please mention the status of Mrs Gs health in your letters as yours come oftener than hers, and I am asked about it, I could not venture to leave all the money in the trunk even to keep the people from talking, indeed what I did leave was because I forgot it, the Express Company at Bermuda Hundreds would not give receipts for any kind of Baggage so that had the Trunk been lost I had no redress at all, money and all would have gone, together you will see that I have to figure pretty loosely about these things in the hurry of moving about,

notwithstanding all that is said by our officers about getting out of the service, four of them Lee[7] Mullins[8] Warner,[9] and the Asst Surgeon, have been at work for three days and have finally succeeded in getting

7. Capt. William A. Lee, Company C.
8. Lt. Michael Mullins, Company E.
9. Lt. David C. Warner, Company I.

mustered out. their promotions on which it is understood they are again holden for three years so that there would seem to be some great inducements.

notwithstanding the hardships to men to have these officers, poor Streit is in trouble. he cannot be mustered in as I have no company full enough for all three officers to be mustered on but I must try to fix it for him, I have not been to Washington as yet but Expect to go about my horse matter if the copy I have will answer the purpose. I wrote Father Hart yesterday. Give him my Respects my Love to Ellen and the Children.

Your Loving Husband
Thos W Cahill

Thomas to Margaret

Head Qrs 9th Conn Vols
in the field 10 miles from Harpers Ferry August 20th 1864

My Dear Wife

I seize the first opportunity offered since we left Washington to drop you a line just to say that we are all alive and well after a tolerably sharp march across the country through Leesburg and Snickers Gap. We Expected some fighting about Snickers Gap but Came through without seeing an Enemy. making 25 miles on the last days March across the mountains and fording the Shenandoah the same night. we have been marching through the most delightfull Country I ever saw. on Every side immense stacks of wheat are to be seen. the appearance of the Houses indicates a rich country and the Landscapes are Magnificient.

I can hardly tell you what we came here for or what we are going to do. there must be a very heavy force of us here now if the Count of Major Generals is any indication of the strength as they are quite numerous. I said I did not know what we were going to do here, but there is one thing we are doing that is destroying immense quantities of wheat. every soldier is actually lying on a foot deep of the finest wheat unthrashed. I suppose this is done to destroy the Enemies supplies.

we are occupying what is said to be a strong position here and I think waiting for an attack. Give my respects to Father Hart. My Love to Ellen. Kiss the Children as Usual for me. make your address 9th Conn Vols 1st Brig 2d Div 19th A.C. Washington and they will be forwarded to us. there is said to be a large mail Came last night for the Div which has not yet

been distributed. I Expect to hear from you by it. The Dr and all others
are well and in good spirits.

Your Loving Husband

Tho W Cahill

Thomas to Margaret

Head Qrs 9th Conn Vols Halltown
Va Aug 24th 1864

My Dear Wife

I take advantage of an hours leisure, after returning from Picket duty
for the last 24 hours to drop you a line just to say that all is well so far,
although we are some what tired of heavy marches and night duty,

The Enemy is *said* to have followed us up continually since we joined
Sheridans Command at Berryville on the 17th August. since which time
we have been continually moving towards Harpers Ferry now some four
miles distant. for what reason unless danger to supply trains I cannot
conceive,

I have been on Picket and on Guard in Every Conceivable place front
and Rear and have heard any amount of Cannon and musquetry fire all
around me and I can safely say that not a man in the Regt knows that he
has seen 10 armed Rebels in all that time and yet the papers say that Early
has 80,000 men in front of us.

Even while I write any amount of Firing is going on our left near where
I came from Picket. this Am I received yours of the 13 3 or 4 days since
but have had no chance to answering till now. do not think of sending
me an Earthly thing as I cannot possibly carry any thing with me Except
on my own and horse pack. hither we have been allowed the miserable
appology of two wagons to a regiment which might allow a very small
valise to each officer.

an hour since I received an order that hereafter but one wagon would
be allowed to a Regiment, and that must carry ten (10) days forage for
the team about all it can carry of itself. I wish I had the little I have with
me in this valise in some safe place. I do not know what to do with my
clothes nor where to send them. We can get no satisfaction to any Enquiries at Hd Qrs about any thing and I really believe they would like to see
us taking out things out and throwing them awawy on the Road.

I will try to send the little I have to Harpers Ferry or to Washington. I
do not want to lose my trops but care but little so my life and health are
spared. notwishstanding all we have been through, the Officer and men

are in good condition for health. I must hurry up this as the messenger is waiting to take it to Harpers Ferry. good bye God Bless you all. I will write at Every opportunity but you need not Expect to hear from me very often. we cannot Carry even papers and Envelopes with us. Give my Respects to Father Hart. Father Leo has broke down and gone to Hospital at Harpers Ferry. Kiss the Babies as usual for me. my Love to Ellen.

    your Loving Husband
    Tho W Cahill

Margaret to Thomas

New Haven August 29th

My Dear Husband

    Yours of the 24th is at hand. you must have one or two more of mine by this time. I sent all those Papers you sent for. They were directed to Tennallytown before we knew of your removal. My Last was dated 25th and directed to Washington.

    How much I do miss your letters Coming almost every day. indeed I was getting quite sick and nervous and I do not know what I should have done if I did not get those few lines from you this morning. although we feel that you are still in great danger and hope for the best always God grant it may turn out well with you but it is so consoling to us to hear from you often.

    I do not believe one word I hear from any person except what you tell me so you must try and keep me well Posted. Father Hart has written or will do so in a day or two. he is suffering some from sore throat. I believe I told you that his Brother William had arrived and is to stay with us.

    I called to see Mrs Galagher this morning. She and her Babies are very well. the little Babe is a Lovely little dear. her name is Julia and I am her mother too and Father Hart her *Other* Papa.

    Our little ones are all well but Master Thomas has hammered his tricks early in life. he took leave of absence yesterday morning and we did not find him until Twelve Oclock. just imagine my feelings and I so worried about not hearing from you in so many days. he went home with Mrs Murphy as she was passing home from first Mass. Mary and Eddy was with him but they returned soon after and said he would not come with them but stayed with Sharlotte. I felt quite easy and went to bring him home about 10 O Clock but there was no Thomas there. they thought he went home with the others he was then gone a good hour and a half.

I can scarsly write about it I will not get over the fright for some time to come. the whole City was Searched in a very little time after we misplaced him every. Mrs Murphys Niece found him in West Water St close by the Dyke. a man and woman had picked him up there nearly exhausted. if it had been a very hot day he would have died from Sun Stroke. he had on that little old straw hat. we have great cause to be thankful that he was not drowned.

I have just recd a few lined from the Lieut Col and Dr McNeil. I am very grateful to them. please tell them so the Col said he would send your mattrass and a Box home by Express. where in name of God are They going to send you two now? write and have others write every oppertunity.

from your Loving Wife

M. E. Cahill

Thomas to Margaret

Head Qrs 9th Conn Vols in
the field on the Winchester Turnpike
Near Charlestown Va August 30th 1864

My Dear Wife

I sent you a halfsheet this AM by a sutler going to Harpers Ferry distant about 8 miles. And am just notified a mail messenger will leave in two hours so lest the other miscarry will send you this. we are all well and in Good spirits so far, and have had as little fighting and as little in prospect immediately as you could desire. The Enemy apparently foiled his attempts to Cross the Potomac in this vicinity. Commenced falling back day before yesterday and yesterday we advanced from our fortifications on the heights at Halltown to the Lines which we threw up a week ago at this place and since our arrival have been busy strengthening them. though for what reason Except to keep us busy I do not know. I do not the Enemy has any notion of attacking us and we will not leave our works to attack him unless a sure thing. If he be really retreating we may possibly follow him somewhat further though not much. It may be he is called for Petersburg and by Grants success on the Weldon Road.[10] if so we may follow him far Enough to be sure he is out of the valley when we too will return to our ships.

---

10. The Battle of Weldon Railroad, August 18–21, 1864, was Grant's successful attempt to cut off Lee's supplies from south of the Richmond-Petersburg lines. Horn, *Petersburg Campaign*, 123–40.

The horse I bought in Washington is doing well. improving rapidly. I picked up another old cripple on whom I manage to pack a tent and some clothes and food so I get along nicely. the weather is delightfull and Roads good and so far horses find plenty. this is a delightfull country full of fine farms and fresh meat plenty. the men and officers are in good health. we get Baltimore papers Every day but have Recd no Mail but once since we left Tennallytown.

To morrow is muster day but the officers have brought no Rolls with them so I do not see how we can muster for pay. I am sorry for this as it will delay the Mens pay though I do not know what they could do with it if they had it here. Capt O Brien joined day before yesterday with all the men from N. Orleans. among them that James Condnon who wrote you about this check. You may as well Enclose it in a letter to me and I will give it to him. The next letter I write will be to Father Hart as I would this but was not sure you had received any from me. I had to borrow this sheet as I had not paper with me. Kiss the babies. as usual my love to Ellen.

Your loving husband
Thos W Cahill

Thomas to Margaret

Hd Qrs 9th Conn Vols in he
field near Charlestown WV
August 30th 1864

My Dear Wife

I dropped a short note to you yesterday by an Ambulance Driver who was returning to Harpers Ferry and I write this Expecting to send it by a sutler going to same place for supplies. We are now behind the same works which we threw up on the night of the 21st of Aug having advanced without any fighting from our Entrenchments on Halltown Heights.

Yesterday A division of Cavalry in our front at a place called Smithville had a Sharp Engagement with the Enemy who is thought to be retiring up the Valley. he has apparently been defeated in his attempt to Cross the River[11] or he may be called to Petersburgh. I think our force is one

---

11. Although Confederate and Union forces had clashed in the Shenandoah Valley during the summer of 1864, the results were inconclusive, and Gen. David Hunter ultimately withdrew his forces back into West Virginia, leaving the valley unguarded. Lee and Jubal Early saw a possible advantage in this unguarded avenue to the north and schemed to move through the Shenandoah, into Maryland, and threaten Washington, D.C., and the Bal-

of Observation and to keep them from dividing up. Evidently our Commanders instructions are to give battle only under the most advantageous circumstances so that we are likely to have as little fighting as Even you could desire. We are constantly at work Entrenching so if they Come at us it must behind breastworks.

all are well and in good spirits. The Dr being senior surgeon has the medical charge of the Brigade. the Lieut Col has gone to Washington with spare baggage and Dr MacNeil for a horse. Capt O Brien joined us yesterday with the Ballance of the New Orleans Men.[12] I have picked up another Old horse for packing my Rations and tent on so I carry all I need with me. the horse I bought in Washington is turning out finely getting as fat as a seal. so I am getting along nicely but we have little or no paper though the newspapers come through regularly. the account in the Baltimore American are very correct of our movements. My Respects to Father Hart as soon as I can get Paper and certain of Going through will write him.

   my love to all
   Thos W Cahill

Father Leo has not yet come back from Harpers Ferry.

---

timore and Ohio Railroad, thereby relieving pressure on Richmond. By July 4 Early's forces controlled the valley and, unable to hold Harpers Ferry due to the strong federal fortifications there, moved to Frederick, Md. Although Union forces put up stiff resistance, by July 11 Early's Confederates were within sight of the capital at Silver Springs, Md. Two days later, though, the Confederates, aware of the arrival of a number of Union regiments, retreated back to the Shenandoah Valley. It is clear that Cahill and his men arrived in the area after Early was pushed away from Washington, D.C., but while he still posed considerable threat to the Union effort in the valley, marked particularly by the burning of Chambersburg on July 30, 1864. Grant gave command of the valley to Gen. Philip Sheridan in early August, and the Union forces immediately began establishing a line at Halltown, which lies along the Shepherdstown Pike and defends the approach to Harpers Ferry. On August 7, Sheridan began his push into the valley. The action Cahill discusses here likely began on August 15 around Cedar Creek, where sharp skirmishing between the Union and Confederate forces ultimately led to the retreat of the Nineteenth Corps. Early pursued, pushing his opponents across the Opequon River and advancing toward Smithfield (Smithville as Cahill notes above), which threatened Charleston. As Early advanced, Sheridan withdrew his entire force back to the fortifications at Halltown. Early stayed outside of Halltown for three days to put pressure on the federal units defending the approach to Maryland before, outnumbered, he determined to fall back to his position west of the Opequon River. Of course, this is a far too brief summary of what was a very complex campaign in the valley in 1864. These movements were summarized from George E. Pond's excellent military analysis of the Shenandoah Valley Campaign. Pond, *Army in the Civil War*; Gallagher, *Shenandoah Valley Campaign of 1864*; Lepa, *Shenandoah Valley Campaign of 1864*; Patchan, *Last Battle of Winchester*.

   12. It seems as though the men who were a part of the regiment's original muster and who reenlisted were granted veteran furlough and those who enlisted later (after the regiment arrived in New Orleans) stayed in Louisiana and rejoined the regiment when the veteran volunteers returned from furlough.

Margaret to Thomas

Monday Sept 5th 1864

My dear Husband

I recd yours of the 29th and 30th this morning I have written to you Since I recd the Lieut Cols and Dr McNeils of the 28th 29th why what does it mean: there is at Least 5 or 6 of my letters on the way to you and all those Papers I send to you before you left Tennallytown. I seems almost usless to write again but you may not get this one first who can tell:

We are all very gloomey at home. poor little Thomas is very sick. he is Cutting his last double teeth, it is the last thing I expected for some months to come. our good old Dr is attending him constantly and I hope will have him under the Mercy of God. he is a great little sufferer. his great fat Limbs and arms are all wasted away. The four Back Teeth are coming through at once.

I do wish you was at home with us. the rest of the Babies are complaining some but nothing of a serious nature. it always seems to me that when one is ailing the rest have to do the same but I have great cause to be Thankful that their health has been so good all Summer when so many Children died around us.

Mrs Galagher and Babies is well. She Complained of some Headache and weakness Last week but was better yesterday morning she tells me she recieves the Drs letters regularly. I hope you will all hear from us soon. I will send you a clean half sheet to write on fill it full and keep writing every chance you have.

Your Loving Wife
M. E. Cahill

Thomas to Margaret

Head Qrs 9th Conn Vols in
the Field near Berryville VA
Sept 10th 1864

My Dear Wife

We are still here taking it very quietly and Comfortably. Our Baggage wagons came up last night. I see no immediate prospect of a move. Early is still some 4 or 5 miles in our front although the papers say he is in Petersburgh but our Commanders say not and that they have felt his lines for 8 or 10 miles in length.

I do not see how he can stay here a great while as our Officers say they destroyed nearly all the forage as they fell back from Winchester and there certainly is not much left within our lines. we live on Commissary stores and mighty dear living it is Ham 29ct Sugar 25 Hard Tack 8ct Port 26ct Potatoes 4c a pound.

There is in Camp two little stragglers. one of them a son of Barney Conlan of Marreca Street. the other name is Robert Fraser who says his mother lives at 136 East Street.[13] I am trying to help them along as the soldiers are not near so lavish with their food as they used to be, in fact they cannot, as they are only furnished a two third ration and Each one Cooks for himself so that stragglers do not fare as well as they used to with the Regiment now. Even the little I give them counts, I intend however to hedge the Expense by carrying their names on my pay Roll as servants so that with a little management every thing helps.

I have not purchased but one Check as yet. I paid 6 dollars for it through Barney. I will buy as many more as I can afford at that rate and send them to you for collection which you only need to present at Fitchs Office to do.

by the by I want you to send me some State Bounty Checks. those for 10 dollars with Fitches name on them. send them in Envelopes as letters putting in as many as you can for letter weight or ask at the Post Office for the weight and put on stamp Enough to carry it, I shall probably send you one from Co K. I could buy more but I have no blanks. I have received no mail for 5 or 6 days but I have written nearly Every day or Every second day.

There is a good deal of Excitement about Officers going out. all whose terms Expire say they are going out but all who have been promoted during their term must remain for three years from date of promotion. O'Brien was a little more than a year. J. G. Healy next April Williams[14] about the same. They are mighty anxious to know what I am going to do.

do not let on to any Except Father Hart what I am to do. of Course you can be as strong as you like about getting me out. of course I went in the second time in good faith and if the government saw fit to hold me they might do so and it was not my fault that they did not see fit to hold me to my bargain. I must say when I hear of them paying 1,500 dollars for substitutes. I think of would pay better to go home and Enlist as a substitute.

---

13. Neither of these men appear in the regiment's muster rolls.
14. Lt. Michael A. Williams, Company A.

All who are present are well Except Dr McNeil who has returned and who is about the sickest man of his bargain as any one I have seen. Garvy Scott has not yet returned. Young Donnelly Richard[15] has returned and looks very well. Dr G. is well and on the Jump all the while doing more work than any six of the other Dr. he is both Division and Brigade surgeon. remember me to Father Hart. I have heard from him. get my Love to Ellen and Kiss the Babies as usual. tell them papa will be coming home in 49 days if God Spares him.

Your Loving husband

Thos W Cahill

Thomas to Margaret

8 P.M. Sept 13th 1864

I have just received official intelligence of the action this P.M. Wilsons Cavalry[16] were out on a Reconaisance and met Kershaws Division[17] of the South Carolina Rebels in Line of Battle charged upon them and captured all there was of the 8th South Carolina Officers and all between two and 300 men.[18]

The News was Read to the men in Camp causing great Cheering. Liet Kenedy has arrived here and sent in an application for leave of absence for twenty to go to New Haven on a surgeons Certificate. do not know whether he will get it. O'Brien the Dr and all others are well. We are getting the Rolls ready for mustering the Non Re Enlisting men out on the 24th. The Dr Recd a letter from Ms G of the 5th. Tell Father Hard I do not think the Army will do much for McClellan rather the contrary. I Ex[pect] long letters by next mail.

TWC

---

15. Richard Donnelly of Company B was one of the few men to enlist in the Ninth Connecticut in 1864, while the regiment was reorganizing in New Haven. He served from May 1864 to October 1864, when he was mustered out of service.

16. Gen. James H. Wilson, commander of the Third Cavalry Division. Army of the Potomac. Longacre, *Grant's Cavalryman*; Keenan, *Wilson's Calvary Corps*.

17. South Carolinian Joseph B. Kershaw, original commander of the Second South Carolina, was promoted to major general in May 1864. Dickert, *History of Kershaw's Brigade*.

18. On September 4, Confederate forces began withdrawing to Winchester. On September 13, cavalry under the command of Gen. James H. Wilson engaged and captured the Eighth South Carolina Infantry along the Berryville Pike. Pond, *Army in the Civil War*, 146.

6–PM Sept 13

Since writing the above Camp rumor says the fighting I spoke of has been successful that an Entire Regiment of South Carolinians has been Captured numbering 250 men and 2 sets of Colors. this is said to have been done by the 3rd New York Cav other say it was the Infantry of the 2d Div 6th Corps.

I am quite certain that the Enemy must have been driven as the firing was first heard a way to the Right near Charles town and Gradually drew towards our center and about five miles in front. while I write an occasional gun is heard but our Infantry have returned to Camp.

TWC

Thomas to Margaret

Head Qrs 9th Conn Vols in the
Field near Charlestown VA Sept 20 1864

My Dear Wife

Yours of the 29th Came to hand to day being the first since leaving Tennallytown with I think one Exception about the 20th. I have not received those papers you sent to me at Tennallytown. I am sorry if you addressed them to any particular *place* as we have no *place* of *address* Except Washington. I hope they will not go astray. They ought to reach me even if they were sent to Tennallytown but the delay may occur in the Post Office of that miserable place. we ought to receive mail matter Every day as Every other Regiment does but mail after mail comes with only one or two letters for the ninth, to day about twenty. among them yours.

So master Tommy has been giving you a lively turn has he, well he could not very well commence much younger. I think you had better get a coil of half inch rope and make it fast inside the house and take a turn around his waist it might keep him in. well he must have had a nice tramp of it down to the Dyke. it is a wonder that no one noticed a child of his age wandering along alone; I think it must be a kind of an Omen that he means to go it alone during his life.

The Dr was quite surprised to hear of the Event at his house. it was the first and only news he had received of it, I mailed you a letter last night so this must be a short one. we have heard nothing of the Enemy for the last two days. in fact very little is said about him any way. we are all behind Entrenchments taking it very Easy indeed.

we have just recd notice that the Head Qrs of the 19th Army Corps at New Orleans which looks as though we might move that way again Ere Long probably as soon as the wet season sets in here. The Dr and Every Body Else in Camp is well. I suppose you know the two Donnelly dropped out for the Hospital the yougest at Tennallytown the other at Halltown. the first is at Washington the other at Sandy Hook so called near Harpers Ferry. I will try to drop you a few lines each day. I have just written to Father Hart. my love to Ellen. Kiss the Babies as usual.

your Loving husband
Thos W Cahill

Thomas to Margaret

In Camp in the Field Near Strasburg Sept 21st 1864

My Dear Wife,

I write this on the second day after one of the severest *Battles* of this dreadfull war, as from the tenor of a dispatch just read to the Line from the secretary of War and also from Liuet Gen Grant it seems to be considered at Head Qrs.[19]

We escaped in a most Wonderfull manner only one slightly wounded. it was a dreadfull scene after the Battle was over on the Field but being victors of course we could manage to take care of our own wounded.

We followed them up immediately and Camped at Winchester that night and continued the pursuit next morning. I have written so far an account sent for to Head Qrs and am informed that I am to make a reconnaisance of the Enemy position.

Sept 22

We made the reconaisance and remained under a severe fire with Cos E and B and part of D four hours and again thanks be to God Escaped

19. On September 18 Sheridan's forces defeated Early's Confederates at Winchester, forcing their withdrawal south up the Valley to a position at Fisher's Hill. It was, according to Early, "the only place where a stand could be made." Early, with approximately 8,500 men, faced Sheridan's advancing force numbering nearly 35,000. A Union victory, the Battle of Fisher's Hill was "key to the Confederate collapse in the Valley." Krick, "A Stampede of Stampedes: The Confederate Disaster at Fisher's Hill" in Gallagher, *Shenandoah Valley Campaign of 1864*, 162, 167. Krick's overview of the battle and the impact of this fight on Union victory in the Shenandoah Valley is helpful to understanding the role of the Ninth Connecticut at this juncture in the war.

without personal injury. on this occasion we lost 3 killed 9 wounded and 1 missing. we were attacked in strong force by the Enemy but being lucky in our position kept them at Bay untill after dark when we succeeded in withdrawing in safety.

This afternoon another Battle as fought beyond Strasbourg and I had a splendid view of it as our Regiment was on Picket and the Country through which the Battle was fought was in full view before me. the Rebels have again been Routed and I suppose we will be in pursuit again to morrow.

Every body is well and in good spirits. I do not know how much further it is intended to pursue Early up this Valley I have just heard of the death of Lt Col Peck of the 12th Conn. I have no means of ascertaining its truth. he was badly wounded in the Battle near Winchester by a fragment of shell.

In the hurry of my writing I forgot to say I received Ellens letter announcing your sickness on the Evening before the battle. I am verry sorry to hear this and am anxiously looking for a letter by the train which should arrive to night and by which I hope to hear that you are well. Ellen says you are fretting for my return on which I hope to do soon. I do not think we can have much more fighting up here now and the time will soon slip by. Give my Respects to Father Hart and say that I have not received the Long promised letter from him. My Love to Ellen and kiss the Babies as usual for me. The Dr is well but I have not seen him since the morning of the fight. he is busy Enough in the Division Hospital.

Good Bye and God Bless you All

Thos W Cahill

Margaret to Thomas

Sept 24th 1864

My dear Husband

I have little courage to write. we are not certain if you are alive and we have no means of finding out the truth. there is no List of names yet Published. God grant nothing has happened to you.

we are all doing nicly at home now. I am getting quite strong. Thomas is well. Mary and Eddy goes to School every day. Liut Kenedy Called to see me. I hear he is Losing the use of his Limbs entirely.

I sent you 12 Blanks on Last Monday as soon as I recd your letter.

Fitch asked no questions and Paid Ellen Ten Dollars. I sent One Hundred Dollars by Express yesterday and F Hart did it for me. I would have sent it sooner but he was away from here. I will enclose more Bounty Check Blanks in this.

your Loving Wife

M E Cahill

Mrs G is well. Katie has a cold is a little unwell.

When I pay out the money for the Horse I will have Three Hundred and fifty Dollars on hand but I will soon have to use some of it for House Expenses. the Prices of eatables is truly frightful. I bought a small tub of butter this week it cost 35 Dollars. everything else the same.

Come home.

I will take up that note for your Horse as soon as I am able to go out. some person called for the money day before yesterday but I was asleep.

yours

M. E. Cahill

Thomas to Margaret

Head Qrs 9th Conn Vols Harrissonburgh
Va Oct 5th 1864

My Dear Wife

Yours of Sept 19th Came to hand Sept 29th I was glad to find you recovering from your severe illness and that all were well at home.

It is all right as to checks from the New Orleans Men although it makes no difference as I have no more. I am in the midst of another discussion about the muster out of the non re Enlisting men. A Division mustering Officer of the 2d Div 19th A.C. who is a Captain of the 13th C.V. named Finlay[20] undertook to make all the men whose term Ended in Sept and Oct wait until the 24th of November as Six men of Co K time is out on that date.

I have appealed last night from his decision to the Corps Mustering Officer and demand that the Men and Officer Mustered in Nov 1st 1861 be Mustered out in New Haven Oct 29th 1864. answer has not been receive at this hour. There are 57 men present who are affected By this

20. Capt. Denison H. Finley, Company G.

decision Myself and the Dr and all officers who have not been *promoted* since the 1st November 1861. should our Rights be given us we should be in New Haven the last week in the Month but I am not certain of it.[21]

the whole question turns on whether we are or are not a *Veteran Regiment.* they now require for this that (¾) three fourths of the whole number of men borne on the Rolls of the Regiment should Re Enlist. ¾ of those *present for duty* with us did Re Enlist but not ¾ of all on the rolls. we needed 176 more to make it a Veteran Regt at least such is the decision here. Being a Veteran Regt would Entitle such of the Officers as would be acceptable to the Corps Commander to be ReMustered as of their Original Grade,

I suspect our Brigade Commander of a desire to consolidate ours with the 13th Conn so as to give Col Blinn[22] of that Regt a friend of his a full Colonelcy. he and others have done their best to draw me out as to my views about continuing service. we should be carefull of saying anything to any one as the Grocers [illegible] on the Corner are friends of Blinns.

My plan is to get home and there if I have a *choice express* it. and taking advantage I may have if any understand that all of us who hold our original position *must* be *mustered out.* Whether *we can if we wish be remustered remains to be seen.* If we cannot of course it is not our fault that we leave the service and will be somewhat in the attitude of injured or wronged me.

I know you and Father Hart will sympathise with me in this case and sympathy is sweet when one feels hurt. I feel some what sore about getting no pay as I wanted to get paid up to the last two months as there is always some trouble about the final payment as to settling accounts and the money I have invested in horses will necessarily cramp me. The

---

21. This deals with the original term of service of the three-year volunteers. Cahill argued that the men who did not reenlist in 1864 should be mustered out of service at the end of October, three years from when they were initially mustered. Confusion ensued because too few men reenlisted and the army could not justify having the number of officers who returned from furlough on the rolls. As colonel, Cahill had the ability to resign his commission and return home, but as so often emerged over the war, such a decision came with consequences; in particular it could create animosity at home. Thus, Cahill argued that his term of original enlistment was up at the end of October 1864 and that he and the other volunteers who did not rejoin the regiment should be released from service.

22. Col. Charles D. Blinn, Thirteenth Connecticut of West Cornwall, Conn., served as the captain of Company C before his promotion. Sprague, *History of the 13th Infantry Regiment*, 21.

horses are good ones though and I look forward to a ride in New Haven with them.

Some of the Officers Williams J G Healy Mullen Connors Wilson Graham[23] Warner[24] while we lay at Berryville before the Winchester Fight Expressed a desire to remain in service. the first has just been to me to beg me to get him out and it is said the second is very weak in the knees. I feel for them *much*. Some will undoubtedly be returned and I have nothing to say in the matter. I suppose if OB does not get out the Devil will be to pay in Hamelton St.

Should we be compelled to wait untill Nov 24th you will see the reasons for it situated as we are many things happen in a day and we can build on noting. The Government clearly has no legal Right to retain us beyond our three years but they have the power. I am in honor bound to fight for the Rights of my men and will do all in my power for them whether I may get in the bad graces of superiors by it remains to be seen.

You speak of sending me money. I do not need any at present and they must give me transportation from Harpers Ferry home. It would take us a week to march from here to Harpers Fery and 3 or 4 days from there home so that we ought to leave here next week but I doubt it. to tell the truth I have no particular desire to go without a strong Escort from here to Winchester and would not go to morrow if I could with out it. there is a story in camp that Frye had ben Gobbled coming up but I do not believe it.

Now Then I think I have defined my position [*illegible*] before me. I think there can be no doubt we will be home Nov 1st but I tell you that I have no desire to be there at the Presidential Election. I mean to dodge it if I can. perhaps I may stop on the way for a few days, but I will send a line to you Every chance we get and when we Reached Harpers Ferry might Telegraph perhaps and perhaps not I might not want the town to know yet.

I must finish this up. give my respects to Father Hart My Love to Ellen. Kiss the babies as usual for me.

> Your Loving husband
> Thos W Cahill

---

23. Lt. James F. Graham, Company I.
24. Lt. David C. Warner (Wainter), Company C.

Thomas to Margaret

Head Qrs 9th Conn Vols
Camp in the field near Cedar Creek
Va Oct 12th 1864

My Dear Wife

This is probably the last letter you will received from me while in the service as I am expecting to proceed home wards tomorrow or the day after with all the non Reenlisting men present and all but ten or twelve officers. you may imagine that there is considerable Excitement among the officers to find out who are to be held and who are to go. I know who they are but as I do not wish to add to the excitement I say nothing. O'B Williams and McK are among them. I expect a deal of trouble in setting up the Regtl affairs and some loss of time. I suppose the papers are full of the Great Race. the Celebrated *Rossers* Rebel Cavalry[25] made away from ours three days since with the loss of Eleven Pieces of Artillery. it was a wonderful affair costing us but four killed and twenty wounded.

I received yours of the 24th Sept and notice about the money at Harpers Ferry. I will try to go that way and get it. I am sorry about our funds as I am afraid it will be a long time before I can get to earn anything at home and it will be some time before I will get the four months pay now due. The mail will close in half an hour so good by until I see you all at home.

Your Loving husband

Thos W Cahill

P.S. Dr is Well and writing now.

---

25. Thomas L. Rosser commanded the Confederate cavalry during the 1864 Valley Campaign. Warner, *Generals in Gray*, 264–65.

Bibliography

PRIMARY SOURCES

Civil War Trust, Washington, D.C.
The Civil War Trust (www.civilwar.org/)

Connecticut State Historical Society, Hartford, Connecticut
MS-73236, Diary of Seneca S. Thresher, dealing with legal affairs of families of soldiers
MS-93558, Charles Frederick Sedgwick to D. W. Gooch
MS-Civil War Box 1, Folder 7, Pay clothing and subsistence voucher for Captain S. W. Sawyer

Connecticut State Library and Archives, Hartford, Connecticut
"Index Books." December 1881. Chronological.
RG-008, Office of the State Comptroller, 1758–1954.
RG-013, Military Department, 1776–1986.
RG-8:67, Paymaster and Quartermaster Accounts, 1861–65.
RG-8:72, Records of Payments to Civil War Soldiers and Families, 1861–66.
RG-13:32, Muster Rolls, Descriptive Lists, Pay Rolls, and Related Papers, 1861–65.
RG-13:49, Incoming Letters Concerning Pensions, November 1864–RG-113, Grand Army of the Republic, 1862–1932.
RG-114, Sons of Union Veterans of the Civil War, 1909–15.

National Archives and Records Administration, Washington, D.C.
M123, Union Veterans Census
M594, Complied Records Showing Service of Military Units in Volunteer Union Organizations
RG-15, Pension Office Files
RG-94, Records of the Adjutant General's Office, 1780s–1917
RG-153 Records of the Judge Advocate General
Seventh Census of the United States (1850)
Eighth Census of the United States (1860)
Ninth Census of the United States (1870)
1890 Veterans Schedule

National Park Service, Washington, D.C.
Civil War Soldiers and Sailors Database (www.nps.gov/civilwar/soldiers-and -sailors-database.htm)

New Haven City Directory of the Year 1860 (www.ancestry.com)

New York State Military Museum, Saratoga Springs
New York Civil War Units: Unit History Project (https://dmna.ny.gov/historic /reghist/civil/)

University of Notre Dame, Indiana, Archives
Calendar of the Catholic Church in the United States (http://archives.nd.edu/)

Private Collections
Cahill Collection, held by Charles Sibley, Hamden, Conn.
Lawrence O'Brien Collection, held by Jeffery Cook, Trumbull, Conn.
Daniel O'Sullivan and George Hill Collection, held by Joseph Kelly, Toms River, N.J.

Published Archival Sources
Adjutant-General's Office of Connecticut. *Catalogue of Connecticut Volunteer Organizations (Infantry, Cavalry and Artillery) in the Service of the United States, 1861– 1865, with Additional Enlistments, Casualties and Brief Summaries, Showing the Operations and Service of the Several Regiments and Batteries.* Hartford: Brown and Gross, 1869.
Official Army Register of the Volunteer Force of the United States Army. Washington D.C.: Adjutant General's Office, 1865.
The War of the Rebellion: A Compilation of the Official Records of Union and Confederate Armies Official Records of Union and Confederate Navies. Washington, D.C.: Government Printing Office, 1898.

Newspapers
Columbian Register (New Haven, Conn.)
Connecticut Courant (Hartford)
Connecticut War Record (New Haven)
Constitution (Middletown, Conn.)
Daily Constitution (Middletown, Conn.)
Hartford Times (Hartford, Conn.)
Lowell Daily Citizen and News (Lowell, Mass.)
New Haven Palladium (New Haven, Conn.)
Phoenix (Brooklyn)
Pilot (Boston)
Republican Farmer (Bridgeport, Conn.)

SECONDARY SOURCES

Alduino, Frank W., and David J. Coles. *Sons of Garibaldi in Blue and Gray: Italians in the American Civil War.* New York: Cambria Press, 2007.

Allardice, Bruce S. *More Generals in Gray.* Baton Rouge: Louisiana State University Press, 1995.

Anbinder, Tyler. *Nativism and Slavery: The Northern Know Nothings and the Politics of the 1850s.* New York: Oxford University Press, 1992.

Arnold, James R. *Grant Wins the War: Decision at Vicksburg.* New York: John Wiley and Sons, 1997.

Ashworth, John. *Slavery, Capitalism, and Politics in the Antebellum Republic.* Vol. 2: *The Coming of the American Civil War, 1851–1861.* New York: Cambridge University Press, 2008.

Attie, Jeanie. *Patriotic Toil: Northern Women and the American Civil War.* Ithaca, N.Y.: Cornell University Press, 1998.

Atwater, Francis. *History of the Town of Plymouth, Connecticut.* Meriden, Conn.: Journal Publishing, 1895.

Ballard, Michael B. *Vicksburg: The Campaign That Opened the Mississippi.* Chapel Hill: University of North Carolina Press, 2004.

Bearss, Edwin C. *The Petersburg Campaign.* Vol. 2: *The Western Front Battles September 1864–April 1865.* El Dorago Hills, Calif.: Savas Beatie, 2014.

Bernstein, Iver. *The New York City Draft Riots: Their Significance for American Society and Politics in the Age of the Civil War.* New York: Oxford University Press, 1990.

Bernstein, Steven. *The Confederacy's Last Northern Offensive: Jubal Early, the Army of the Valley and the Raid on Washington.* Jefferson, N.C.: McFarland, 2010.

Bowen, James Lorenzo. *Massachusetts at War: 1861–1865.* Springfield, Mass.: Clark W. Bryan, 1889.

Brady, Kevin T. "Fenians and the Faithful: Philadelphia's Irish Republican Brotherhood and the Diocese of Philadelphia, 1859-1870." Diss., Temple University, 1999

Bremner, Robert H. *The Public Good: Philanthropy and Welfare in the Civil War Era.* New York: Alfred A. Knopf, 1980.

Brown, Dee. *Grierson's Raid.* Urbana: University of Illinois Press, 1954.

Burton, Brian K. *Extraordinary Circumstances: The Seven Days Battles.* Bloomington: Indiana University Press, 2001.

Burton, William. *Melting Pot Soldiers.* New York: Fordham University Press, 1998.

Byrne, William. *History of the Catholic Church in the New England States.* Boston: Hurd and Everts, 1899.

Callaghan, James. "The San Patricios." *American Heritage* 46, no. 7 (1995).

Casey, Marion, and J. J. Lee. *Making the Irish American: History and Heritage of the Irish in the United States.* New York: New York University Press, 2006.

Clinton, Catherine, and Nina Silber. *Divided Houses: Gender and the Civil War.* New York: Oxford University Press, 1992.

Coffey, David. *Sheridan's Lieutenants: Phil Sheridan, His Generals, and the Final Year of the Civil War.* Latham, Md.: Rowman and Littlefield, 2005.

Collections of the New Haven Colony Historical Society. New Haven: New Haven Colony Historical Society, 1907.

Conyngham, Daniel. *The Irish Brigade and Its Campaigns.* London: F. Pitman, 1866.

Corby, William. *Memoirs of Chaplain Life.* New York: Fordham University Press, 1992.

Costa, Debra, and Matthew Kahn. *Heroes and Cowards: The Social Face of War.* Princeton, N.J.: Princeton University Press, 2008.

Cotham, Edward T., Jr. *Sabine Pass: The Confederacy's Thermopylae.* Austin: University of Texas Press, 2004.

Cozzens, Peter. *Shenandoah 1862: Stonewall Jackson's Valley Campaign.* Chapel Hill: University of North Carolina Press, 2008.

Crafts, James Monroe, and William Francis Crafts. *The Crafts Family: A Genealogical and Biographical History of the Descendants of Griffin and Alice Craft of Roxbury, Mass, 1630–1890.* Northampton, Mass.: Gazette Printing, 1893.

Daniel, Larry J. *The Battle of Stones River: The Forgotten Conflict between the Confederate Army of Tennessee and the Union Army of the Cumberland.* Baton Rouge: Louisiana State University Press, 2012.

Dickert, D. Augustus. *History of Kershaw's Brigade.* Newberry, S.C: Elbert H. Aull, 1899.

Diner, Hasia R. *Erin's Daughters in America: Irish Immigrant Women in the Nineteenth Century.* Baltimore, Md.: Johns Hopkins University Press, 1983.

Dodge, Andrew R., and Betty K Koed. *Biographical Directory of the United States Congress, 1774–2005.* Washington, D.C.: U.S. Government Printing Office, 2005.

Dorsey, Sarah A. *Recollections of Henry Watkins Allen: Brigadier-General Confederate States Army Ex-Governor of Louisiana.* New Orleans: M. Doolady, 1866.

Dougherty, Kevin. *The Peninsula Campaign of 1862: A Military Analysis.* Jackson: University Press of Mississippi, 2005.

———. *The Vicksburg Campaign: Strategy, Battles, and Key Figures.* Jefferson, N.C.: McFarland, 2015.

Duncan, Jason K. *Citizens or Papists: The Politics of Anti-Catholicism in New York, 1685–1821.* New York: Fordham University Press, 2005.

Erie, Steven P. *Rainbow's End: Irish-Americans and the Dilemmas of Urban Machine Politics, 1840–1985.* Los Angeles: University of California Press, 1988.

Ewer, James Kendall. *The Third Massachusetts Cavalry in the War for the Union.* Maplewood, Mass.: Wm. G. J. Perry Press, 1903.

Faller, Phillip E. *The Indiana Jackass Regiment in the Civil War: A History of the 21st Infantry/1st Regiment Heavy Artillery Regiment, with a Roster.* Jefferson, N.C.: McFarland, 2013.

Fallows, Marjorie R. *Irish Americans: Identity and Assimilation.* Englewood Cliffs, N.J.: Prentice-Hall, 1979.

Fitzharris, Joseph C. "Field Officer Courts and U.S. Civil War Military Justice," *Journal of Military History* 68, no. 1 (January 2004): 47–72.

Forbes, Edwin, ed. *Thirty Years After: An Artist's Memoir of the Civil War.* Baton Rouge: Louisiana State University Press, 1993.

Foreman, Amanda. *World on Fire: Britain's Crucial Role in the American Civil War.* New York: Random House, 2012.

Friend, Jack. *West Wind, Flood Tide: The Battle of Mobile Bay.* Annapolis, Md.: Naval Institute Press, 2004

Gallagher, Gary W., ed. *Chancellorsville.* Chapel Hill: University of North Carolina Press, 1996.

———. *The Richmond Campaign of 1862: The Peninsula and the Seven Days.* Chapel Hill: University of North Carolina Press, 2000.

———, ed. *The Shenandoah Valley Campaign of 1864.* Chapel Hill: University of North Carolina Press, 2006.

Geary, James W. *We Need Men: The Union Draft in the Civil War.* DeKalb: Northern Illinois University Press, 1991.

Giesberg, Judith Ann. *Army at Home: Women and the Civil War on the Northern Home Front.* Chapel Hill: University of North Carolina Press, 2009.

———. *Civil War Sisterhood: The U.S. Sanitary Commission and Women's Politics in Transition.* Boston: Northeastern University Press, 2000.

Grant, Ulysses S. *Personal Memoirs of U. S. Grant.* Vol. 1 and 2. New York: Century, 1895.

Green, Francis Vinton. *Campaigns of the Civil War: The Mississippi.* New York: Charles Scribner's Sons, 1892.

Guelzo, Allen C. *Gettysburg: The Last Invasion.* New York: Alfred A. Knopf, 2013.

Hargrove, Hondon B. *Black Union Soldiers in the Civil War.* Jefferson, N.C.: McFarland, 1988.

Hearn, Chester G. *When the Devil Came Down to Dixie: Ben Butler in New Orleans.* Baton Rouge: Louisiana State University Press, 1997.

Hewitt, Lawrence Lee. *Port Hudson: Confederate Bastion on the Mississippi.* Baton Rouge: Louisiana State University Press, 1987.

Hewitt, Lawrence Lee, and Arthur W. Bergeron, eds. *Confederate Generals in the Western Theater: Essays on America's Civil War.* Vol. 3. Knoxville: University of Tennessee Press, 2011.

Hill, Everett Gleason. *A Modern History of New Haven and Eastern New Haven County.* Vol. 2. New York: S. J. Clarke Publishing, 1918.

Hirst, Benjamin. *The Boys From Rockville: The Civil War Narratives of Sgt. Benjamin Hirst, Company D, 14th Connecticut Volunteers.* Edited by Robert L. Bee. Knoxville: University of Tennessee Press, 1998.

Hollandsworth, James G., Jr. *Pretense of Glory: The Life of General Nathaniel P. Banks.* Baton Rouge: Louisiana State University Press, 1998.

Horn, John. *The Petersburg Campaign: June 1864–April 1865.* Boston, Mass.: Da Capo Press, 1993.

Hutton, Paul Andrew. *Phil Sheridan and His Army*. Lincoln: University of Nebraska Press, 1985.

Jones, Howard. *The Union in Peril: The Crisis over British Intervention in the Civil War*. Chapel Hill: University of North Carolina Press, 1992.

Jones, Wilmer L. *Generals in Blue and Gray: Davis's Generals*. Mechanicsburg, Pa.: Stackpole Books, 2004.

———. *Generals in Blue and Gray: Lincoln's Generals*. Westport, Conn.: Praeger, 2004.

Kee, Robert. *The Green Flag: A History of Irish Nationalism*. New York: Penguin Books, 1972.

Keenan, Jerry. *Wilson's Calvary Corps: Union Campaigns in the Western Theater, October 1864 through Spring 1865*. Jefferson, N.C.: McFarland, 1998.

Kohl, Lawrence, and Margaret Richard, eds. *Irish Green and Union Blue: The Civil War Letters of Peter Walsh*. New York: Fordham University Press, 1986.

Kurtz, William. "'Let Us Hear No More of "Nativism"'": The Catholic Press in the Mexican and Civil Wars." *Civil War History* 60, no. 1 (2014).

Lamers, William M. *The Edge of Glory: A Biography of General William S. Rosecrans, U.S.A.* Baton Rouge: Louisiana State University Press, 1961.

Lardas, Mark. *Roughshod through Dixie: Grierson's Raid, 1863*. Oxford: Osprey Publishing, 2010.

Lawson, Melinda. *Patriot Fires: Forging a New American Nationalism in the Civil War*. Lawrence: University Press of Kansas, 2002.

Lepa, Jack H. *The Shenandoah Valley Campaign of 1864*. Jefferson, N.C.: McFarland, 2003.

Longacre, Edward G. *General Ulysses S. Grant: The Soldier and the Man*. Boston, Mass.: Da Capo Press, 2006.

———. *Grant's Cavalryman: The Life and Wars of General James H. Wilson*. Mechanicsburg, Pa.: Stackpole, 2000.

———. *The Man behind the Guns: A Military Biography of General Henry J. Hunt, Commander of Artillery, Army of the Potomac*. Boston: Da Capo Press, 2003.

Lonn, Ella. *Foreigners in the Union Army*. Baton Rouge: Louisiana State University Press, 1951.

Lynch, Timothy G. "'Erin's Hope': the Fenian brotherhood of New York City, 1858-1886." Diss., City University of New York, 2004.

Lynch-Brennan, Margaret. *The Irish Bridget: Irish Immigrant Women in Domestic Service in America, 1840–1930*. Syracuse, N.Y.: Syracuse University Press, 2009.

Marszalek, John F. *Commander of All Lincoln's Armies: A Life of General Henry W. Halleck*. Cambridge, Mass.: Harvard University Press, 2004.

Massachusetts Adjutant General's Office. *Massachusetts Soldiers, Sailors, and Marines in the Civil War: Index to Army Records*. Boston: Wright and Potter Printing, 1937.

McKean, Cornelius. *McKean Genealogies, from the Early Settlement of McKeans or McKeens in America to the Present Time, 1902*. Des Moines, Iowa: Kenyon Printing and Manufacturing, 1902.

McPherson, James. *Battle Cry of Freedom: The Civil War Era*. New York: Oxford University Press, 1988.

Milburn, William Henry. *The Pioneers, Preachers and People of the Mississippi Valley*. New York: Derby and Jackson, 1860.

Miller, Kerby. *Emigrants and Exiles: Ireland and the Irish Exodus to North America*. New York: Oxford University Press, 1995.

Mindell, David A. *Iron Coffin: War, Technology and Experience Aboard the USS Monitor*. Baltimore: Johns Hopkins University Press, 2012.

Moore, David G. *William S. Rosecrans and the Union Victory: A Civil War Biography*. Jefferson, NC: McFarland and Company, 2014.

Murray, Thomas Hamilton. *The History of the Ninth Regiment, Connecticut Volunteer Infantry "The Irish Regiment" in the War of the Rebellion, 1861–65*. New Haven, Conn.: Price, Lee and Adkins, 1903.

Niven, John, *Connecticut for the Union: The Role of the State in the Civil War*. New Haven, Conn.: Yale University Press, 1965.

Nolan, Janet A. *Ourselves Alone: Women's Emigration from Ireland, 1885–1920*. Lexington: University of Kentucky Press, 1989

Norris, L. David, James C. Mulligan, and Odie B. Faulk. *William H. Emory: Soldier and Scientist*. Tucson: University of Arizona Press, 1998.

Oakes, James. *Freedom National: The Destruction of Slavery in the United States, 1861–1865*. New York: W. W. Norton, 2013.

O'Broin, Leon. *Fenian Fever: The Anglo-American Dilemma*. London: Chatto and Windus, 1971.

Öfele, Martin W. *True Sons of the Republic: European Immigrants in the Union Army*. Westport, Conn.: Greenwood Publishing Group, 2008.

Orcutt, Samuel. *The History of the Old Town of Derby, Connecticut, 1642–1880*. Derby, Conn.: Springfield Printing, 1880.

Oxford Dictionary of English. 3rd ed. New York: Oxford University Press, 2010.

Paine, Halbert E. *A Wisconsin Yankee in Confederate Bayou Country: The Civil War Reminiscences of a Union General*. Baton Rouge: Louisiana State University Press, 2009.

Palladino, Grace. *Another Civil War: Labor, Capital, and the State in the Anthracite Regions of Pennsylvania, 1840–1868*. New York: Fordham University Press, 2006.

Park, Carl D. *Ironclad Down: USS Merrimack-CSS Virginia from Construction to Destruction*. Annapolis, Md.: Naval Institute Press, 2007.

Patchan, Scott C. *The Last Battle of Winchester: Phil Sheridan, Jubal Early, and the Shenandoah Valley Campaign, August 7–September 19, 1864*. El Dorado Hills, Calif.: Savas Beatie, 2013.

Pena, Christopher G. *Scarred by War: Civil War in Southeast Louisiana*. Bloomington, Ind.: AuthorHouse, 2004.

Pierson, Michael D. *Mutiny at Fort Jackson: The Untold Story of the Fall of New Orleans*. Chapel Hill: University of North Carolina Press, 2008.

Pinheiro, John. "Religion without Restriction: Anti-Catholicism, All Mexico, and the Treaty of Guadalupe Hidalgo." *Journal of the Early Republic* 3, no. 1 (2003).

Piston, William Garrett, and Richard W. Hatcher. *Wilson's Creek: The Second Battle of the Civil War and the Men Who Fought It.* Chapel Hill: University of North Carolina Press, 2000.

Pond, George E. *The Army in the Civil War: The Shenandoah Valley in 1864.* New York: Charles Scribner's Sons, 1882.

Quinter, Edwin B. *Military History of Wisconsin.* Chicago: Clarke, 1866.

Rable, George C. *Fredericksburg! Fredericksburg!* Chapel Hill: University of North Carolina Press, 2002.

Ramold, Steven J. *Across the Divide: Union Soldiers View the Northern Home Front.* New York: New York University Press, 2013.

Ramon, Marta. *A Provisional Dictator: James Stephens and the Fenian Movement.* Dublin: University College Dublin Press, 2007.

Reid, Brian Holden. *America's Civil War: The Operational Battleground.* New York: Prometheus Books, 2008.

Reid, Whitlaw. *Ohio in the War: Her Generals, and Soldiers.* Vol. 1: *History of the State during the War and the Lives of Her Generals.* New York: Moore, Wilstach, and Baldwin, 1868.

Richter, William L. *Historical Dictionary of the Civil War and Reconstruction.* Lanham, Md.: Scarecrow Press, 2012.

Rightor, Henry, ed. *Standard History of New Orleans.* Chicago: Lewis Publishing, 1900.

Rockey, John. *History of New Haven County, CT.* Vol 1. New York: W. W. Preston, 1892.

Sadliers' Catholic Dictionary and Ordo for the Year of Our Lord 1864. New York: J. Sadlier, 1864.

Samito, Christian G., ed. *Commanding Boston's Irish Ninth: The Civil War Letters of Colonel Patrick R. Guiney, Ninth Massachusetts Volunteer Infantry.* New York: Fordham University Press, 1998.

Sandow, Robert M. *Deserter Country: Civil War Opposition in the Pennsylvania Appalachians.* New York: Fordham University Press, 2009.

Sears, Stephen W. *To the Gates of Richmond: The Peninsula Campaign.* New York: Ticknor and Fields, 1992.

Shahan, Thomas J. ed. *The Catholic Historical Review: For the Study of the Church History of the United States.* Vol. 1. Washington, D.C.: Catholic University of America, 1916.

Silber, Nina. *Daughters of the Union: Northern Women Fight in the Civil War.* Cambridge, Mass.: Harvard University Press, 2005.

———. *Gender and the Sectional Conflict.* Chapel Hill: University of North Carolina Press, 2008.

Smith, Derek. *The Gallant Dead: Union and Confederate Generals Killed in the Civil War.* Mechanicsburg, Pa.: Stackpole Books, 2005.

Snay, Mitchell. *Fenians, Freedmen, and Southern Whites: Race and Nationality in the Era of Reconstruction.* Baton Rouge: Louisiana State University Press, 2007.

Snell, Mark A. *From First to Last: The Life of Major General William B. Franklin.* New York: Fordham University Press, 2002.

Sprague, Homer B. *History of the 13th Infantry Regiment of Connecticut Volunteers during the Great Rebellion.* Hartford, Conn.: Case, Lockwood, 1867.

Steward, Patrick, and Brian P. McGovern. *The Fenians: Irish Rebellion in the North Atlantic World, 1858–1876.* Knoxville: University of Tennessee Press, 2013.

Stoker, Donald. *The Grand Design: Strategy and the U.S. Civil War.* New York: Oxford University Press, 2010.

Sylvester, Nathaniel Bartlett. *History of Rensselaer Co., New York.* Philadelphia: Everts and Peck, 1880.

Symonds, Craig L. *Lincoln and His Admirals: Abraham Lincoln, the U.S. Navy, and the Civil War.* New York: Oxford University Press, 2008.

Thorpe, Sheldon B. *The History of the Fifteenth Connecticut Volunteers in the War for the Defense of the Union, 1861–1865.* New Haven, Conn.: Price, Lee and Adkins, 1893.

Tidball, Eugene C. *No Disgrace to My Country: The Life of John C. Tidball.* Kent, Ohio: Kent State University Press, 2002.

Tucker, Spencer, ed. *The Civil War Naval Encyclopedia.* Vol. 1. Santa Barbara, Calif.: ABC-CLIO Press, 2011.

Ural, Susannah, ed. *Civil War Citizens: Race, Ethnicity, and Identity in America's Bloodiest Conflict.* New York: New York University Press, 2010.

———. *The Harp and the Eagle.* New York: New York University Press, 2006.

———. "'Remember Your Country and Keep Up Its Credit': Irish Volunteers and the Union Army, 1861–1865." *Journal of Military History* 69, no. 2 (2005): 331–59.

Walker, Mabel Gregory. *The Fenian Movement.* Colorado Springs: Ralph Myles Publisher, 1969.

Warner, Ezra J. *Generals in Blue: Lives of the Union Commanders.* Baton Rouge: Louisiana State University Press, 1964.

———. *Generals in Gray: Lives of the Confederate Commanders.* Baton Rouge: Louisiana State University Press, 1959.

Warshauer, Matthew. *Connecticut in the American Civil War: Slavery, Sacrifice, and Survival.* Middletown, Conn.: Wesleyan University Press, 2011.

Waugh, Joan. *U. S. Grant: American Hero, American Myth.* Chapel Hill: University of North Carolina Press, 2009.

Weber, Jennifer L. *Copperheads: The Rise and Fall of Lincoln's Opponents in the North.* New York: Oxford University Press, 2006.

Williams, David. *I Freed Myself: African American Self-Emancipation in the Civil War Era.* New York: Cambridge University Press, 2014.

Williams, T. Harry. *P. G. T. Beauregard: Napoleon in Gray.* Baton Rouge: Louisiana State University Press, 1955.

Winters, John D. *The Civil War in Louisiana.* Baton Rouge: Louisiana State University Press, 1963.

Wise, Stephen R. *Gate of Hell: Campaign for Charleston Harbor, 1863*. Columbia: University of South Carolina Press, 1994.

Witcomb, Caroline Elizabeth. *History of the Second Massachusetts Battery (Nims' Battery) of Light Artillery, 1861–1865*. Concord, N.H.: Rumsford Press, 1912.

Woodworth, Steven E. *Northing but Victory: The Army of the Tennessee, 1861–1865*. New York: Random House, 2005.

Young, Bette Roth. *Emma Lazarus and Her World: Life and Letters*. Philadelphia: Jewish Publishing Society, 1995.

Index

New Perspectives on the Civil War Era

CPSIA information can be obtained
at www.ICGtesting.com
Printed in the USA
LVOW11s2001190917
549285LV00004B/435/P

9 780820 351551